Architectural Drawings

PAULO ZAVALA

INK START MEDIA
5710 W Gate City Blvd Ste K #284
Greensboro, NC 27407

PAULO ZAVALA Architectural and Interior Design
Phone:
Email:

design by	drawn by	date	scale	job number

ARCHITECTURAL DRAWINGS

INTRODUCTION

I was designing for years, then my Art Professor in my last year of High School, suggested that I became an Architect. I took his advice and since then, there is not a day that I do not design something.

At this time I want to share with you a few Architectural Drawings from Projects produced from the very beginning of my professional practice, until now.

You will see many different techniques of drafting in this book. Drawings are the medium in Architectural practice to communicate an idea. Those drawings are the answers to the challenges I went though, to solve Architectural issues that came with the practice of the profession.

These drawings were produced under very different approaches to the main subject, and go from Sketches to Renderings.

A few of my Renderings pictured here, are not my own designs, but are the solutions to Realtors, Builders, Modular Housing Industries and Private Investors, all of them trying to put a product on the market.

PAULO ZAVALA Architectural and Interior Design
Phone: Email:

design by	drawn by	date	scale	job number

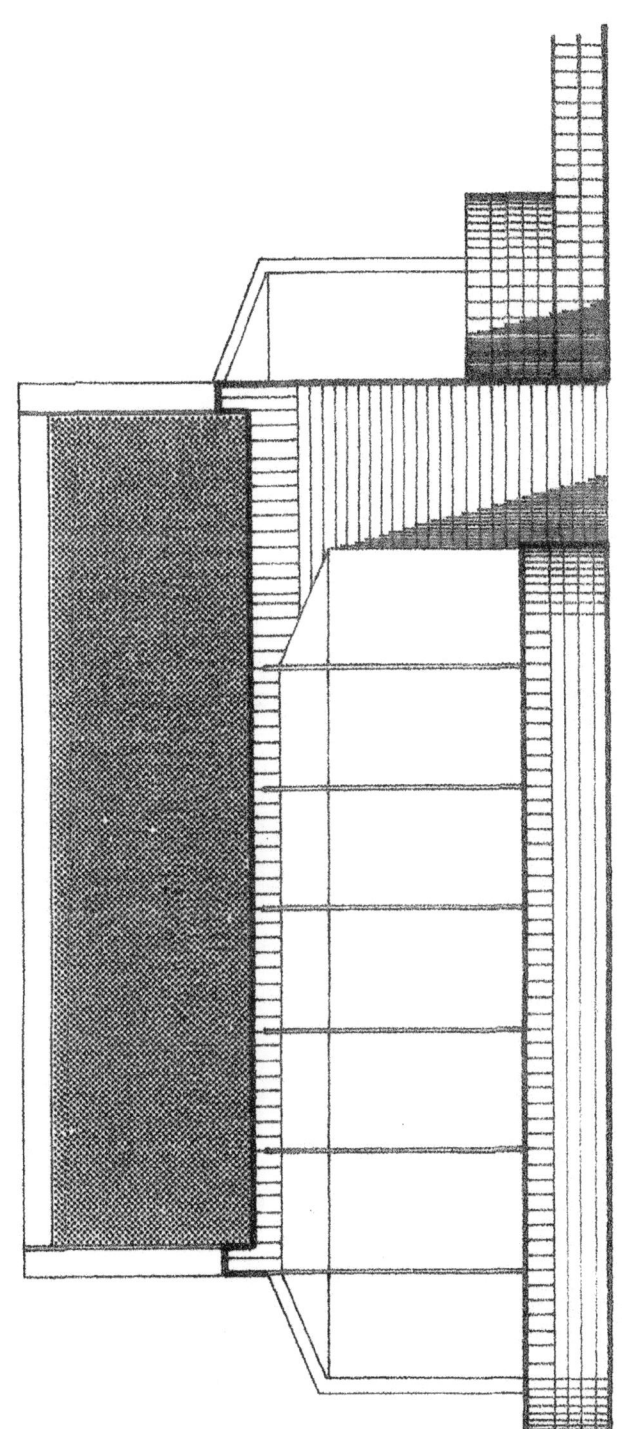

PAULO ZAVALA Architectural and Interior Design
Phone:
Email:

design by	drawn by	date	scale	job number

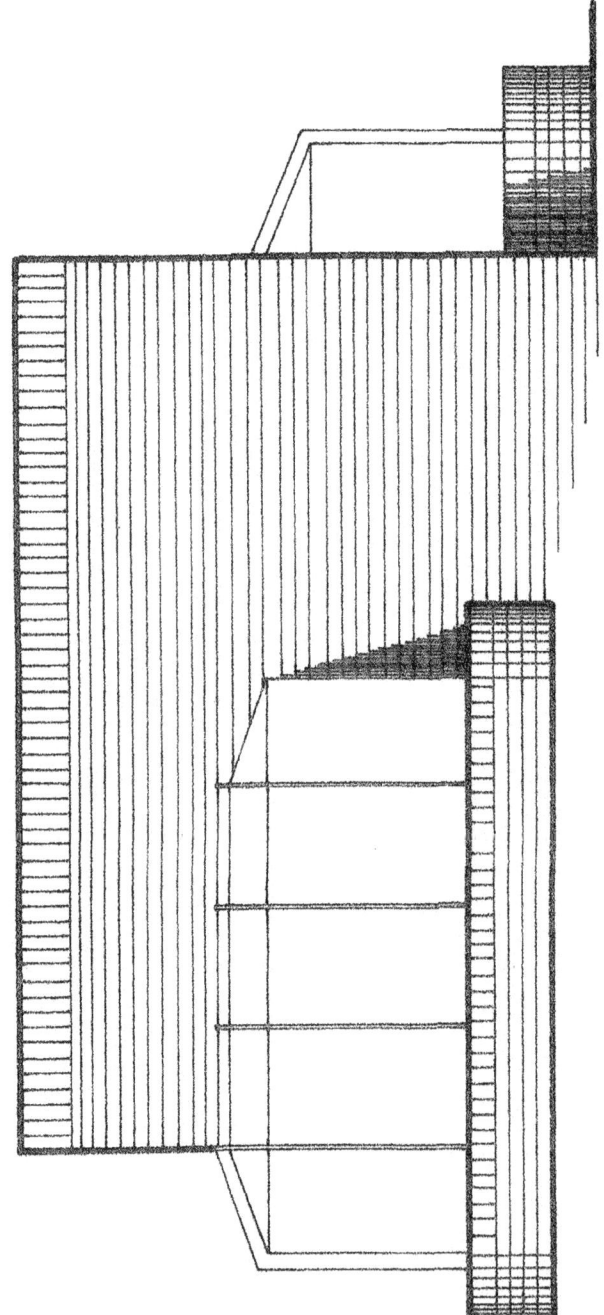

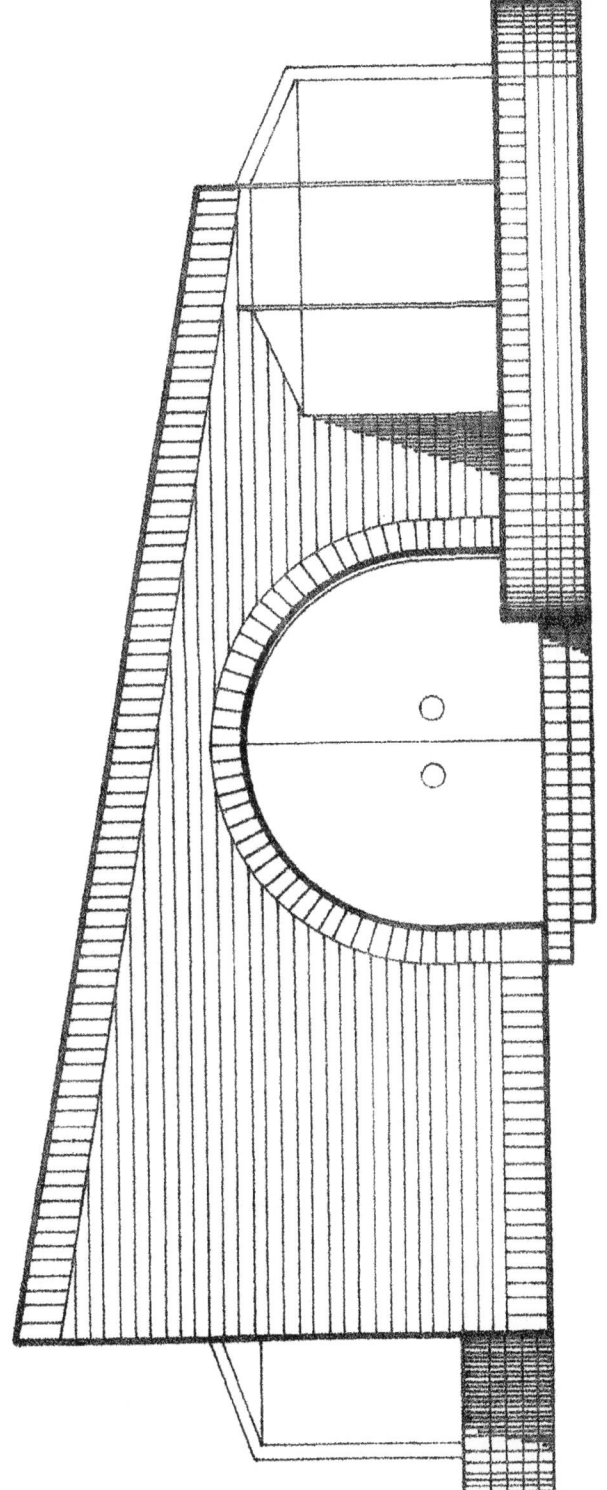

PAULO ZAVALA Architectural and Interior Design
Phone: Email:

design by	drawn by	date	scale	job number

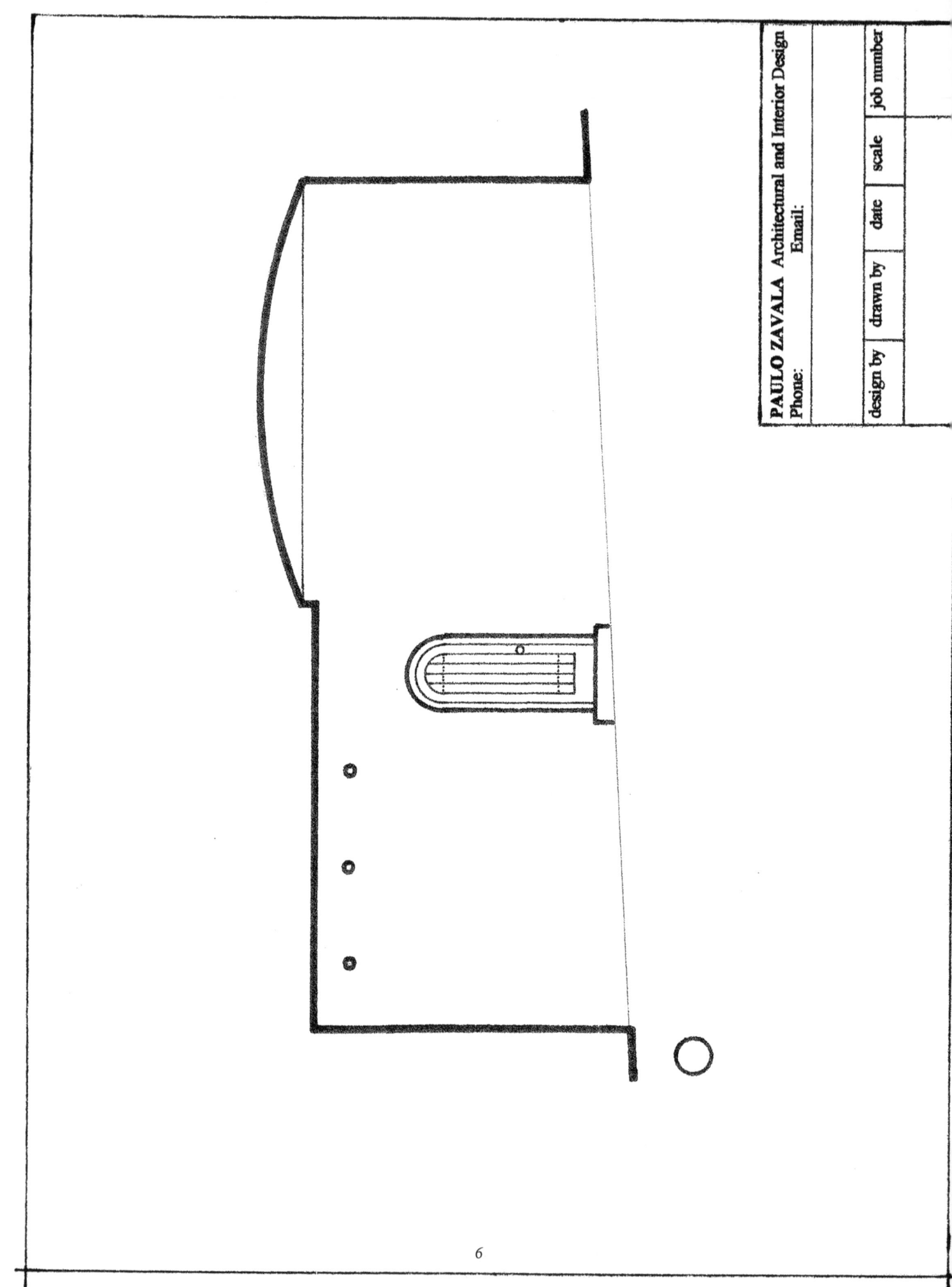

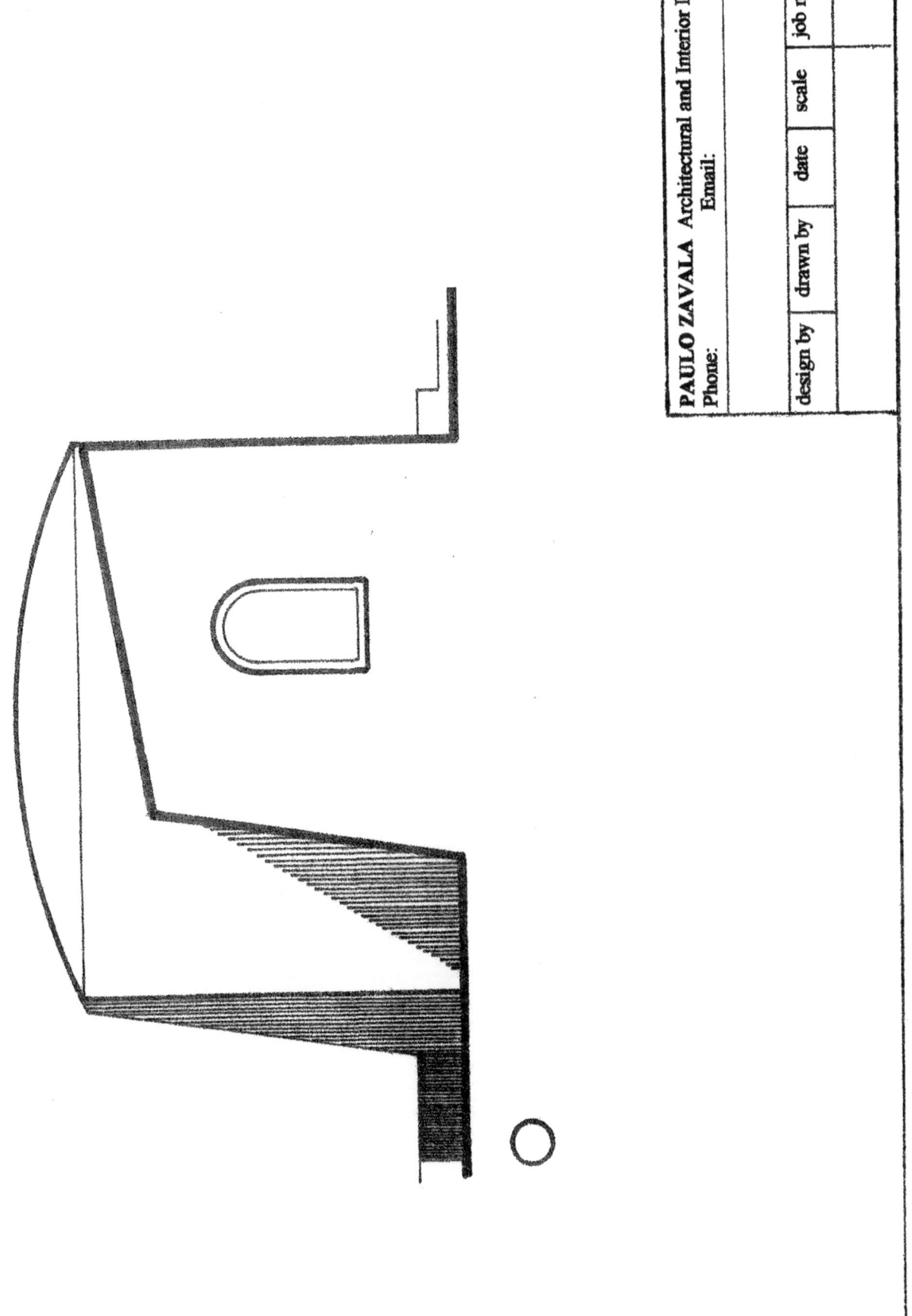

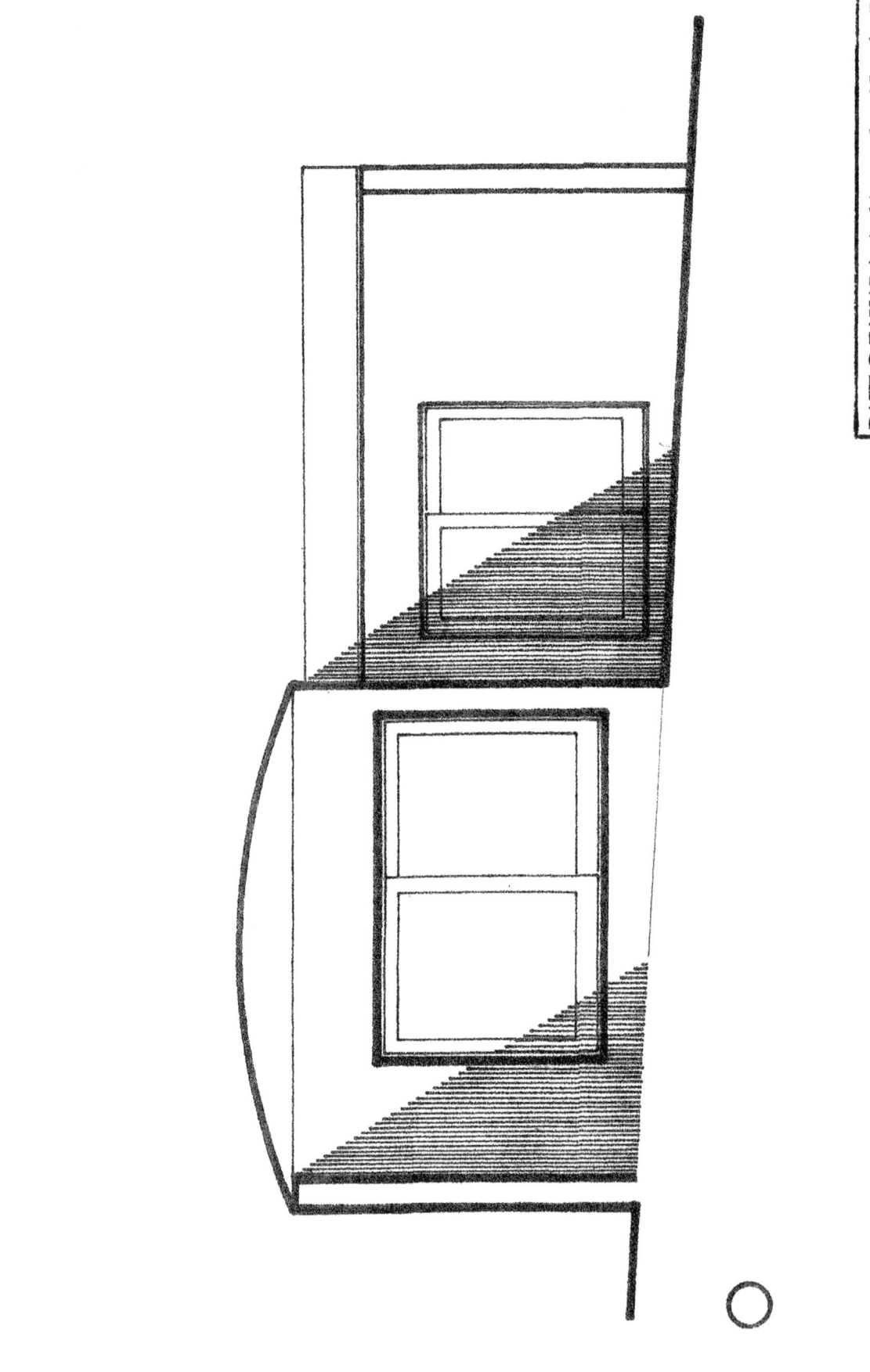

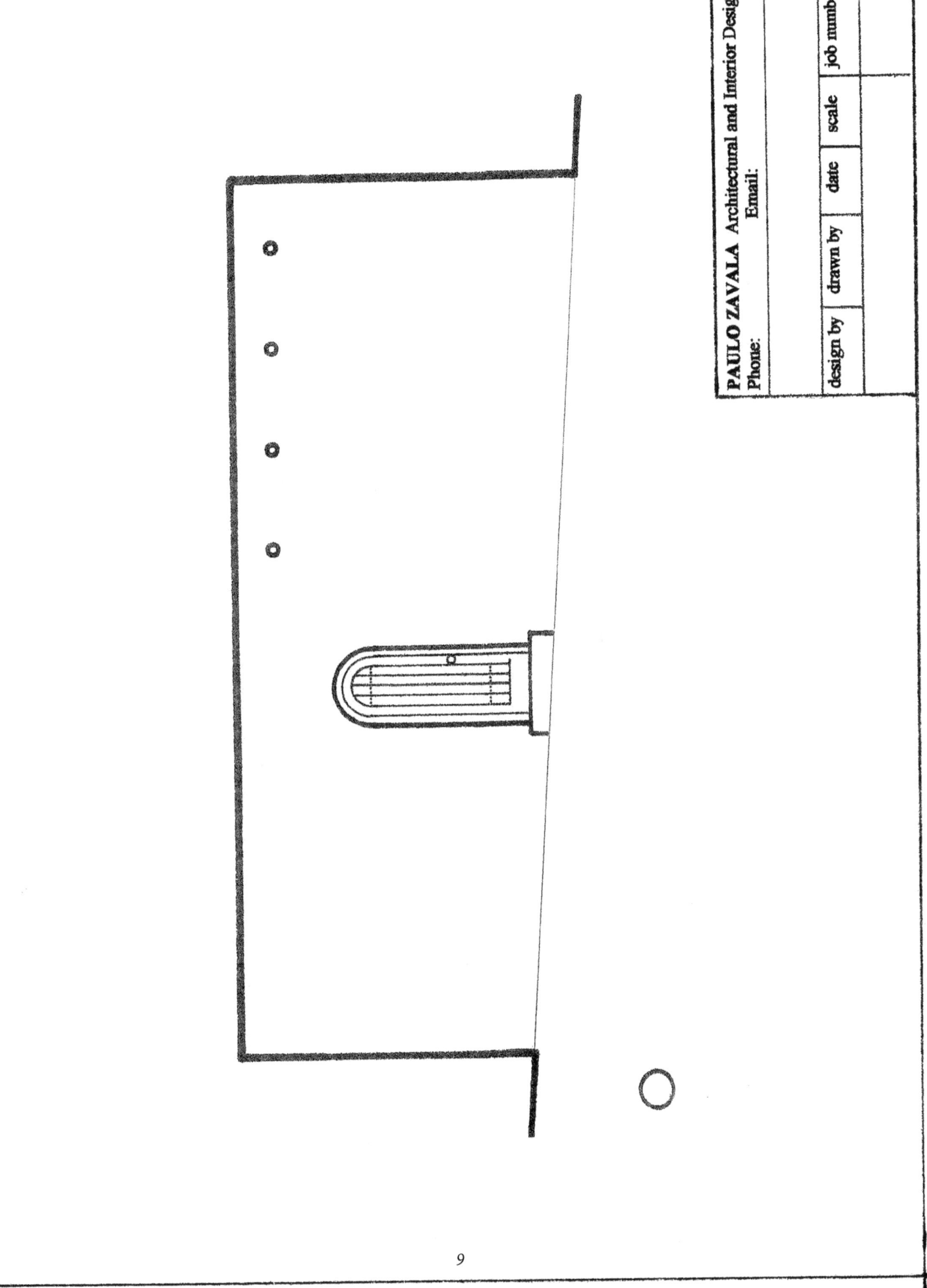

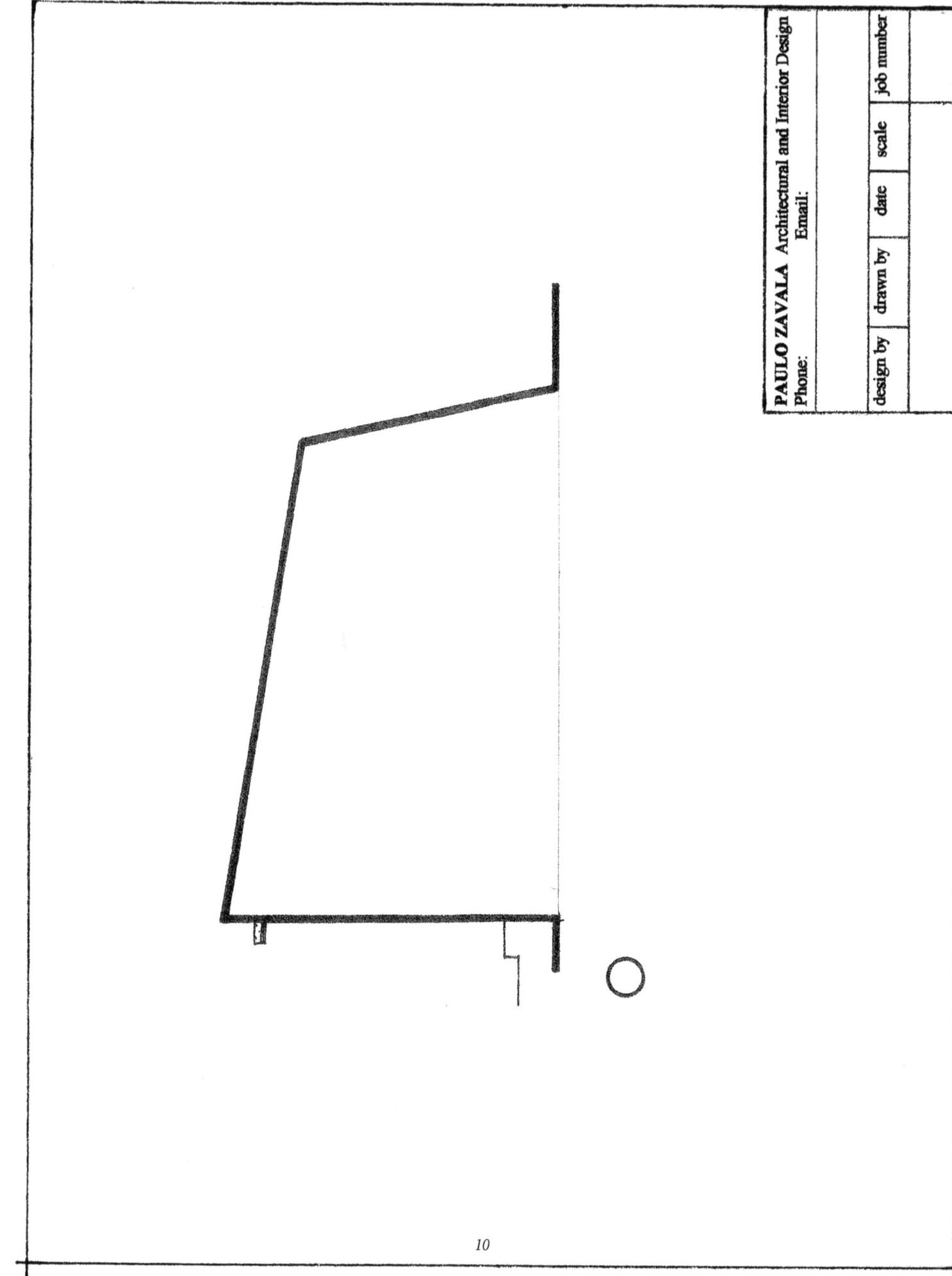

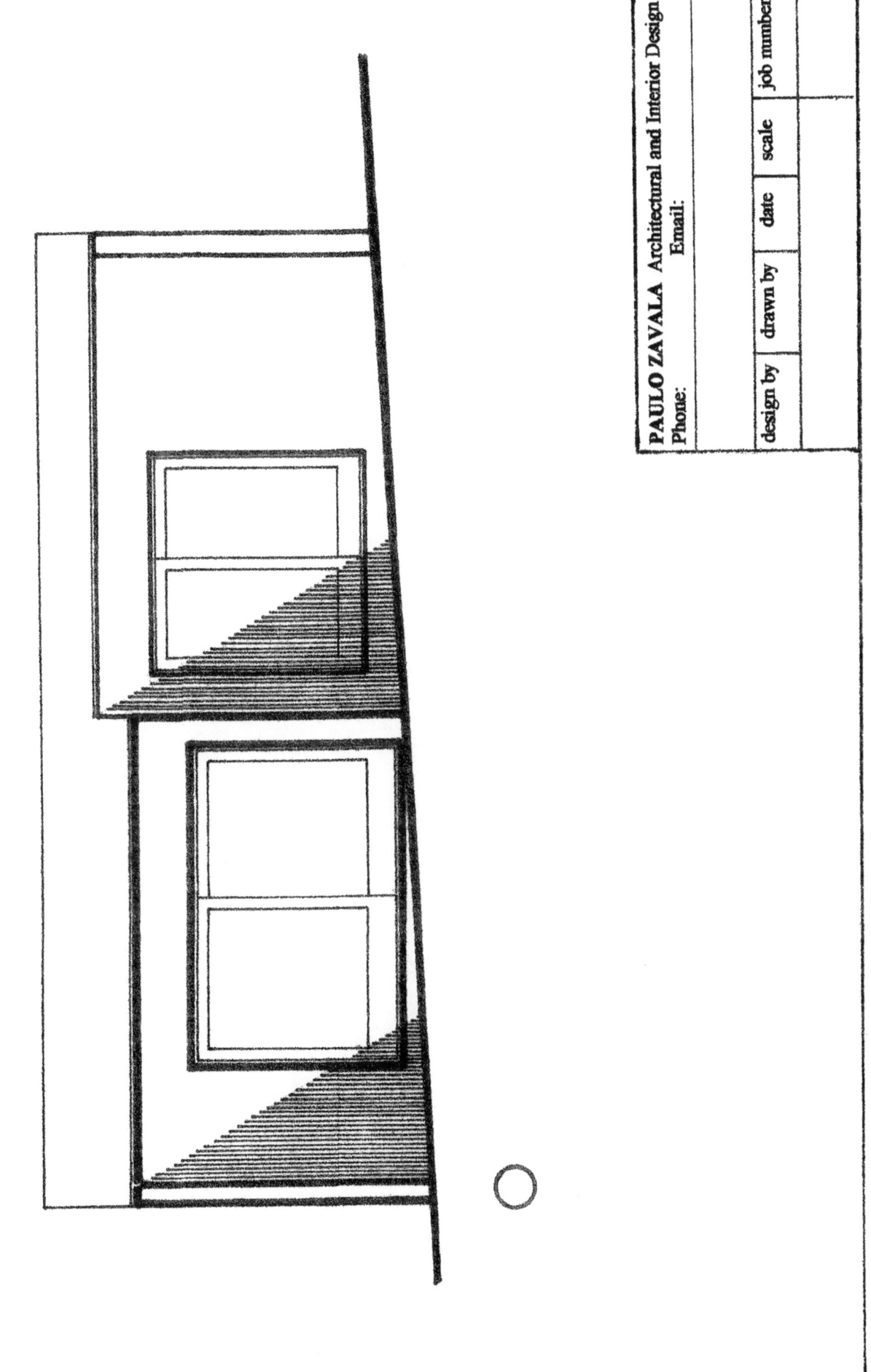

PAULO ZAVALA Architectural and Interior Design
Phone: Email:

design by	drawn by	date	scale	job number

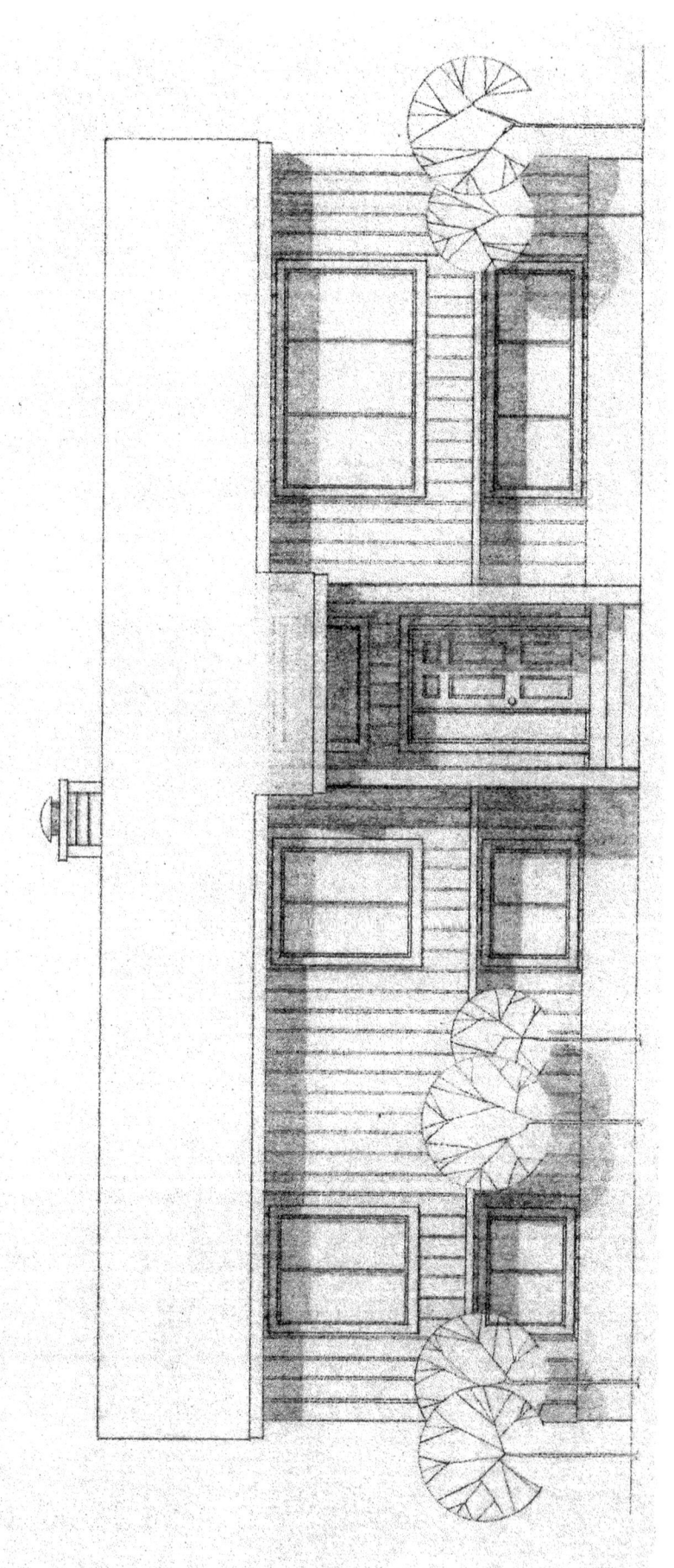

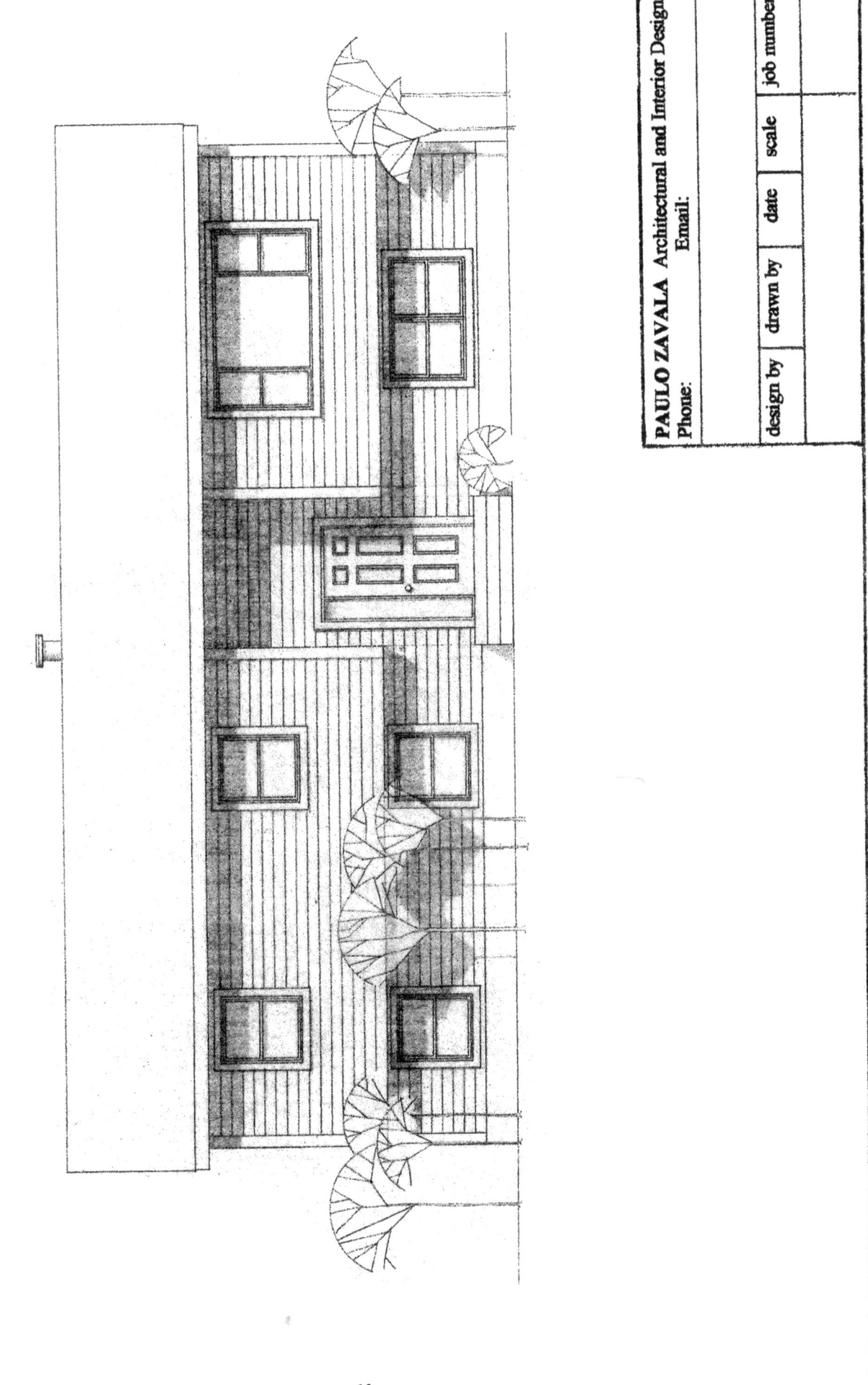

PAULO ZAVALA Architectural and Interior Design
Phone: Email:

design by	drawn by	date	scale	job number

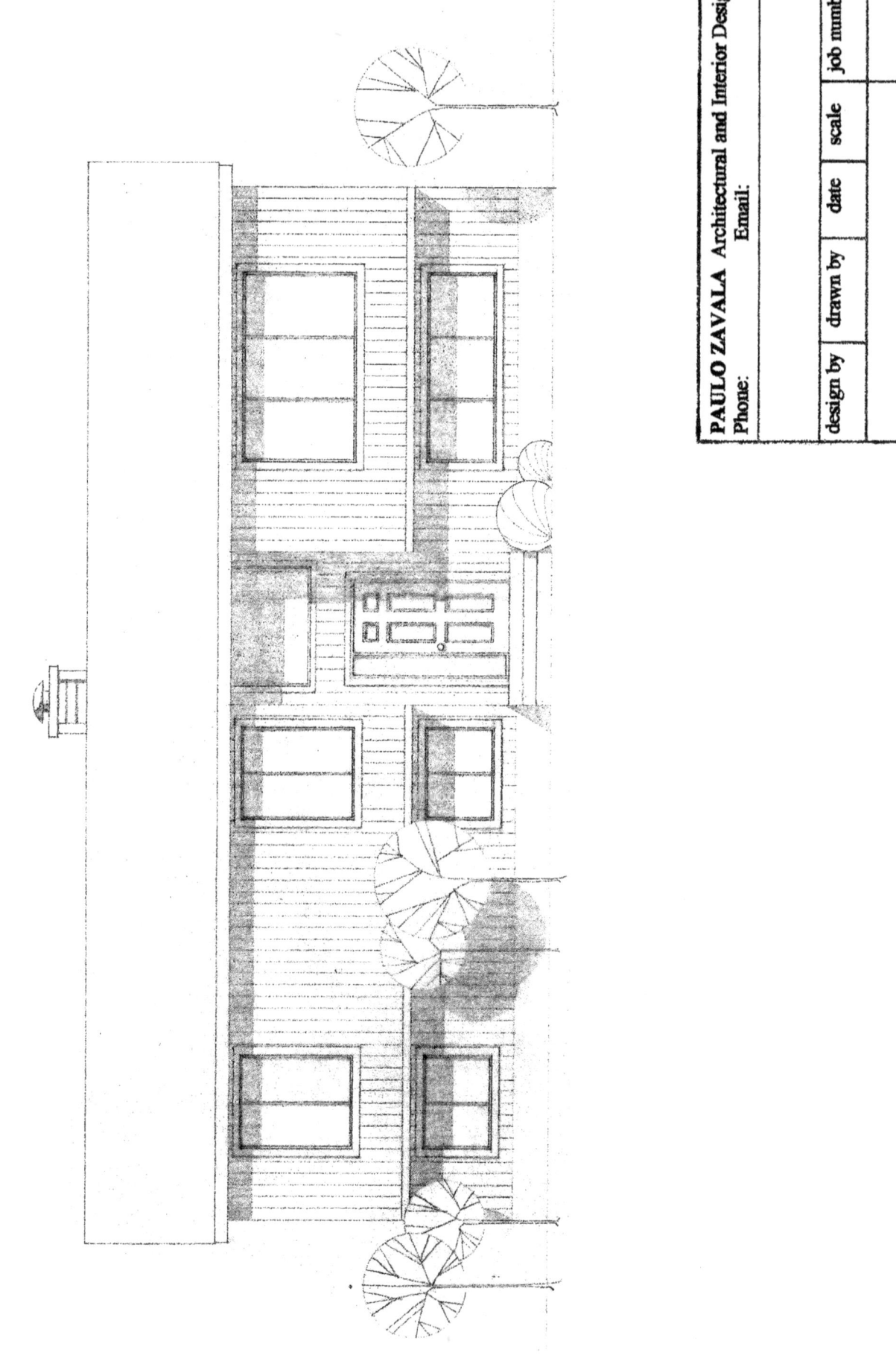

PAULO ZAVALA Architectural and Interior Design
Phone:
Email:

design by | drawn by | date | scale | job number

PAULO ZAVALA Architectural and Interior Design
Phone:
Email:

design by	drawn by	date	scale	job number

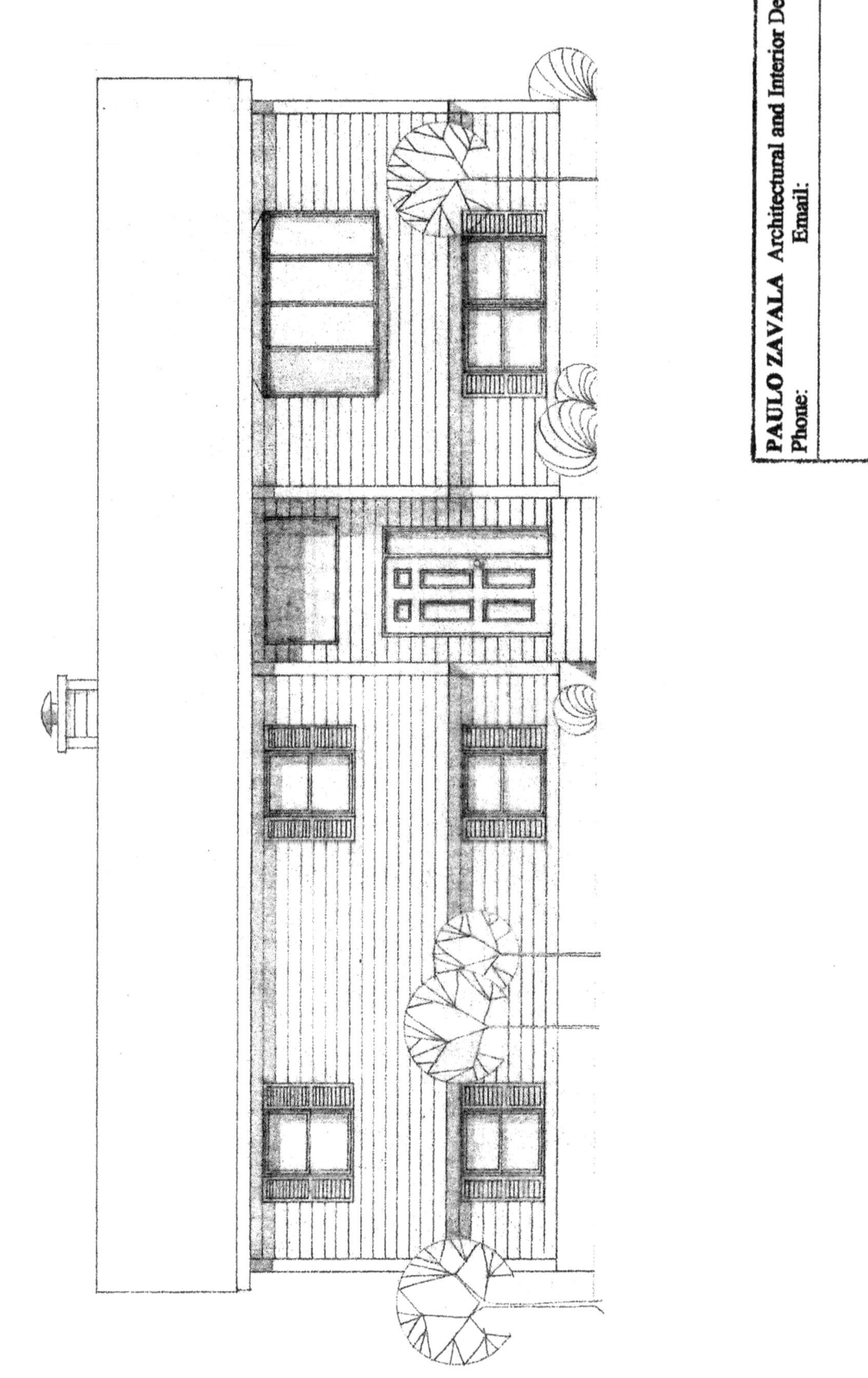

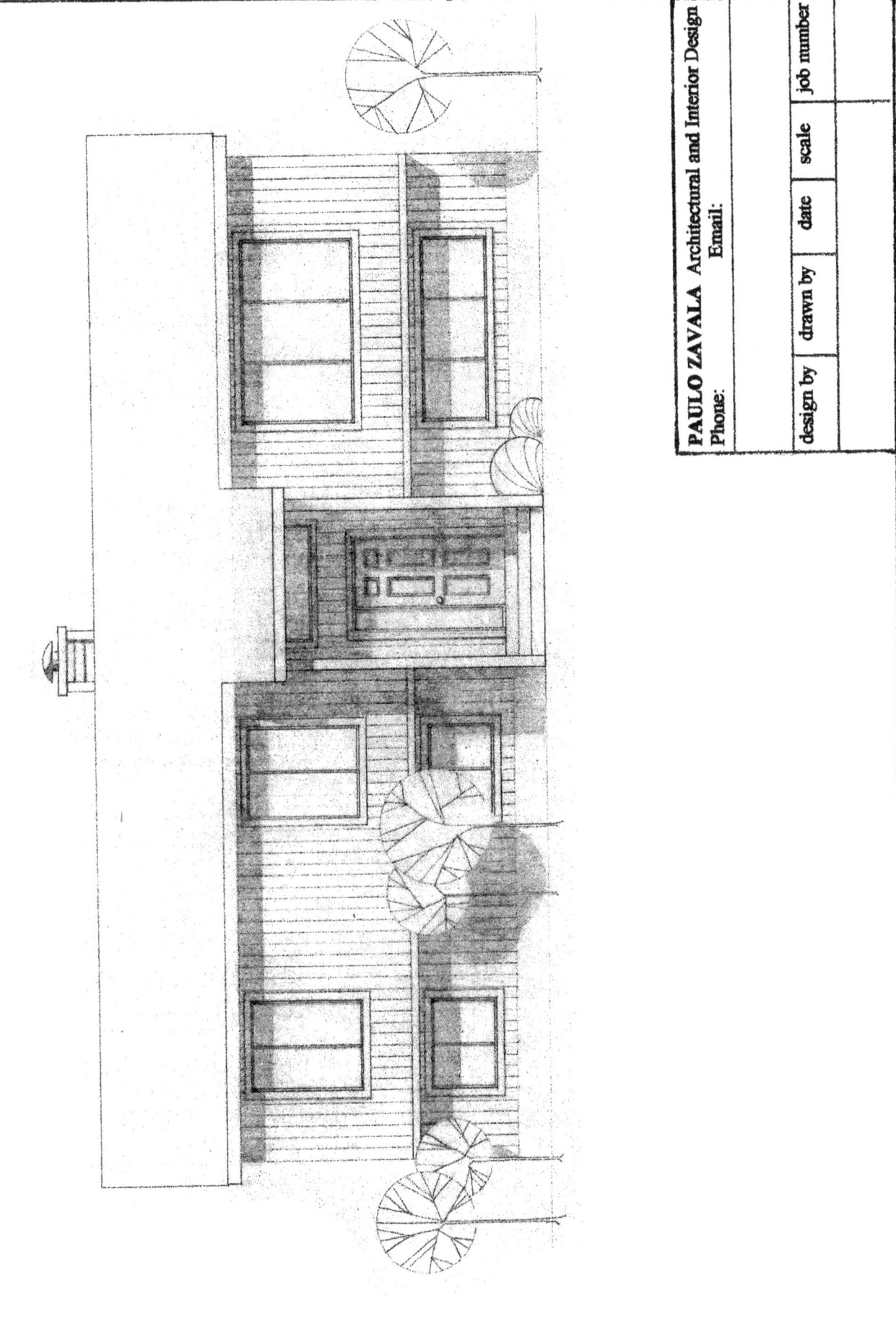

PAULO ZAVALA Architectural and Interior Design
Phone:
Email:

design by	drawn by	date	scale	job number

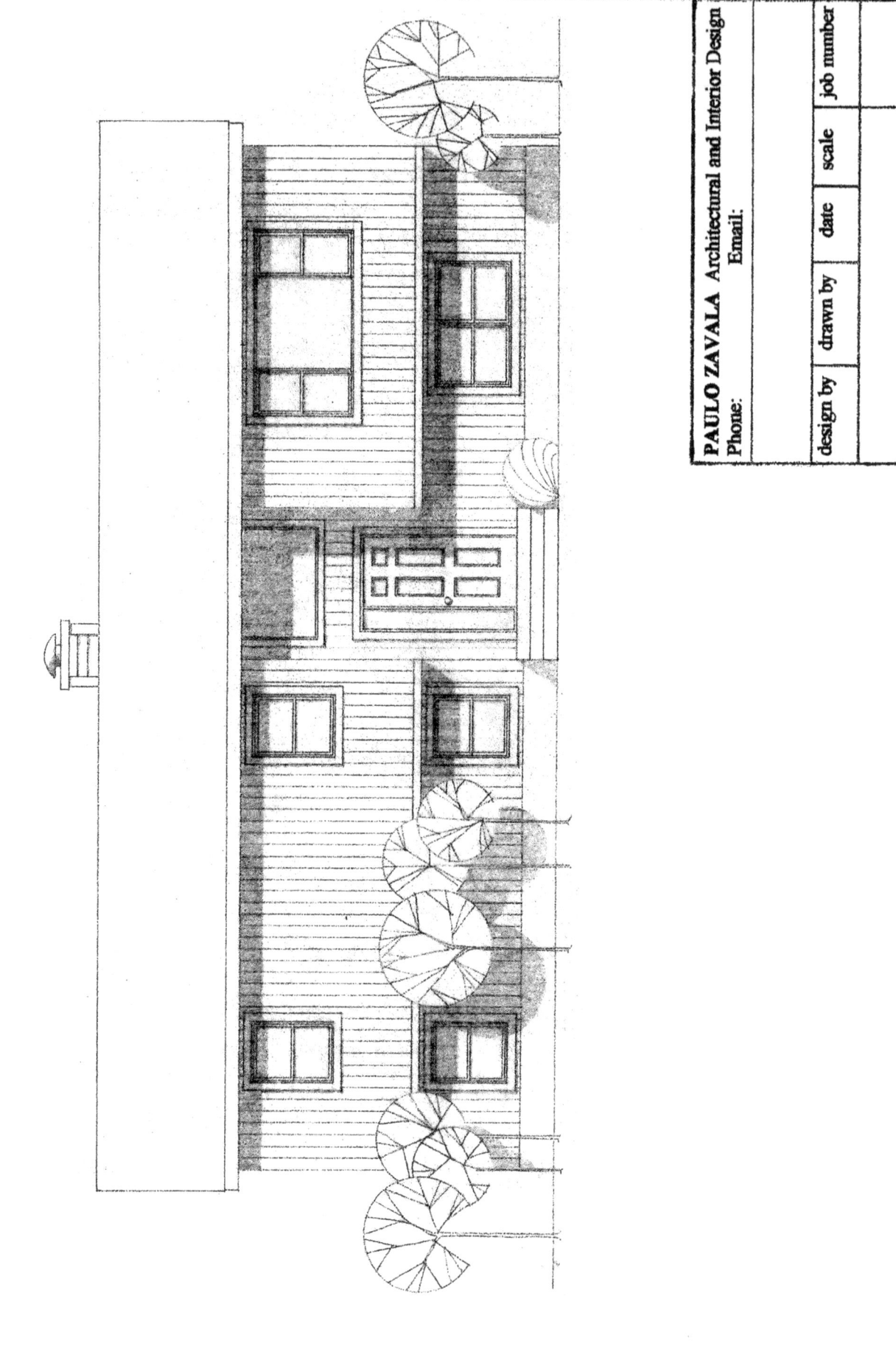

PAULO ZAVALA Architectural and Interior Design
Phone:
Email:

design by	drawn by	date	scale	job number

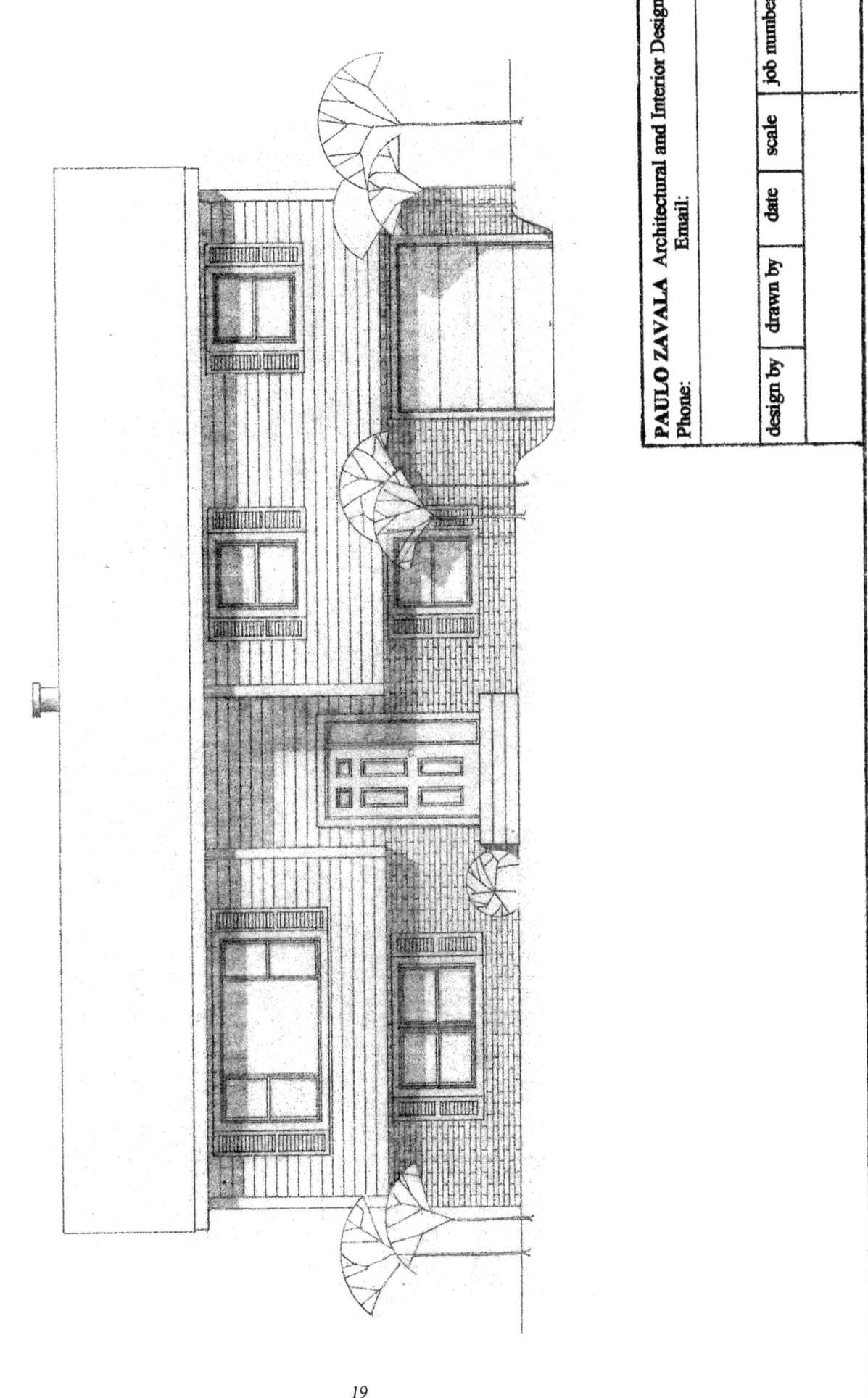

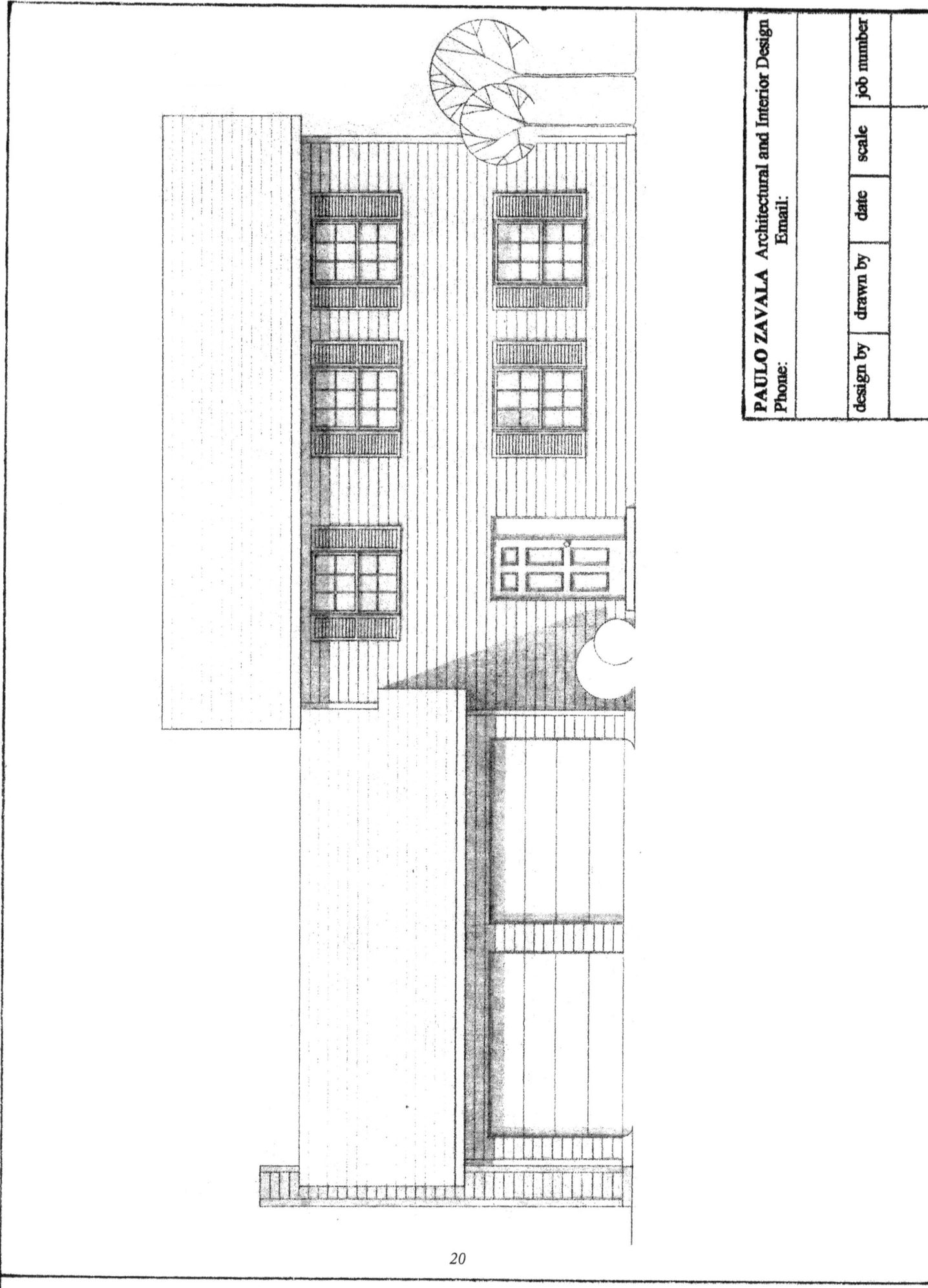

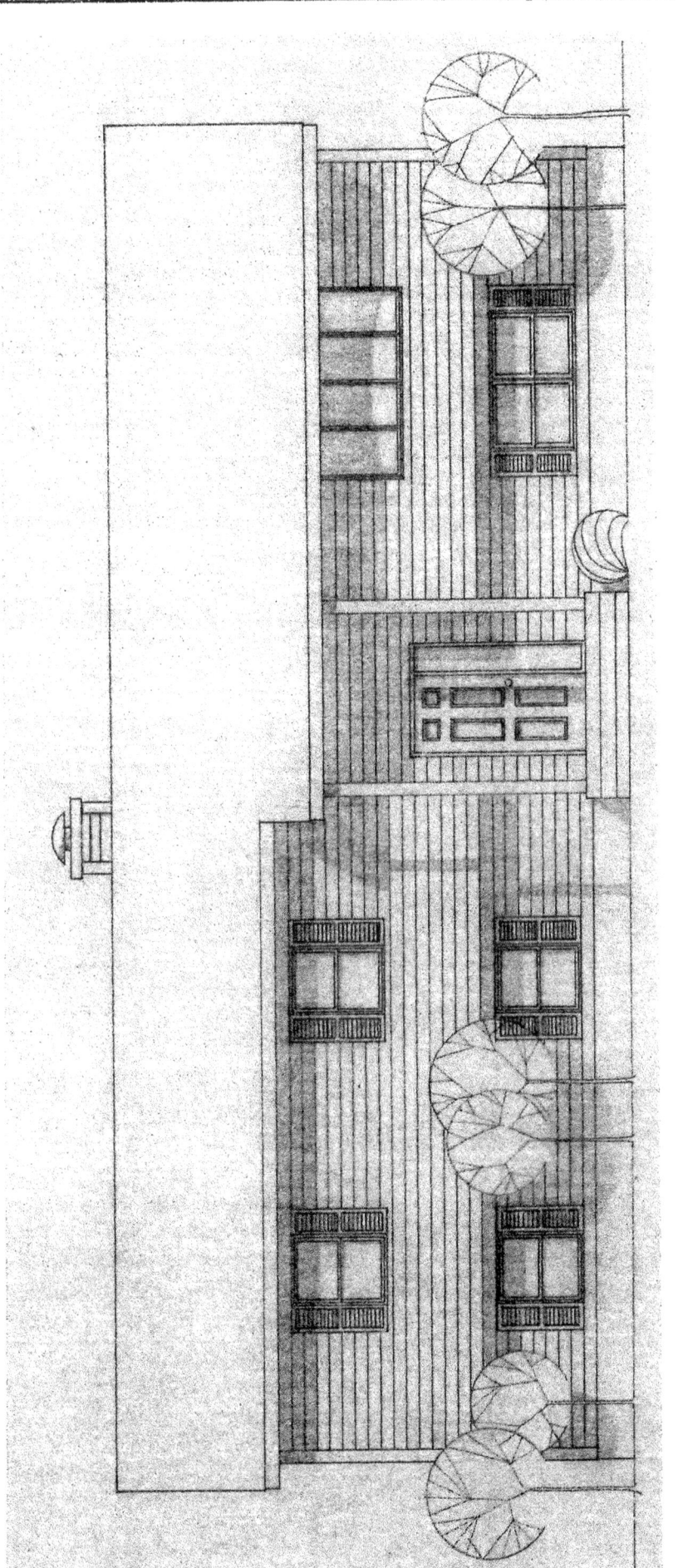

PAULO ZAVALA Architectural and Interior Design
Phone:
Email:

design by	drawn by	date	scale	job number

PAULO ZAVALA Architectural and Interior Design
Phone:
Email:

design by | drawn by | date | scale | job number

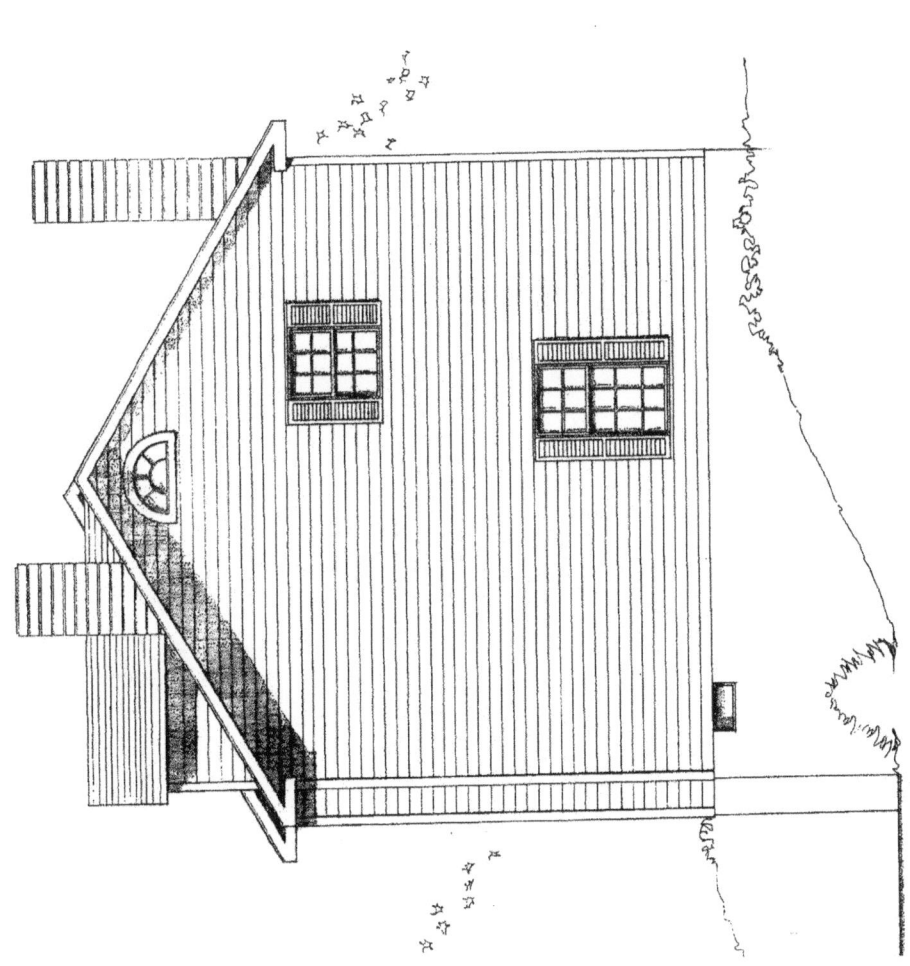

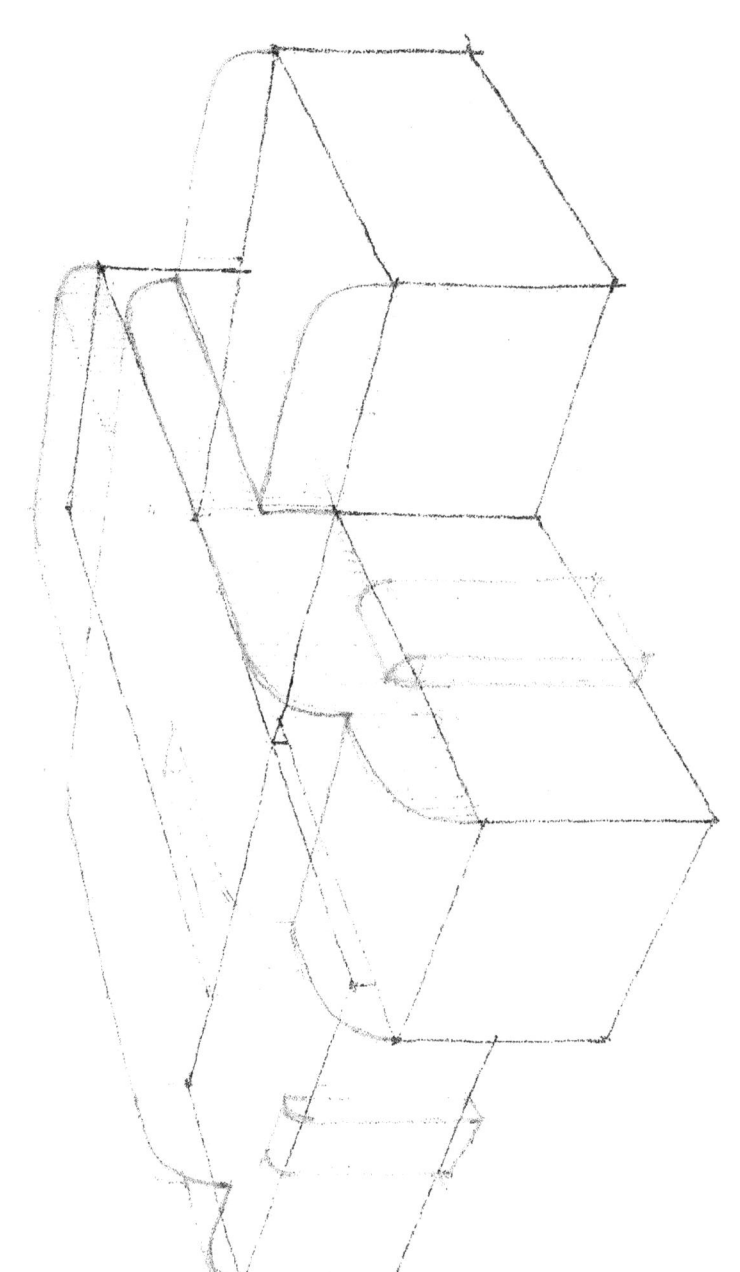

PAULO ZAVALA Architectural and Interior Design
Phone: Email:

design by	drawn by	date	scale	job number

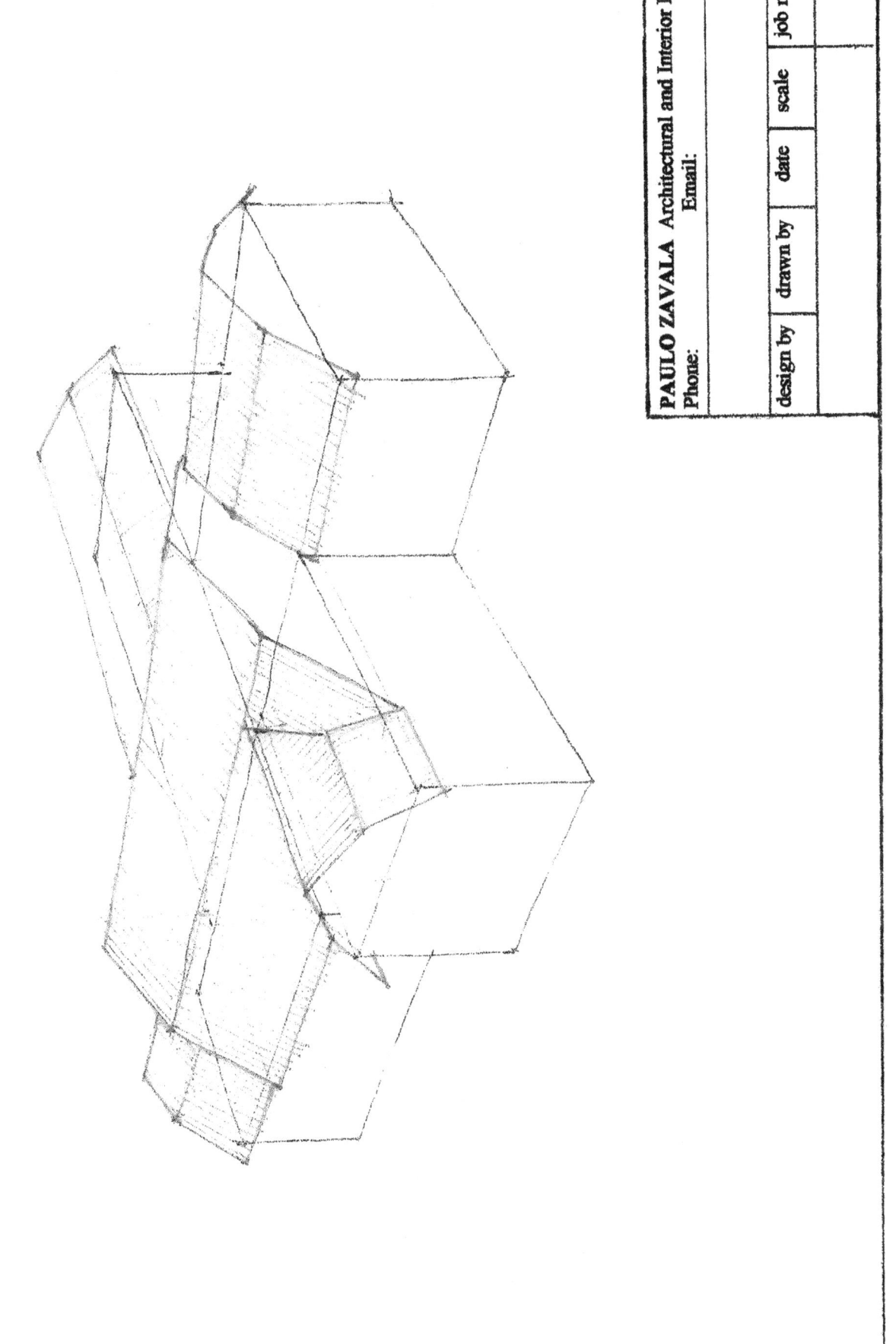

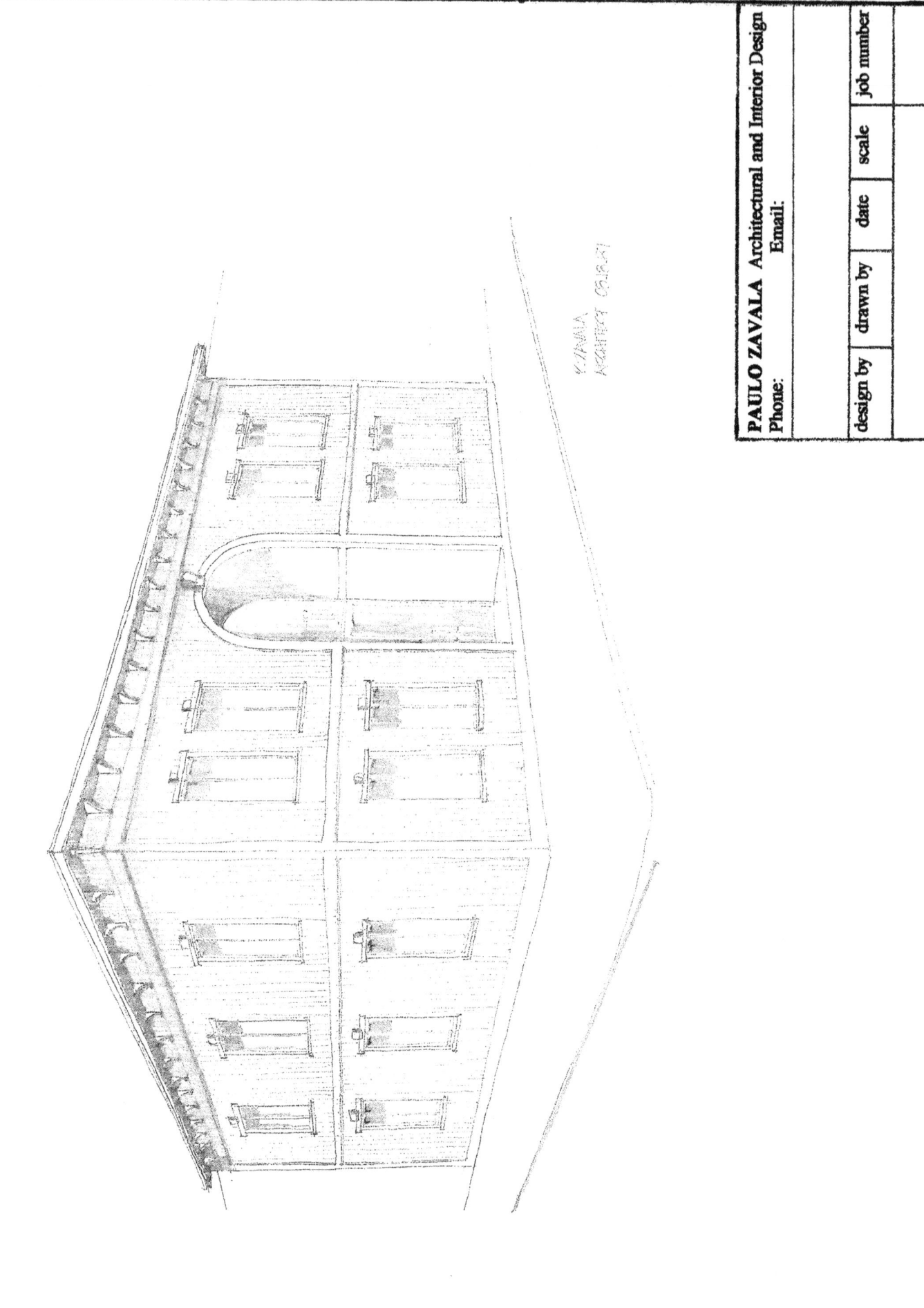

PAULO ZAVALA Architectural and Interior Design

Phone: Email:

design by	drawn by	date	scale	job number

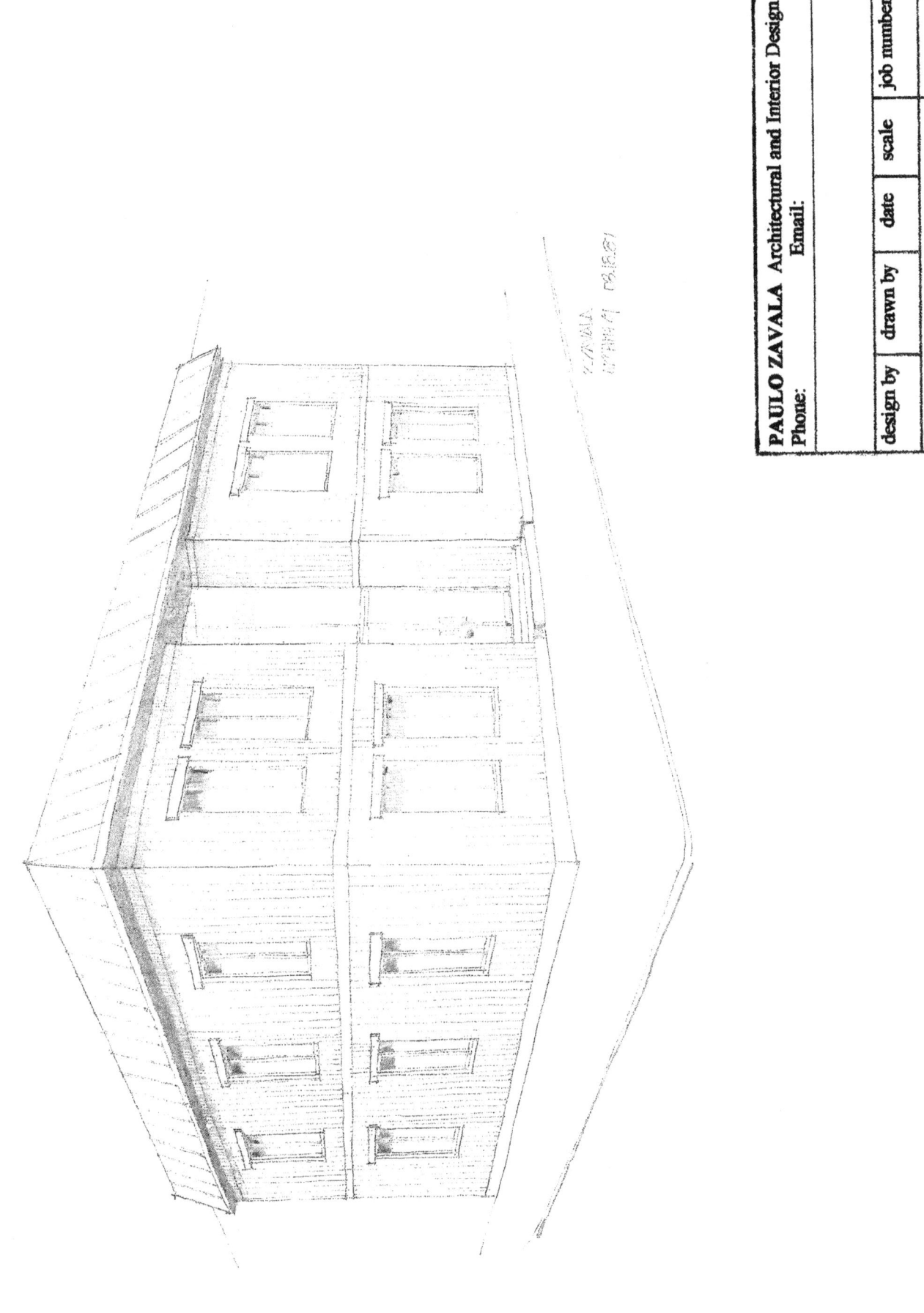

PAULO ZAVALA Architectural and Interior Design
Phone:
Email:

design by	drawn by	date	scale	job number

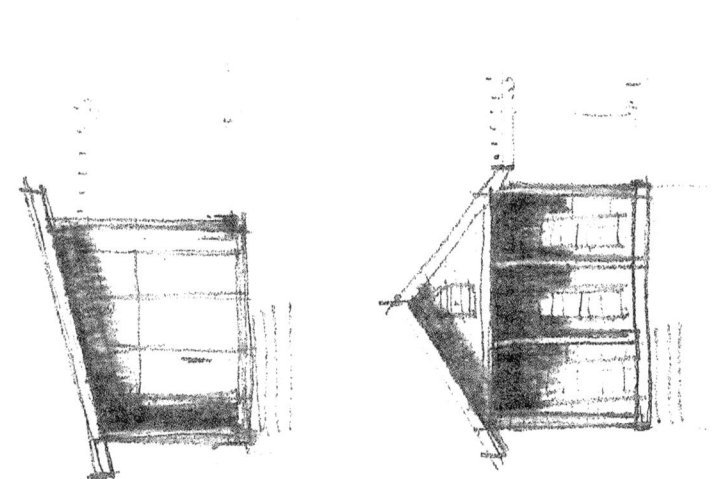
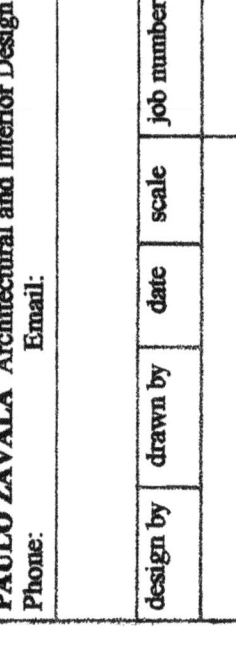

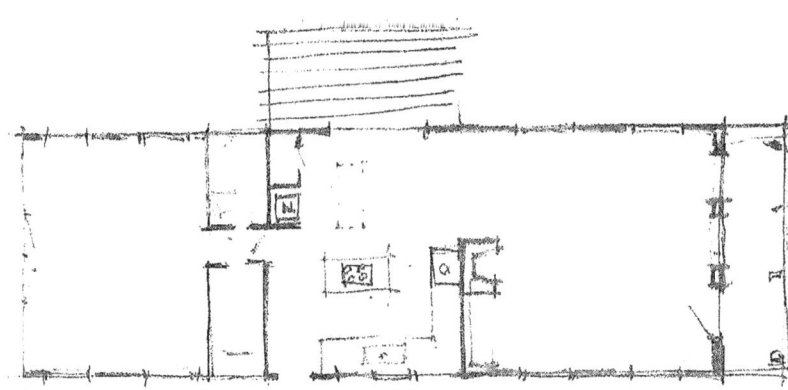

PAULO ZAVALA Architectural and Interior Design
Phone:
Email:

design by | drawn by | date | scale | job number

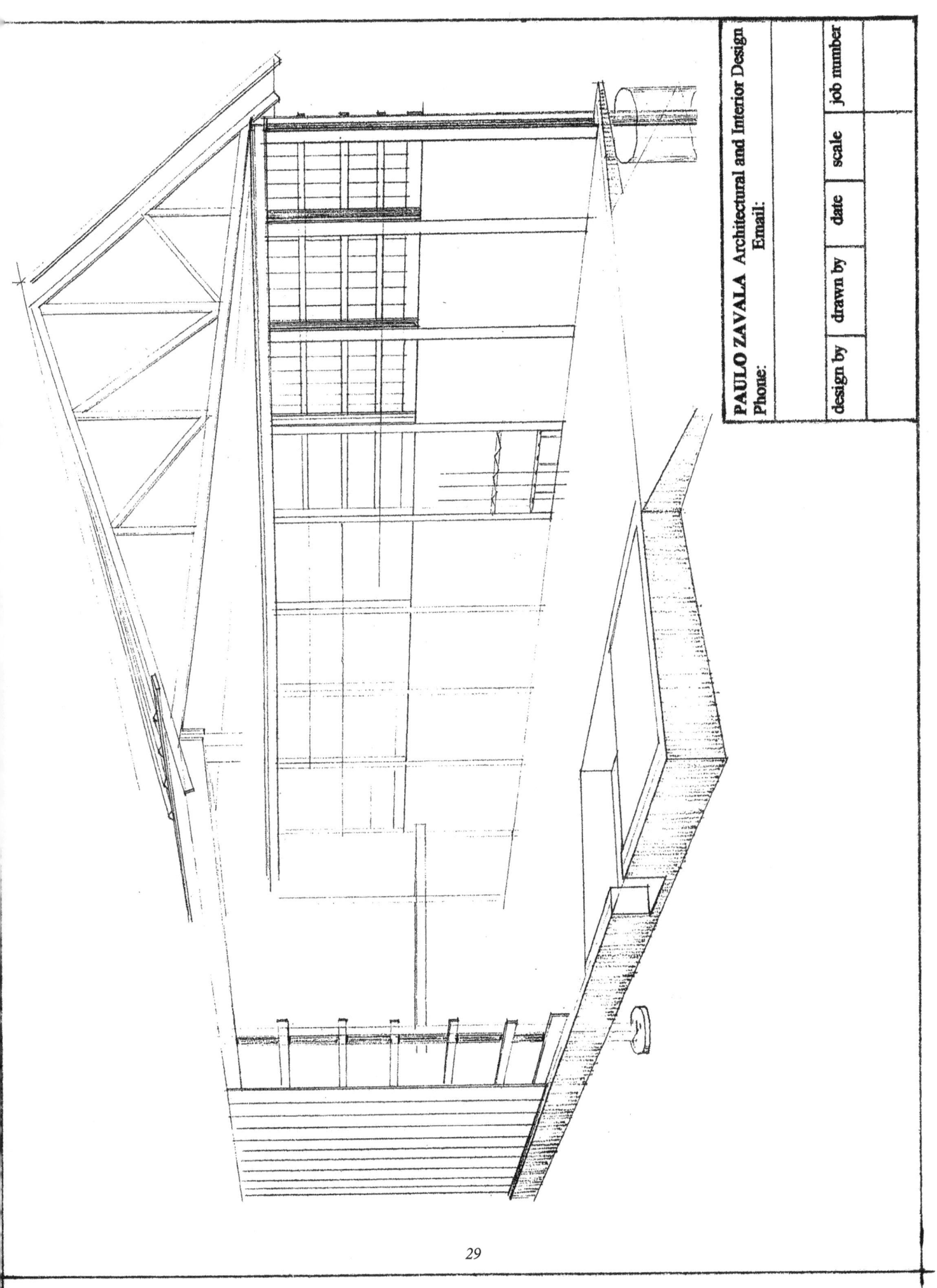

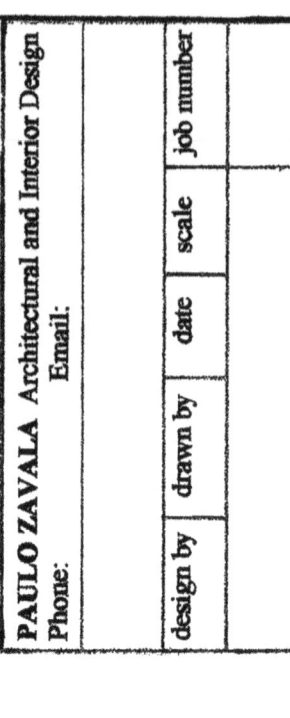

PAULO ZAVALA Architectural and Interior Design
Phone: Email:

design by	drawn by	date	scale	job number

ELEVATION EAST

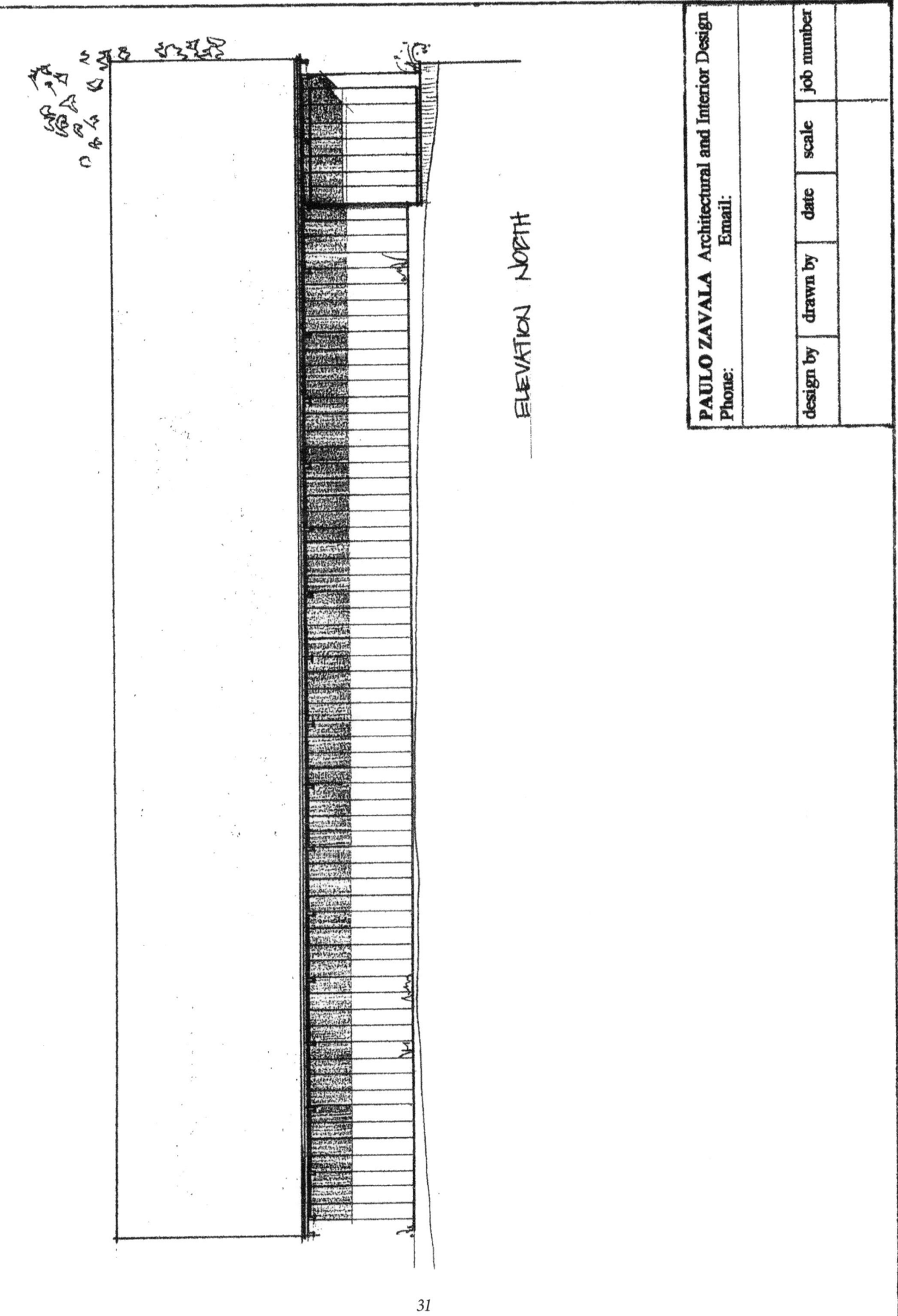

ELEVATION NORTH

PAULO ZAVALA Architectural and Interior Design
Phone: Email:

design by	drawn by	date	scale	job number

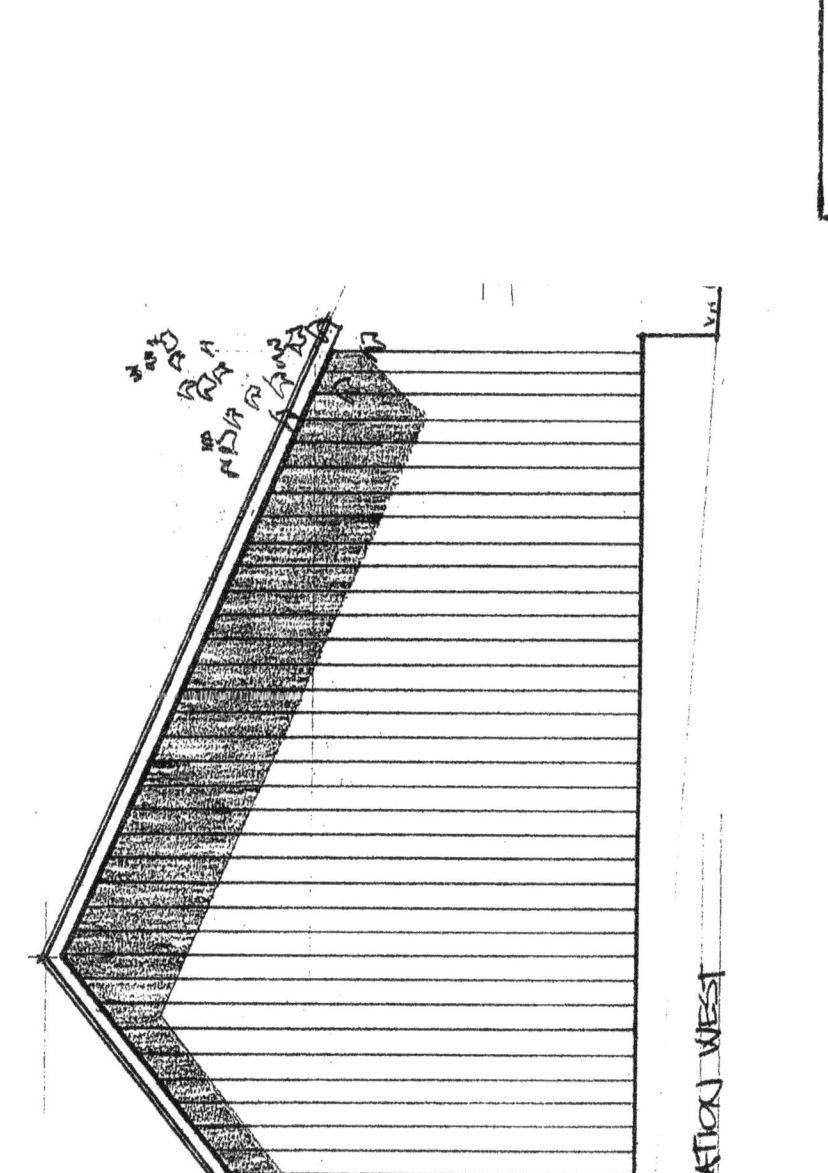

ELEVATION WEST

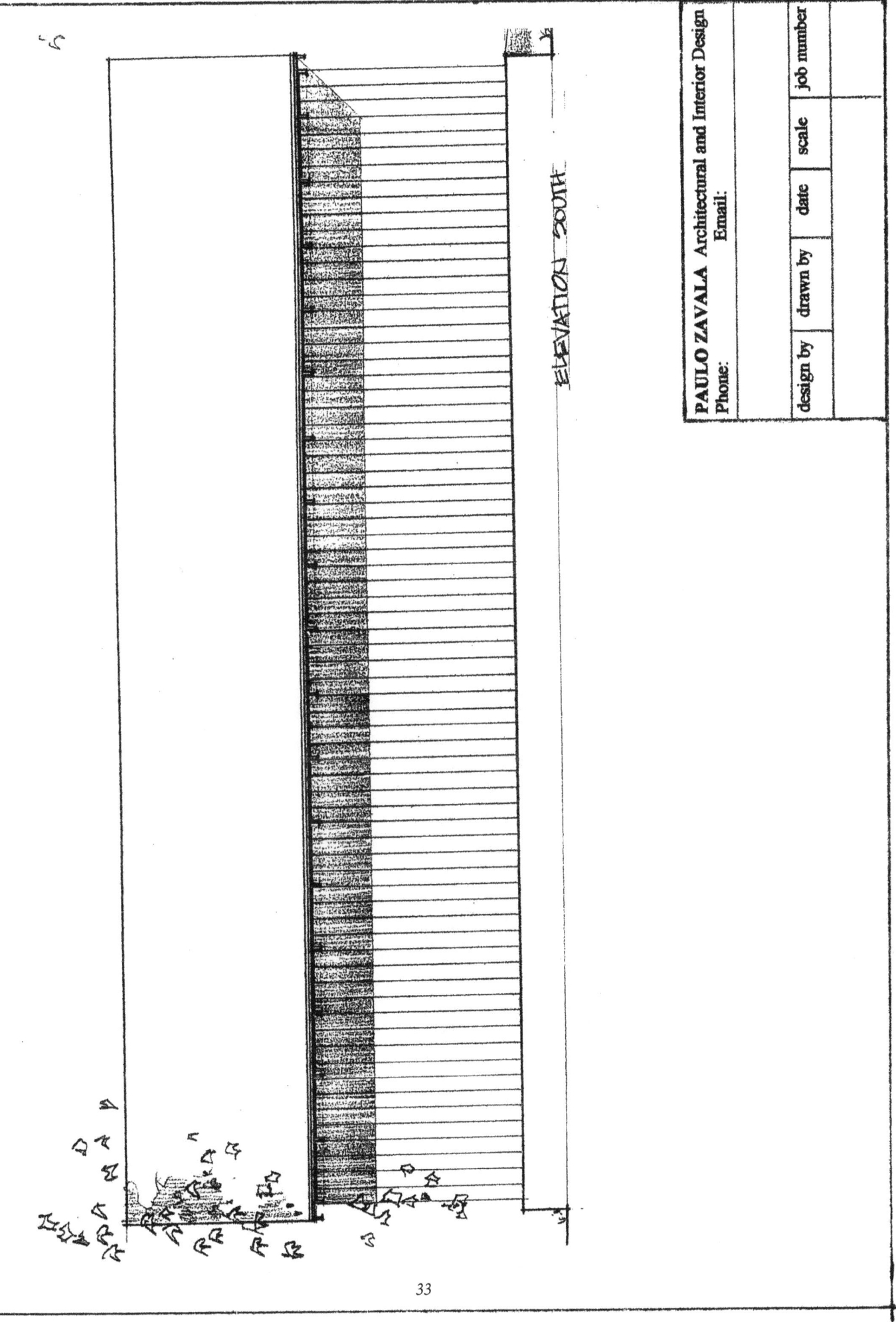

ELEVATION SOUTH

PAULO ZAVALA Architectural and Interior Design
Phone: Email:

design by	drawn by	date	scale	job number

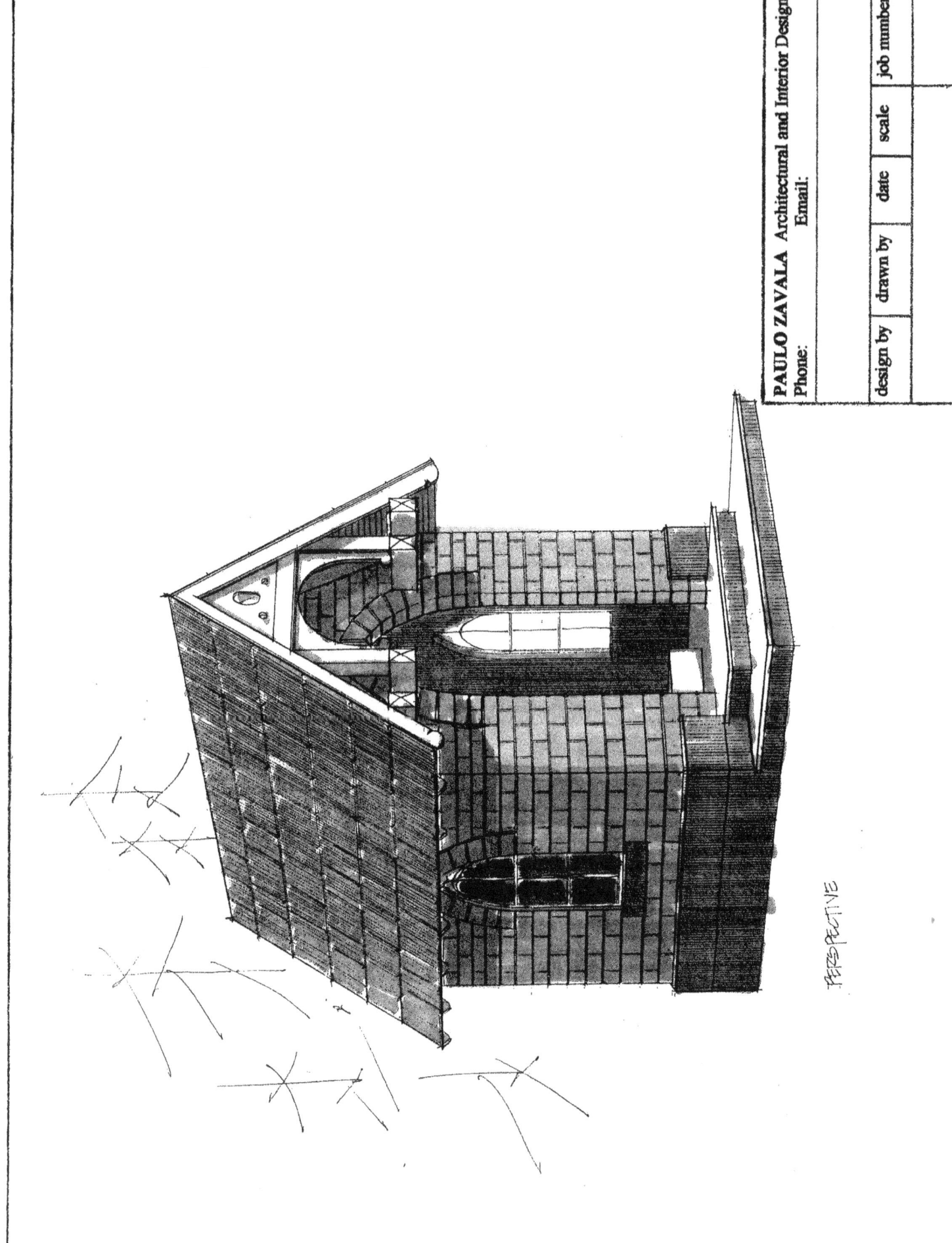

PERSPECTIVE

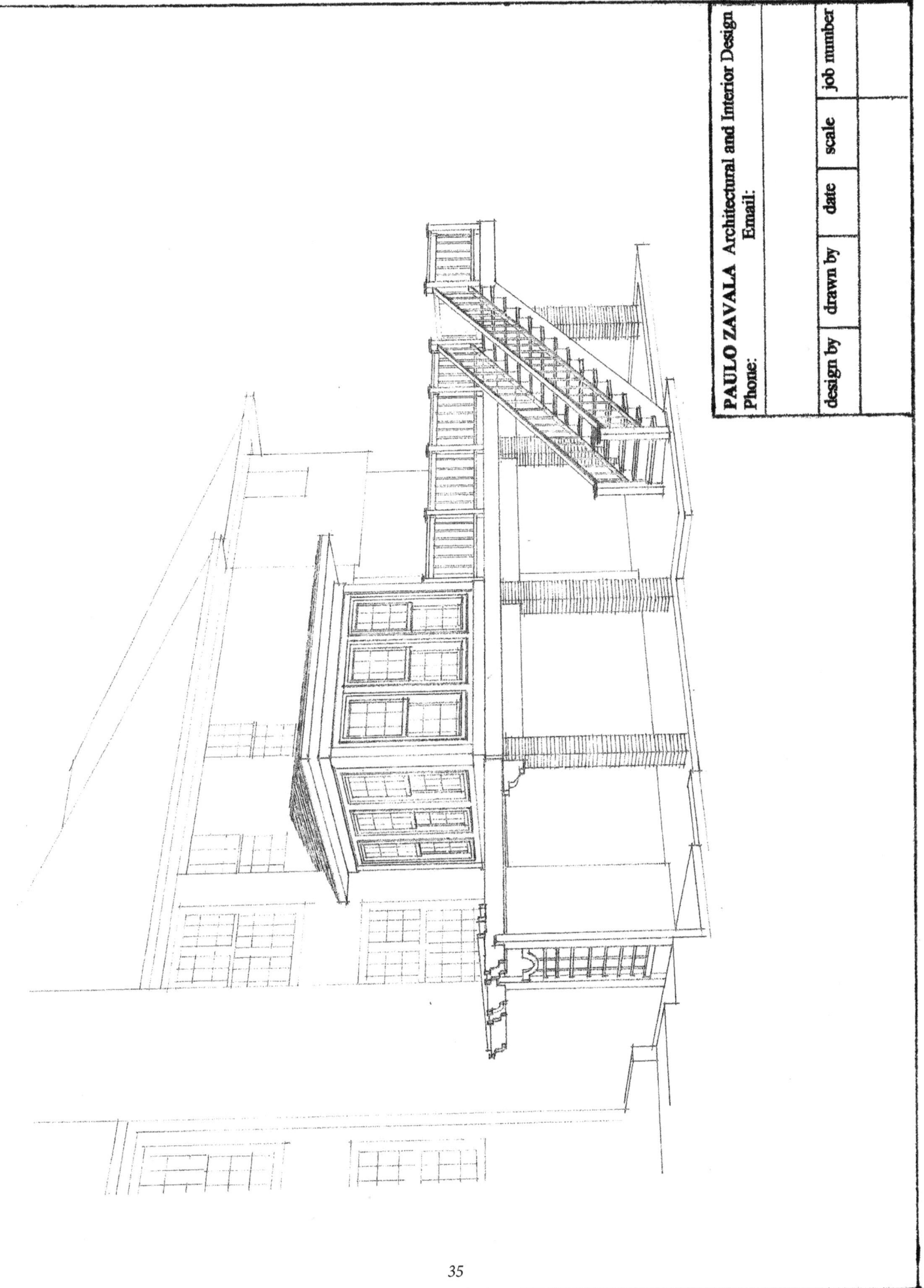

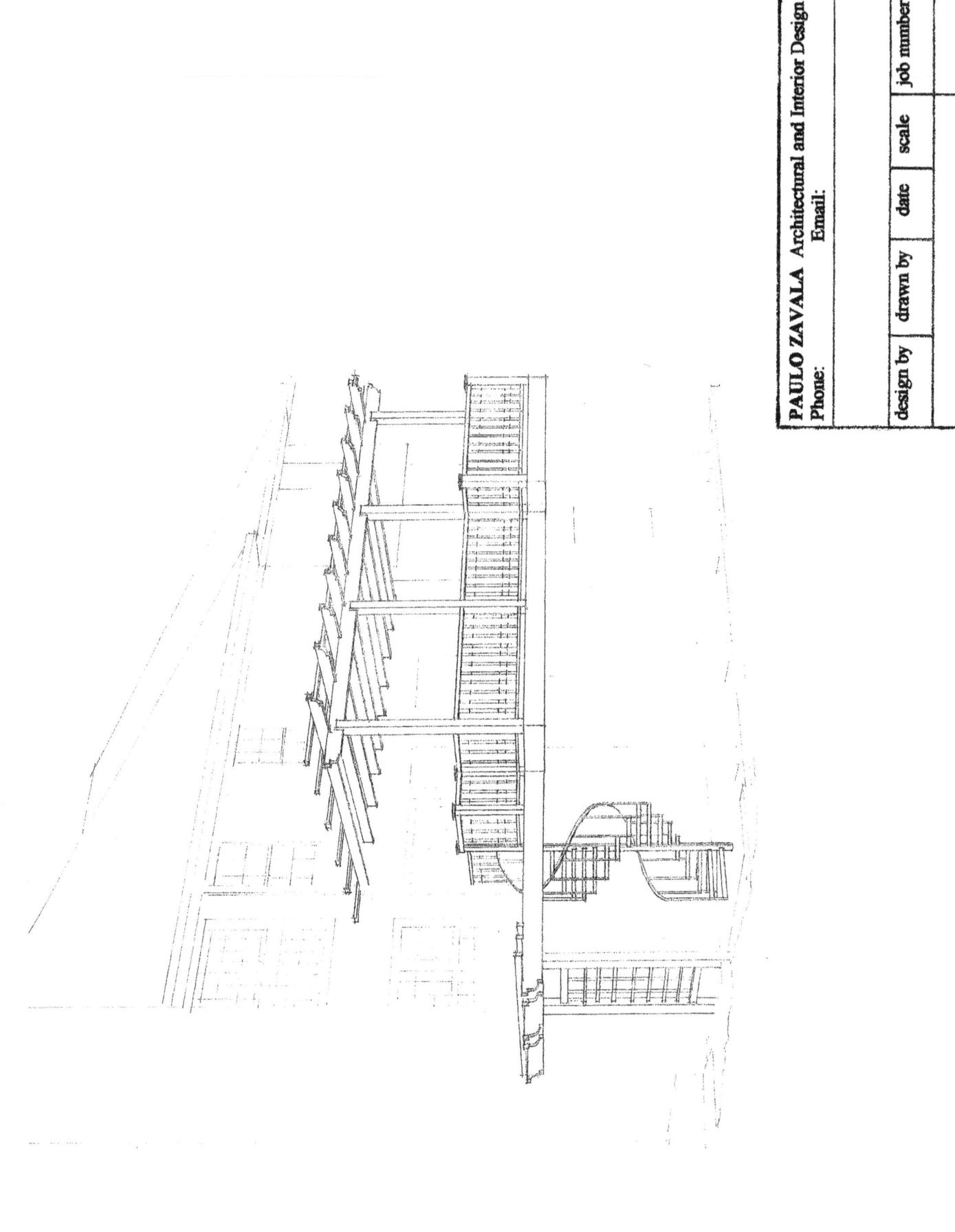

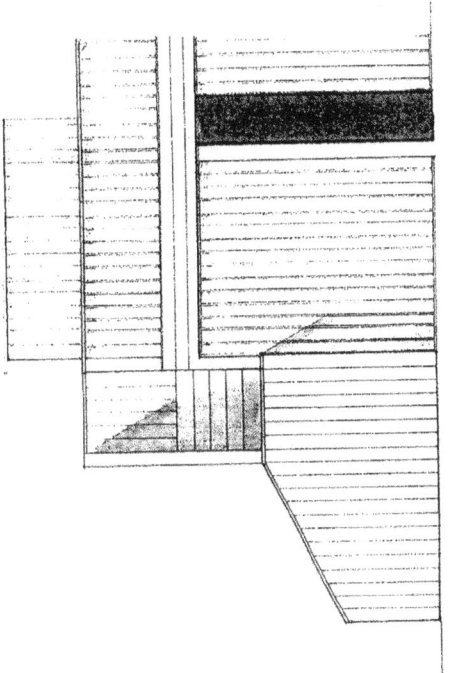

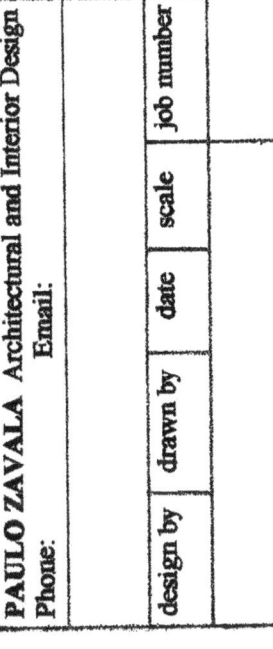

PAULO ZAVALA Architectural and Interior Design
Phone:
Email:

design by	drawn by	date	scale	job number

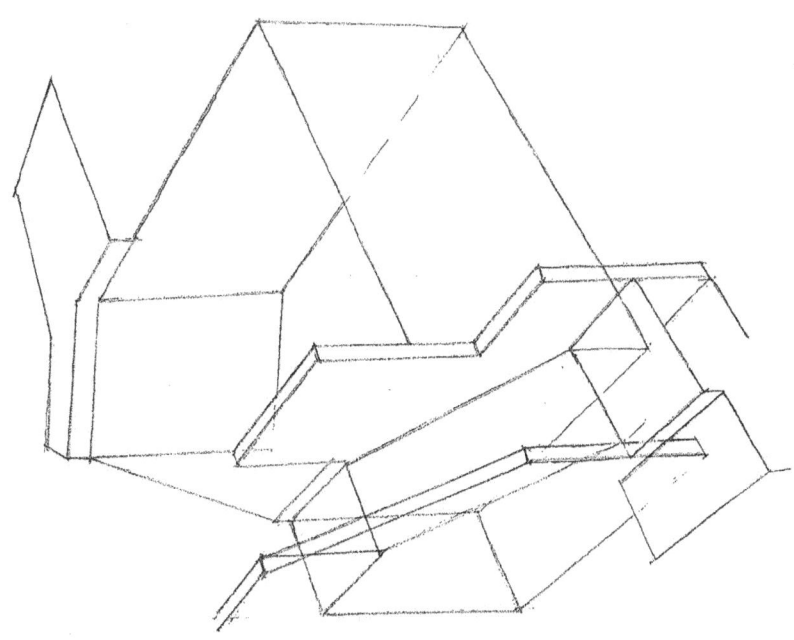

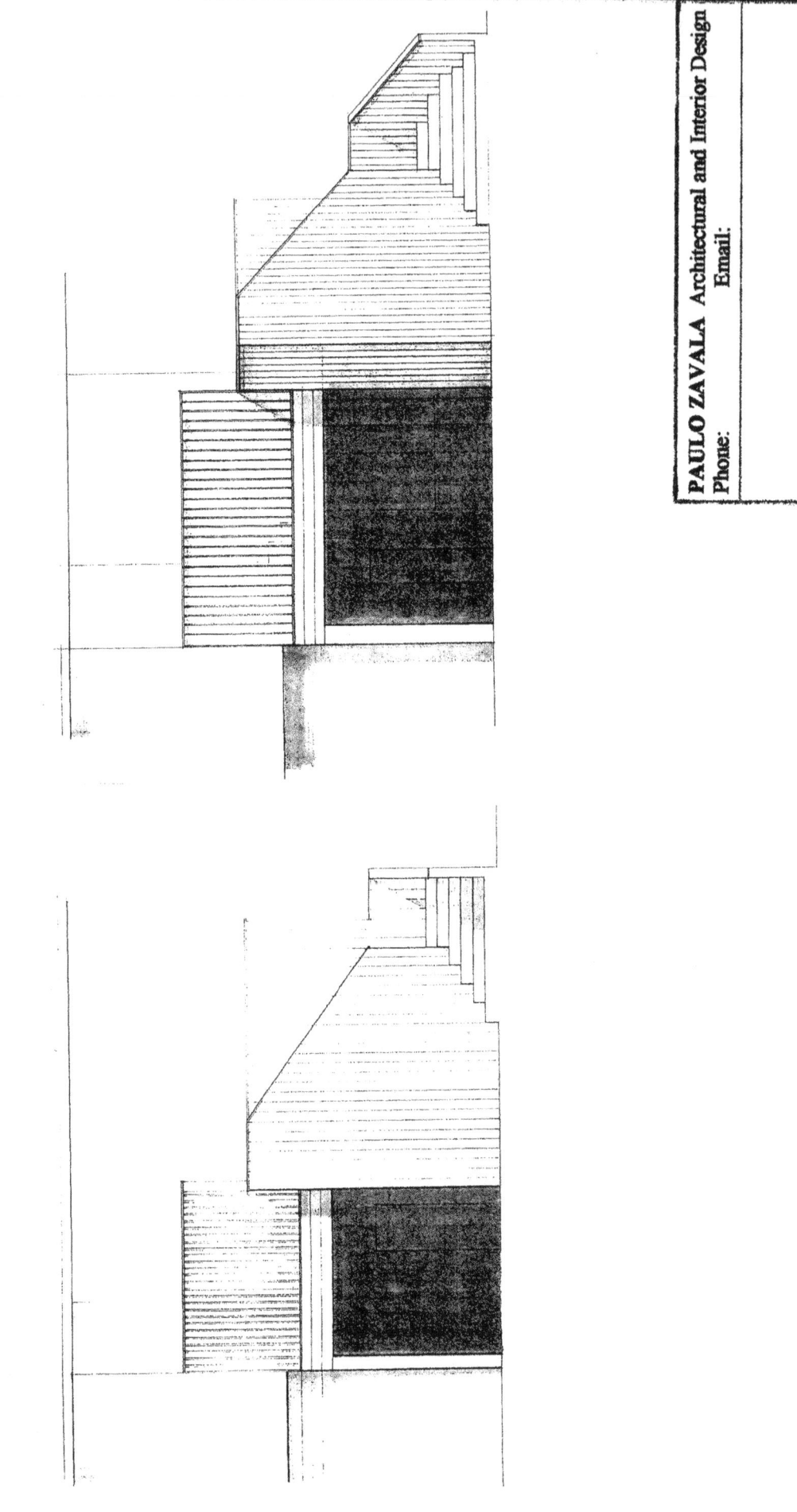

PAULO ZAVALA Architectural and Interior Design
Phone:
Email:

design by	drawn by	date	scale	job number

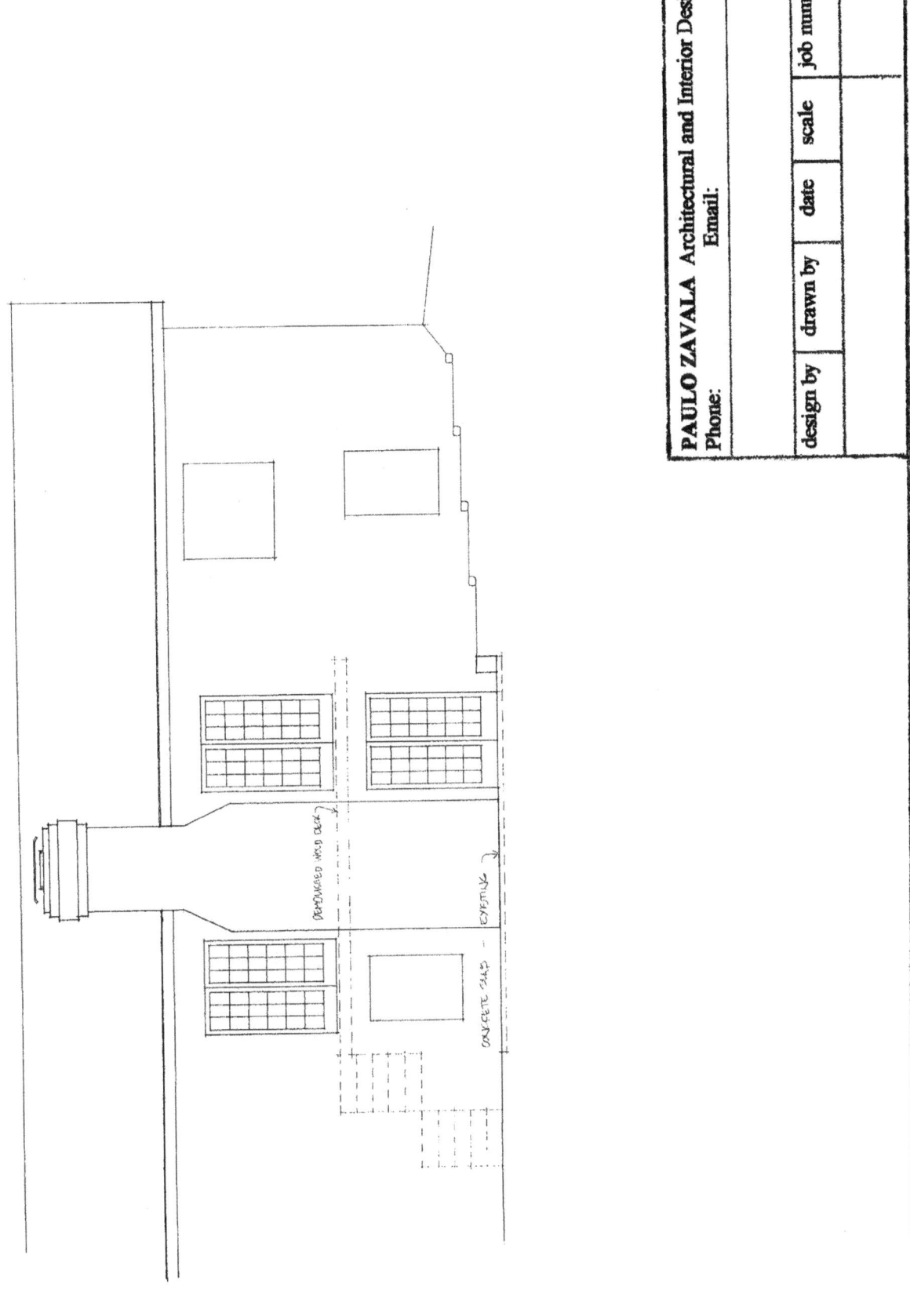

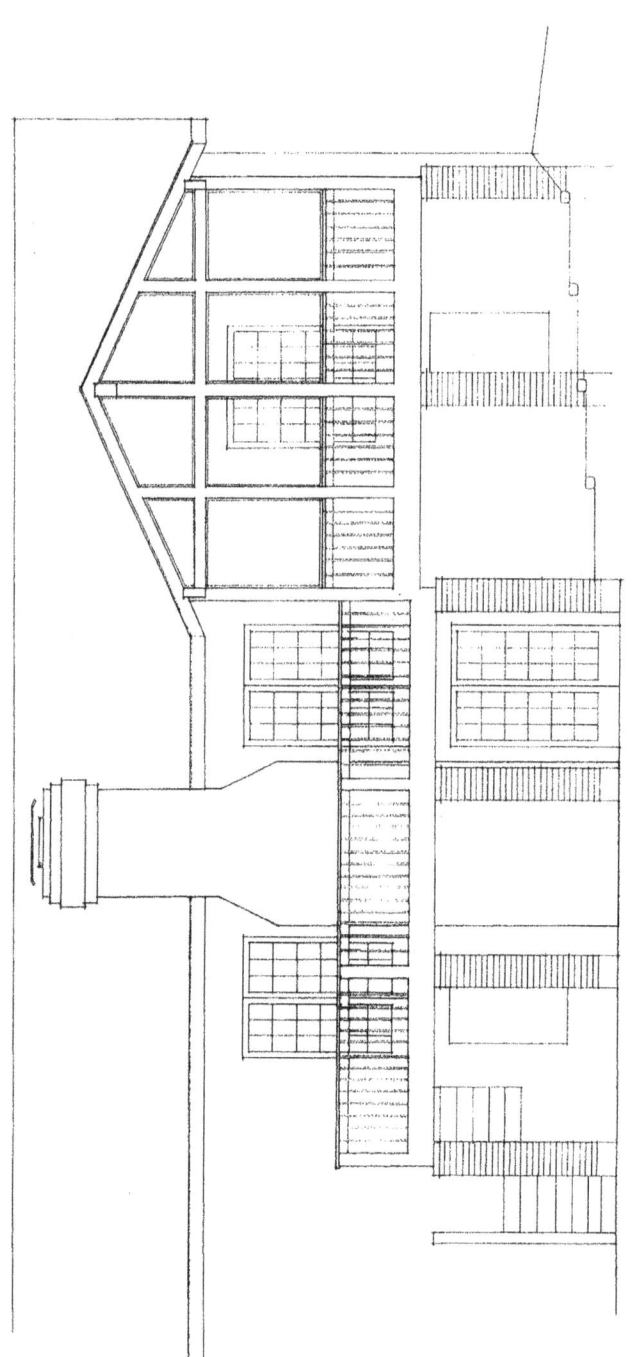

PAULO ZAVALA Architectural and Interior Design
Phone:
Email:

design by	drawn by	date	scale	job number

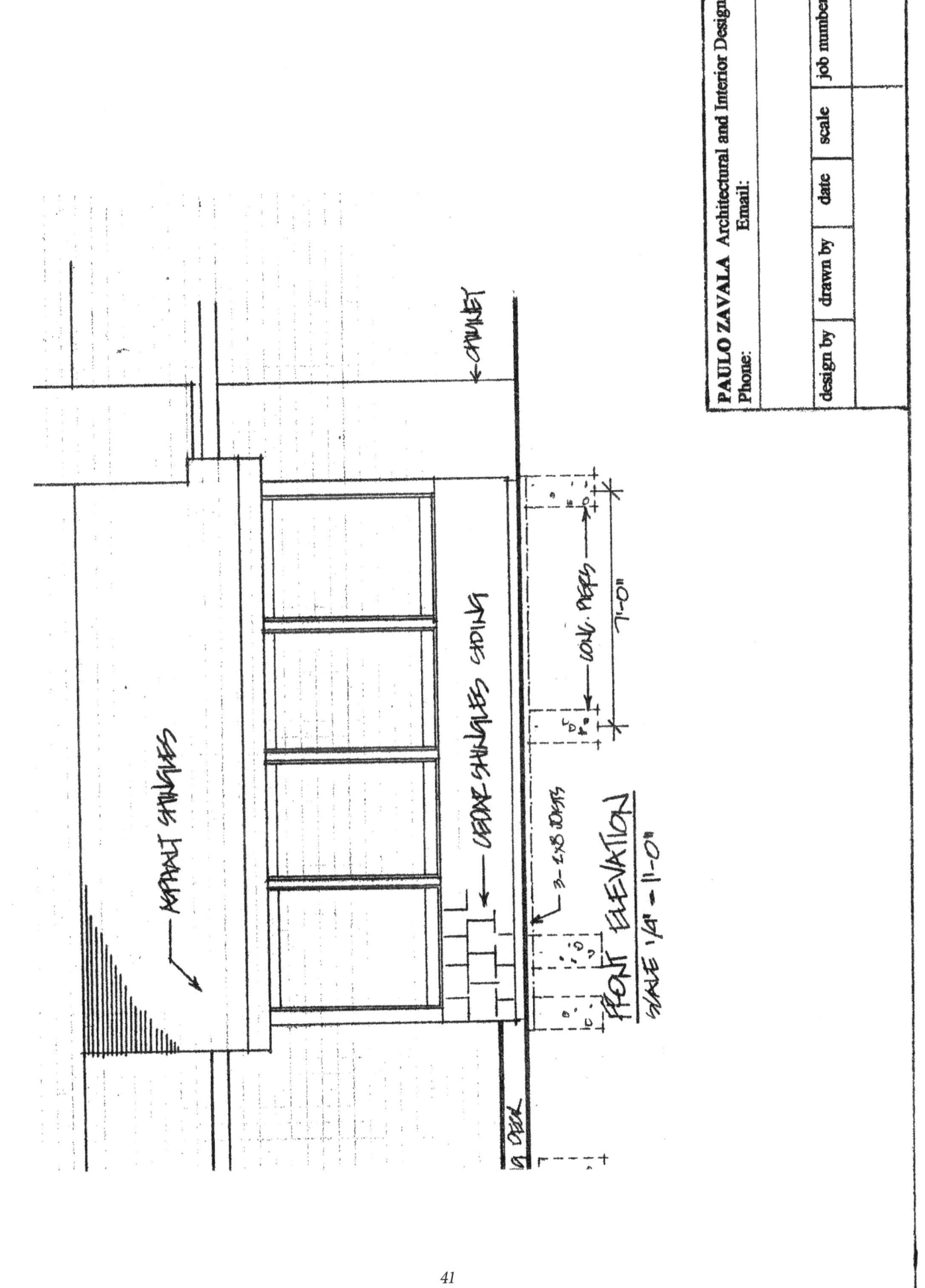

FRONT ELEVATION

SCALE 1/4" = 1'-0"

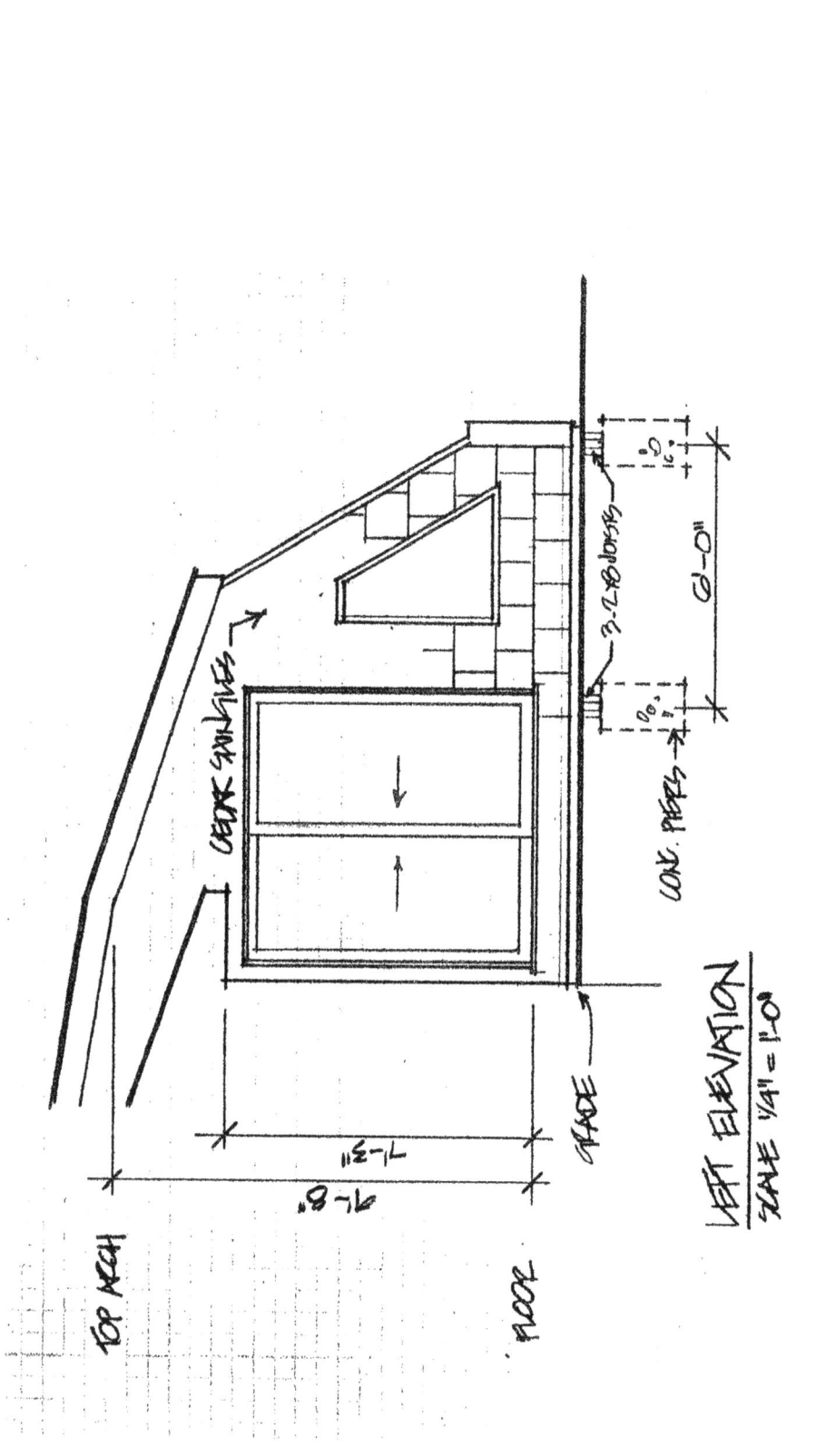

LEFT ELEVATION
SCALE 1/4" = 1'-0"

PAULO ZAVALA Architectural and Interior Design
Phone: Email:

design by	drawn by	date	scale	job number

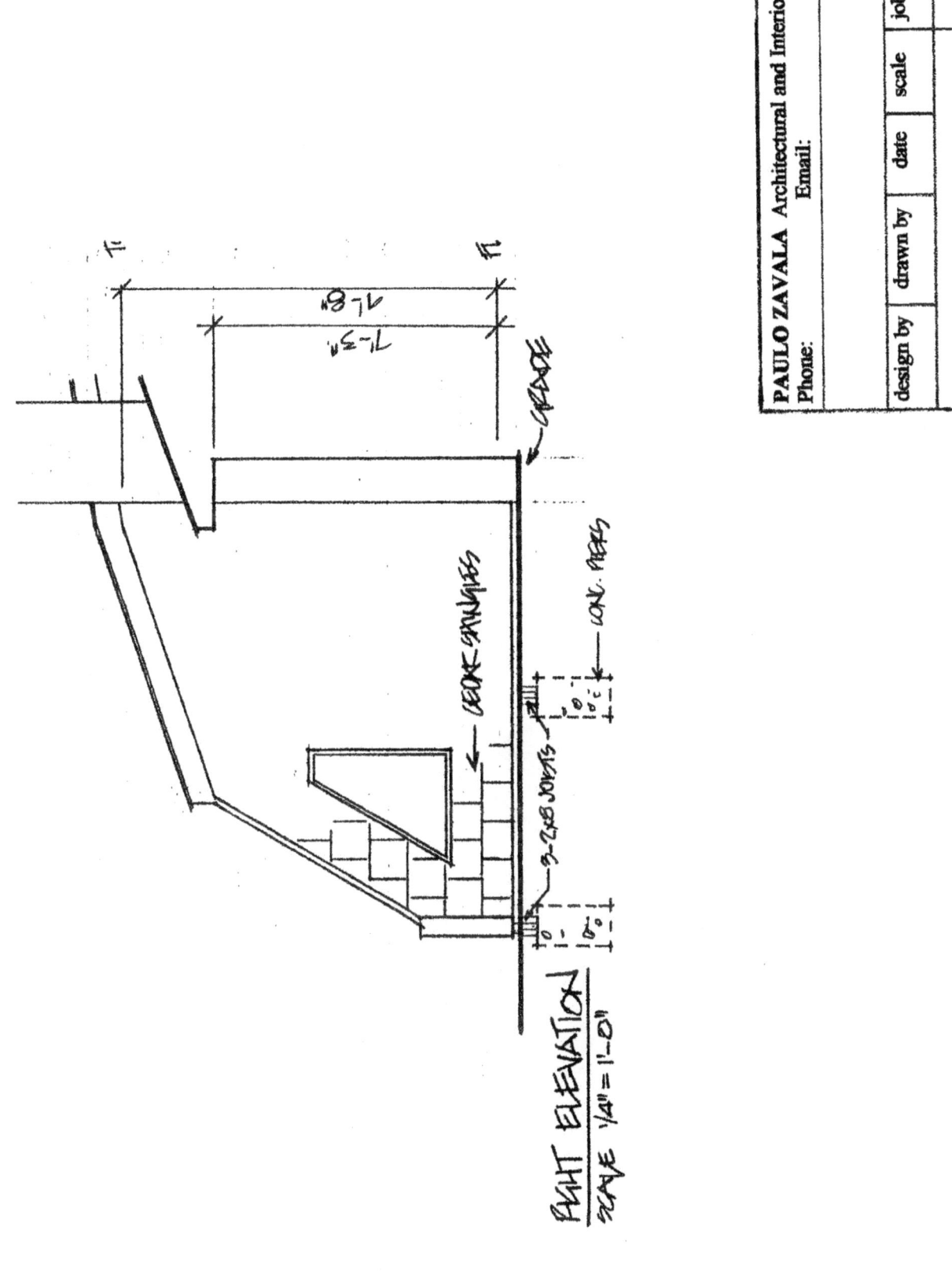

FRONT ELEVATION
SCALE 1/4" = 1'-0"

7'-3"

7'-8"

GRADE

CEDAR SHINGLES

3-2x8 JOISTS

CONC. PIERS

PAULO ZAVALA Architectural and Interior Design
Phone:
Email:

design by	drawn by	date	scale	job number

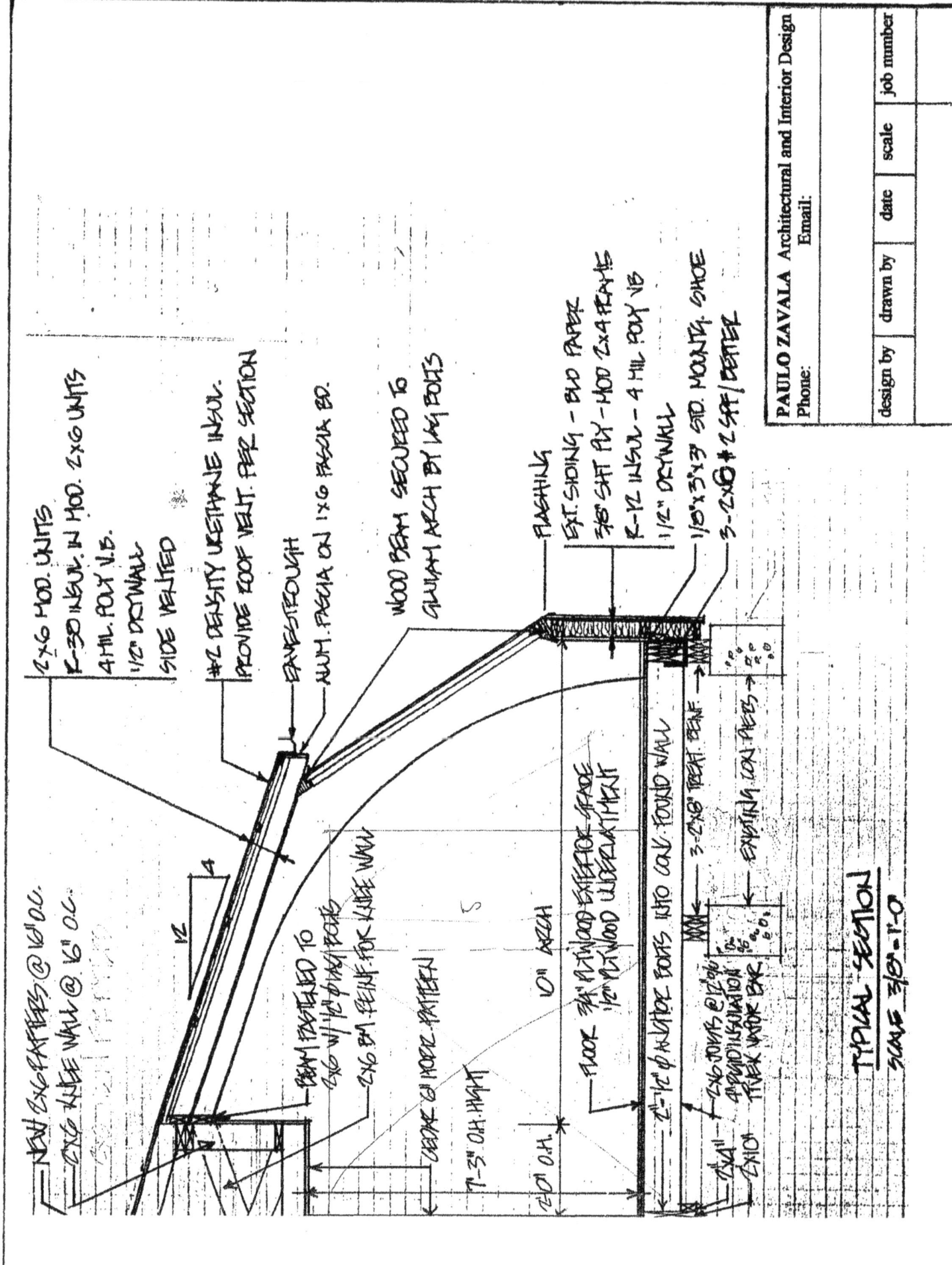

2×6 MOD. UNITS
R-30 INSUL IN MOD. 2×6 UNITS
4 MIL POLY V.B.
1/2" DRYWALL
SIDE VENTED

#2 DENSITY URETHANE INSUL.
PROVIDE ROOF VENT. PER SECTION

BREAK THROUGH
ALUM. FASCIA ON 1×6 FASCIA BD.

WOOD BEAM SECURED TO
GLULAM ARCH BY 1/4 BOLTS

FLASHING
EXT. SIDING - BLD PAPER
5/8 EXT PLY - MOD 2×4 PLATE
R-12 INSUL - 4 MIL POLY VB
1/2" DRYWALL
1/8"×3"×3" STD. MOUNT'G SHOE
3-2×6 #2 SPF/BETTER

NEW 2×6 RAFTERS @ 16" O.C.
2×6 KNEE WALL @ 16" O.C.

BEAM FASTENED TO
2×6 W/ 1/2" PLY PLATE
2×6 BM BEAM FOR KNEE WALL

GRADE OR MODE PATTERN

7'-3" O.H. HIGHT

12
4

5

10" ARCH

7'-0" O.H.

FLOOR 3/4" PLYWOOD SUBFLOOR SPACE
1/2" PLYWOOD UNDERLAYMENT

2'-1/2" Ø ANCHOR BOLTS INTO CONC. FOUND WALL

3-2×8" TREAT. BEAM

EXISTING CONC. PIERS

#4 DOWEL @ 16"
2'-0" DEPTH/INSULATION
THICK VAPOR BAR.

2×4 #
#4
2'-4"
EPDM

TYPICAL SECTION
SCALE 3/8" = 1'-0"

PAULO ZAVALA Architectural and Interior Design
Email:
Phone:

design by   drawn by   date   scale   job number

44

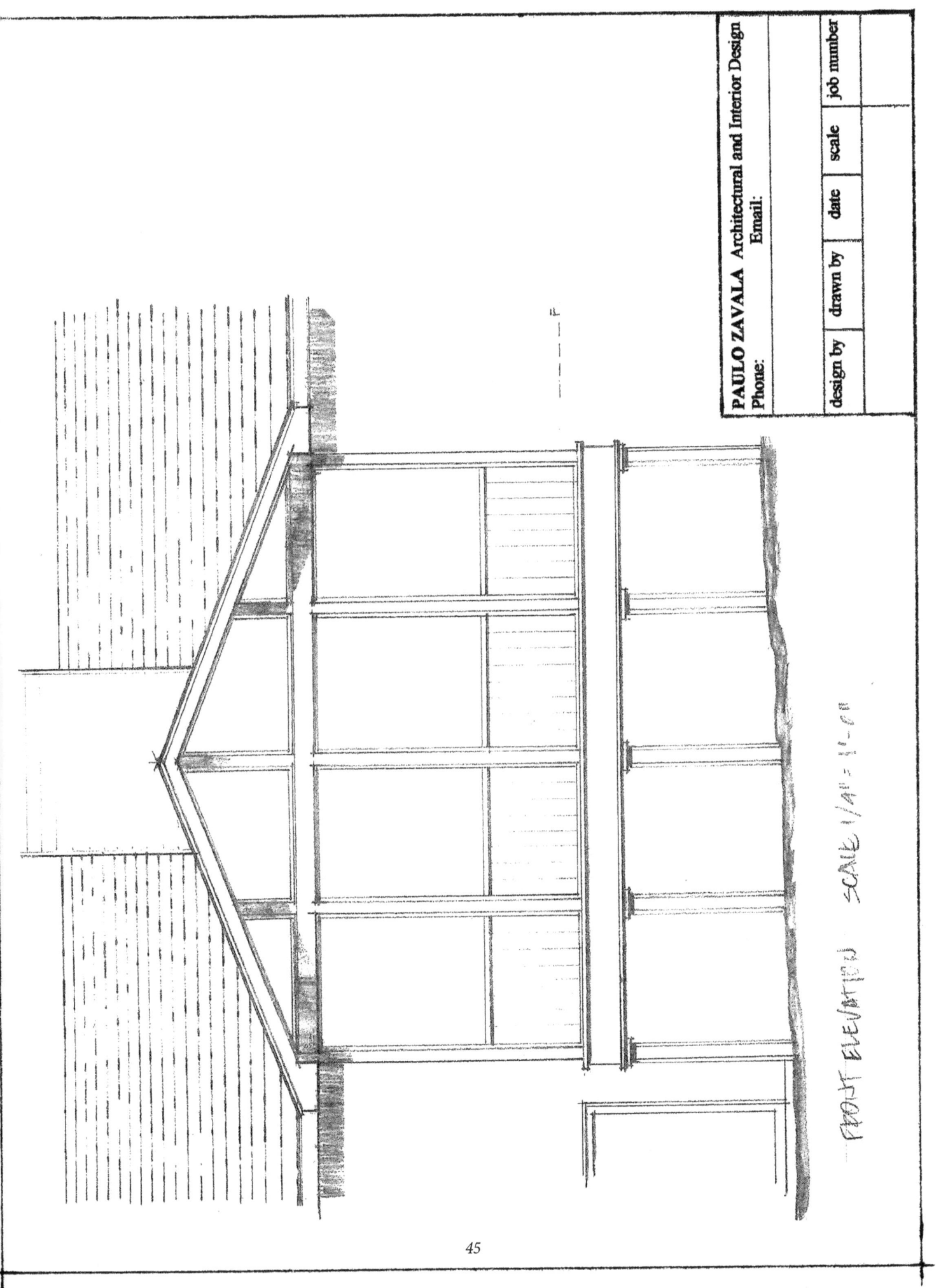

FRONT ELEVATION SCALE 1/4" = 1'-0"

PAULO ZAVALA Architectural and Interior Design
Phone: Email:

design by	drawn by	date	scale	job number

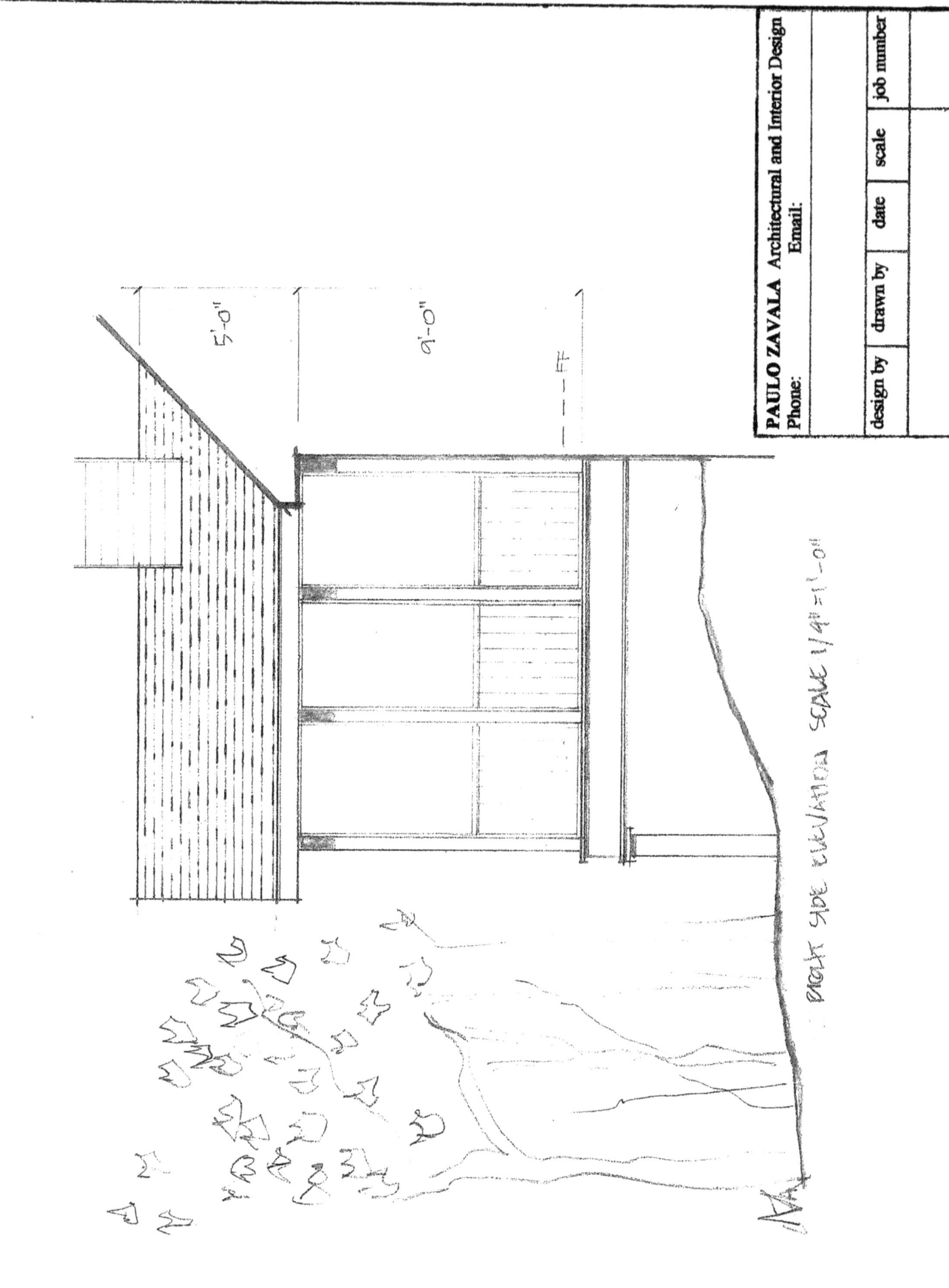

RIGHT SIDE ELEVATION SCALE 1/4"=1'-0"

5'-0"

9'-0"

PAULO ZAVALA Architectural and Interior Design
Phone:
Email:

design by	drawn by	date	scale	job number

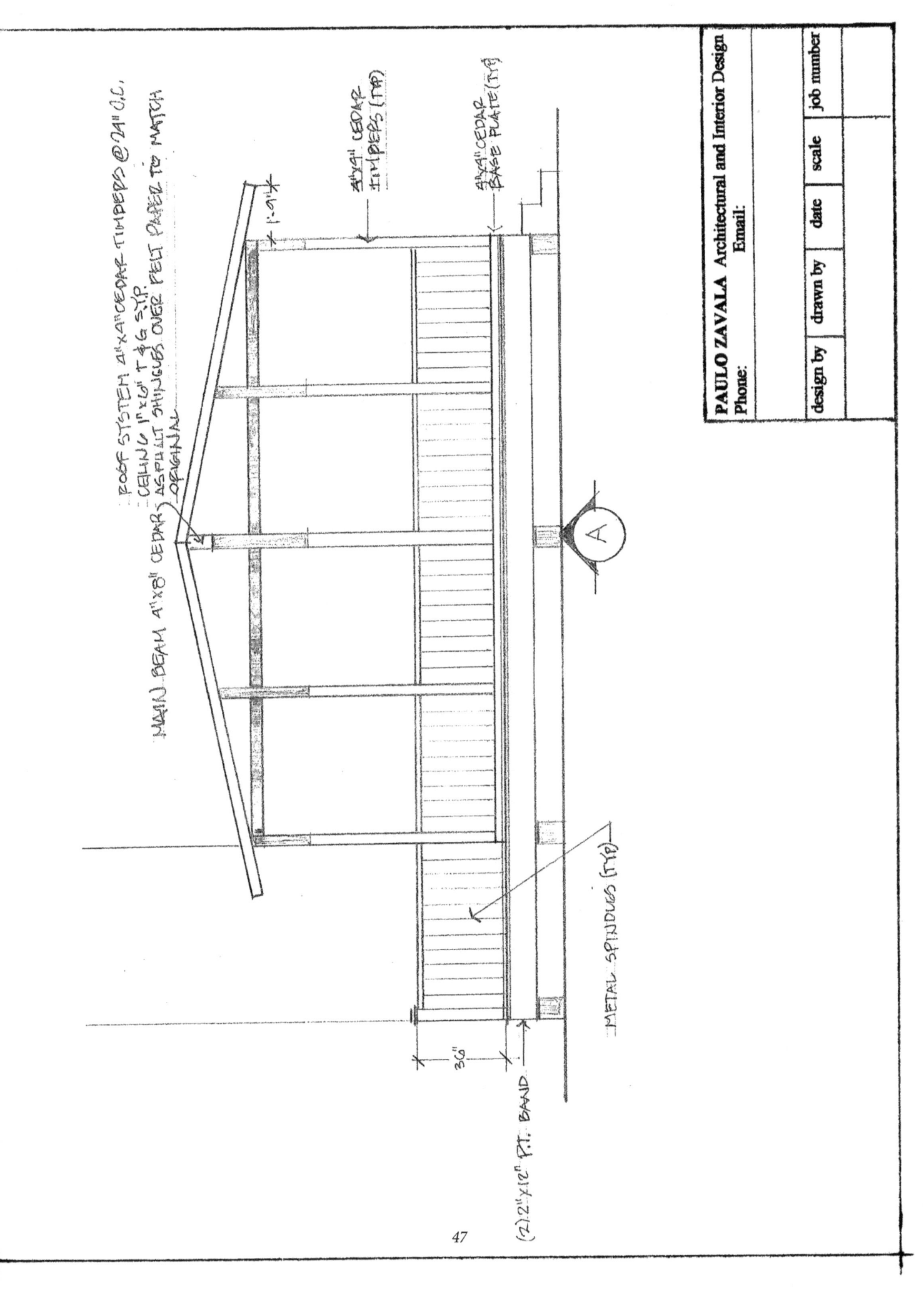

ROOF SYSTEM 4"X4" CEDAR TIMBERS @ 24" O.C.
- CEILING 1"X6" T&G SYP.
- ASPHALT SHINGLES OVER FELT PAPER TO MATCH ORIGINAL

4"X4" CEDAR TIMBERS (TYP)

4"X4" CEDAR BASE PLATE (TYP)

MAIN BEAM 4"X8" CEDAR

1'-9"

A

METAL SPINDLES (TYP)

3'-6"

(2) 2"X 12" P.T. BAND

47

PAULO ZAVALA Architectural and Interior Design
Phone: Email:

design by	drawn by	date	scale	job number

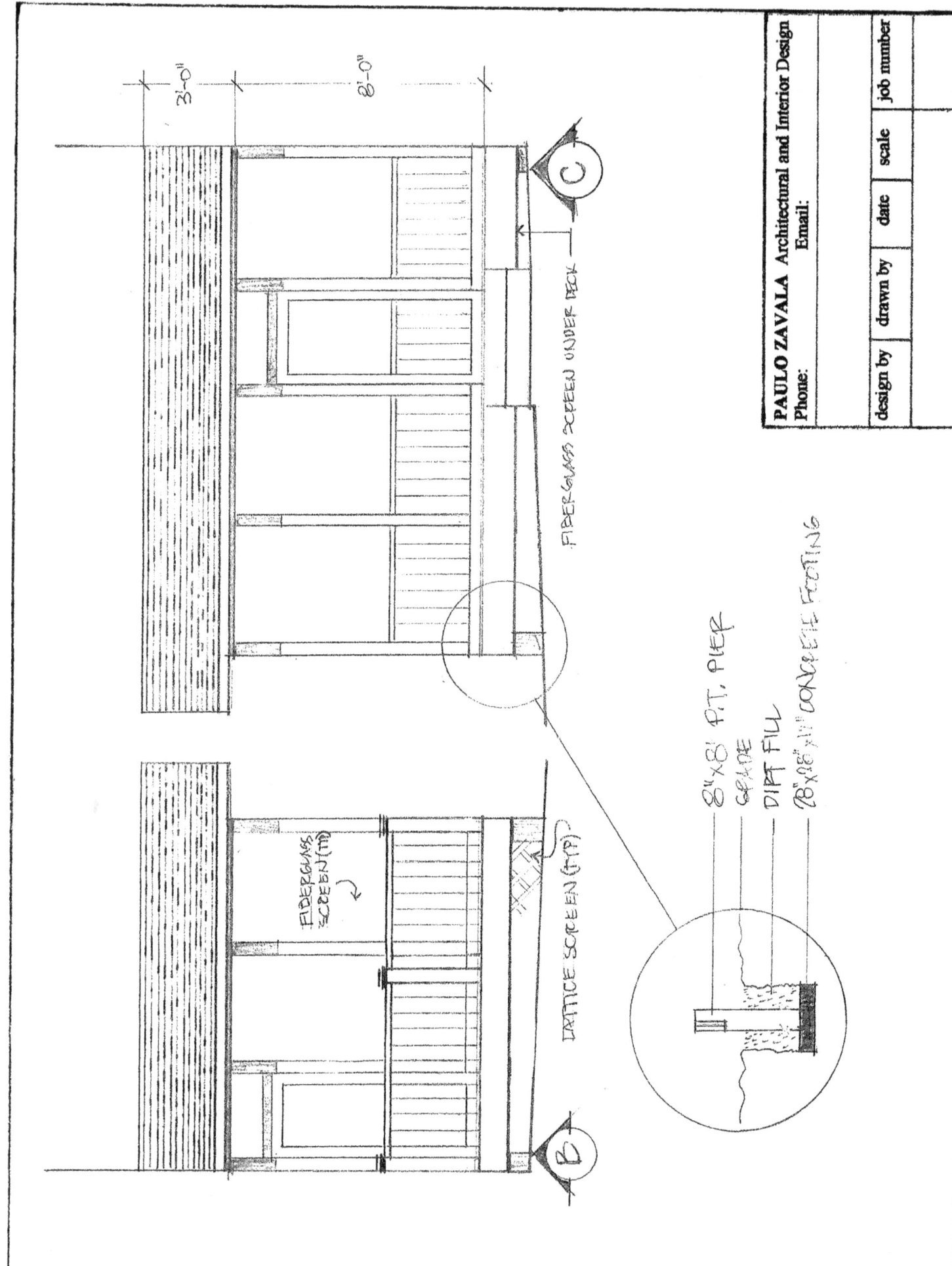

FIBERGLASS SCREEN UNDER DECK

FIBERGLASS SCREEN (TYP)

LATTICE SCREEN (TYP)

3'-0"

8'-0"

8"x8' P.T. PIER
GRADE
DIRT FILL
28"x28"x1" CONCRETE FOOTING

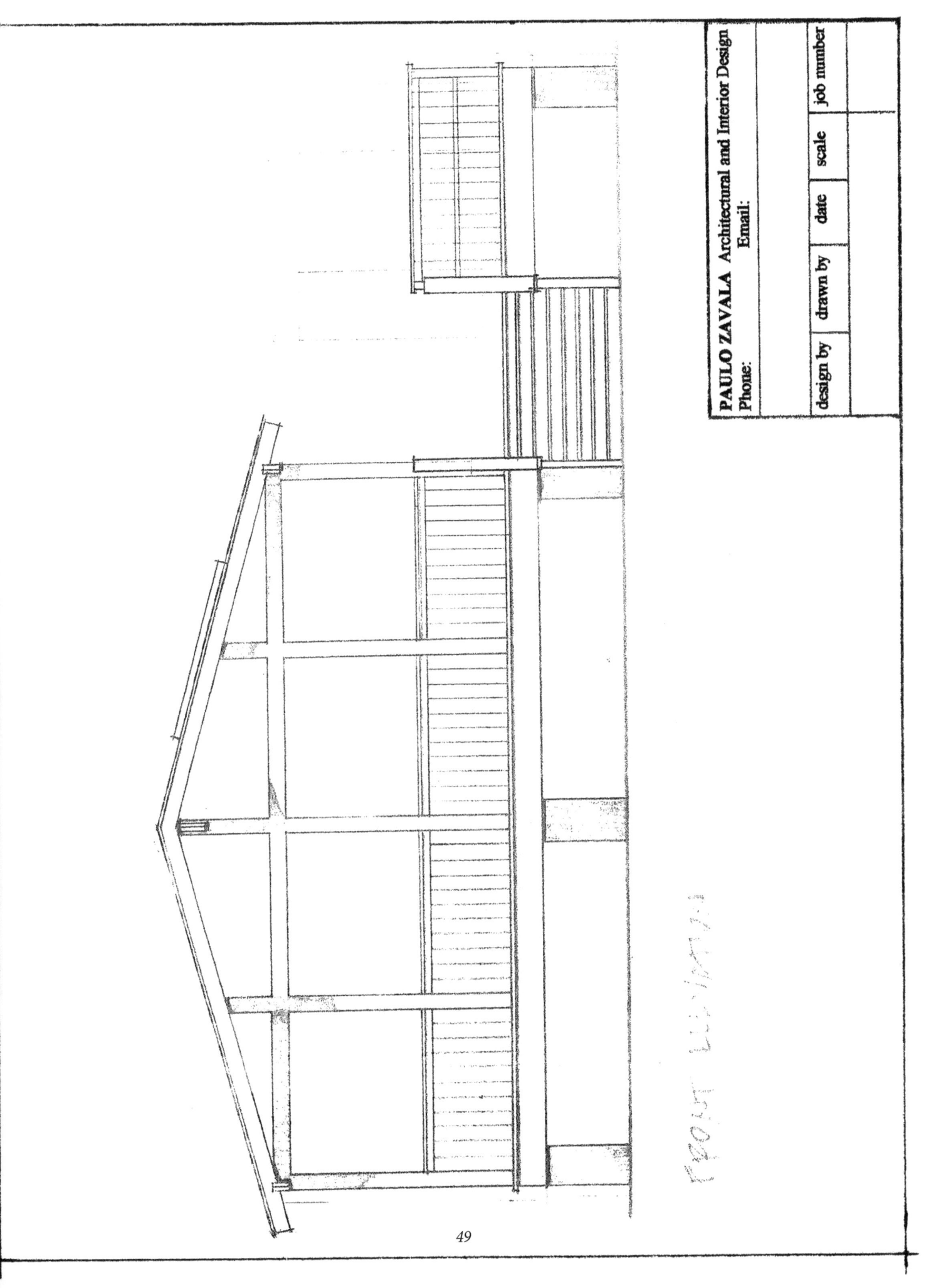

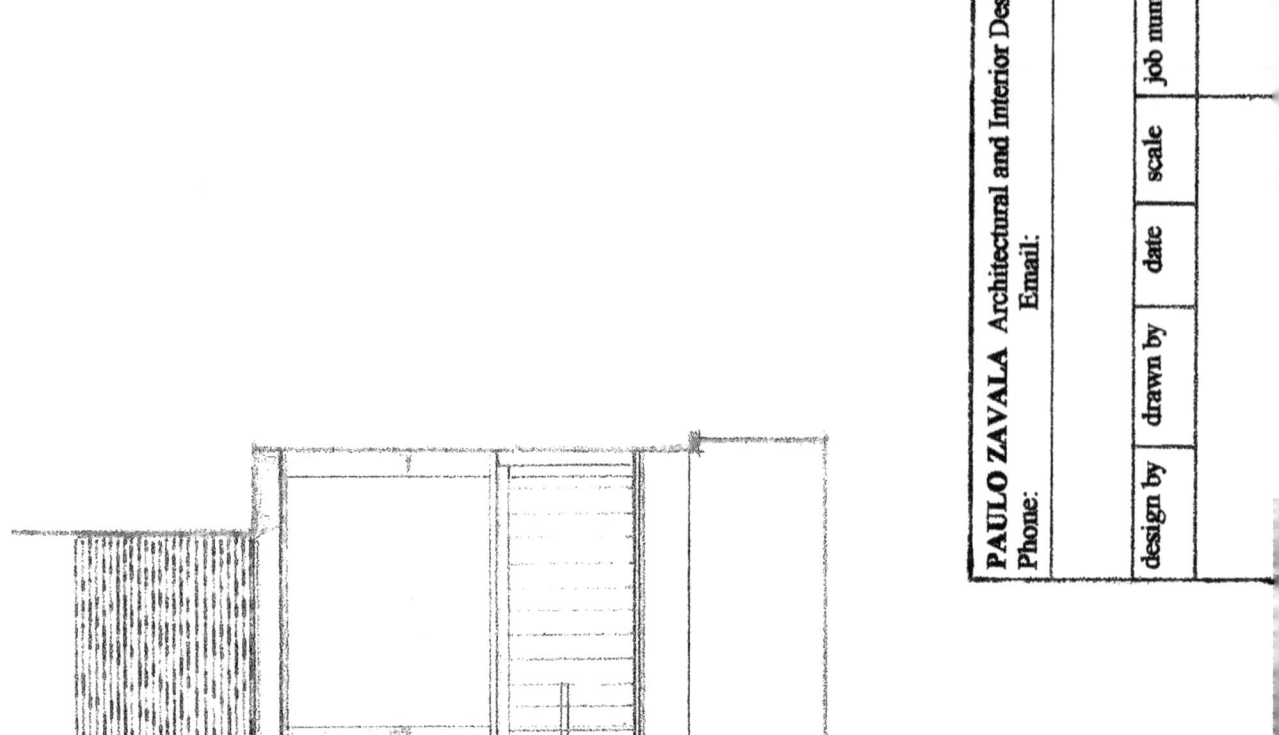

FRONT SIDE ELEVATION

PAULO ZAVALA Architectural and Interior Design
Phone: Email:

design by	drawn by	date	scale	job number

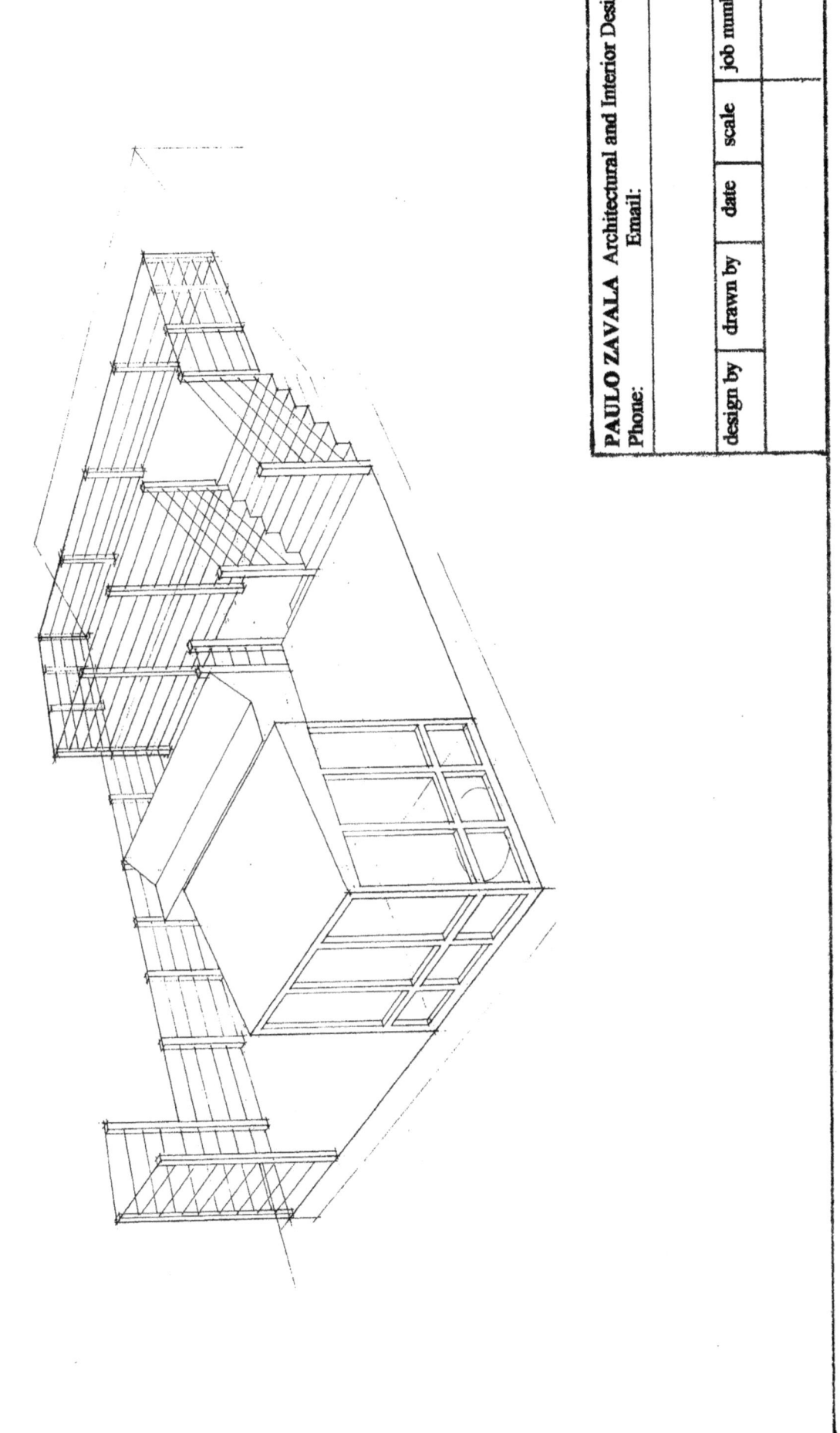

PAULO ZAVALA Architectural and Interior Design
Phone:
Email:

design by | drawn by | date | scale | job number

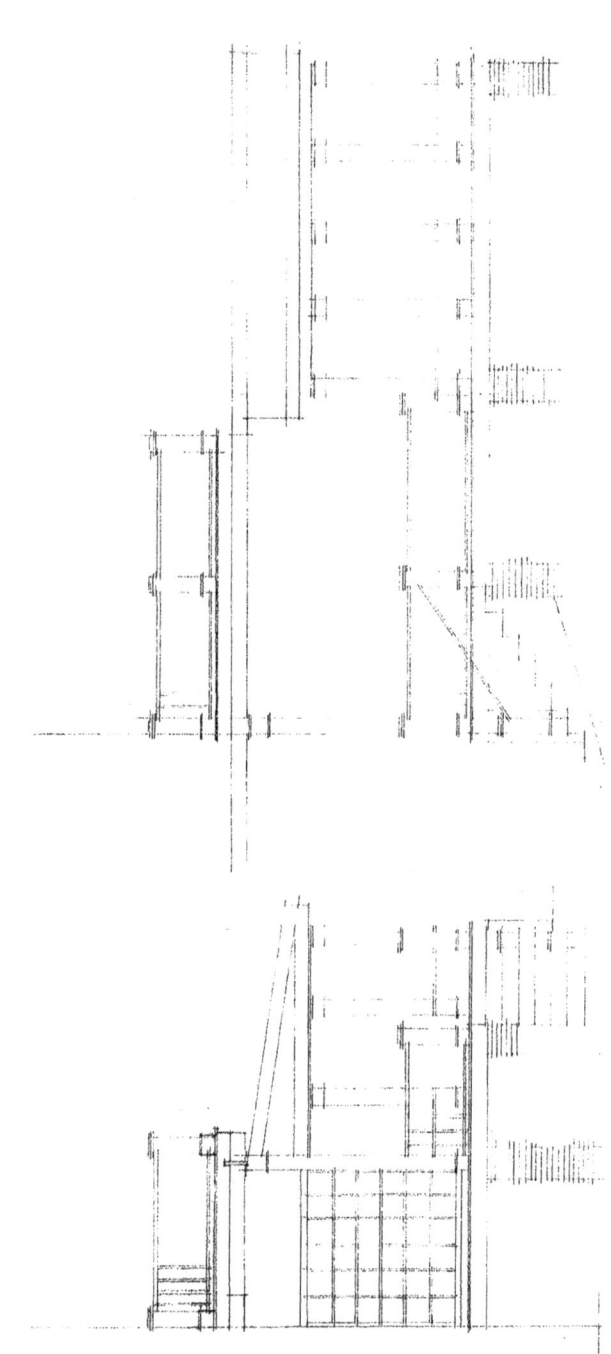

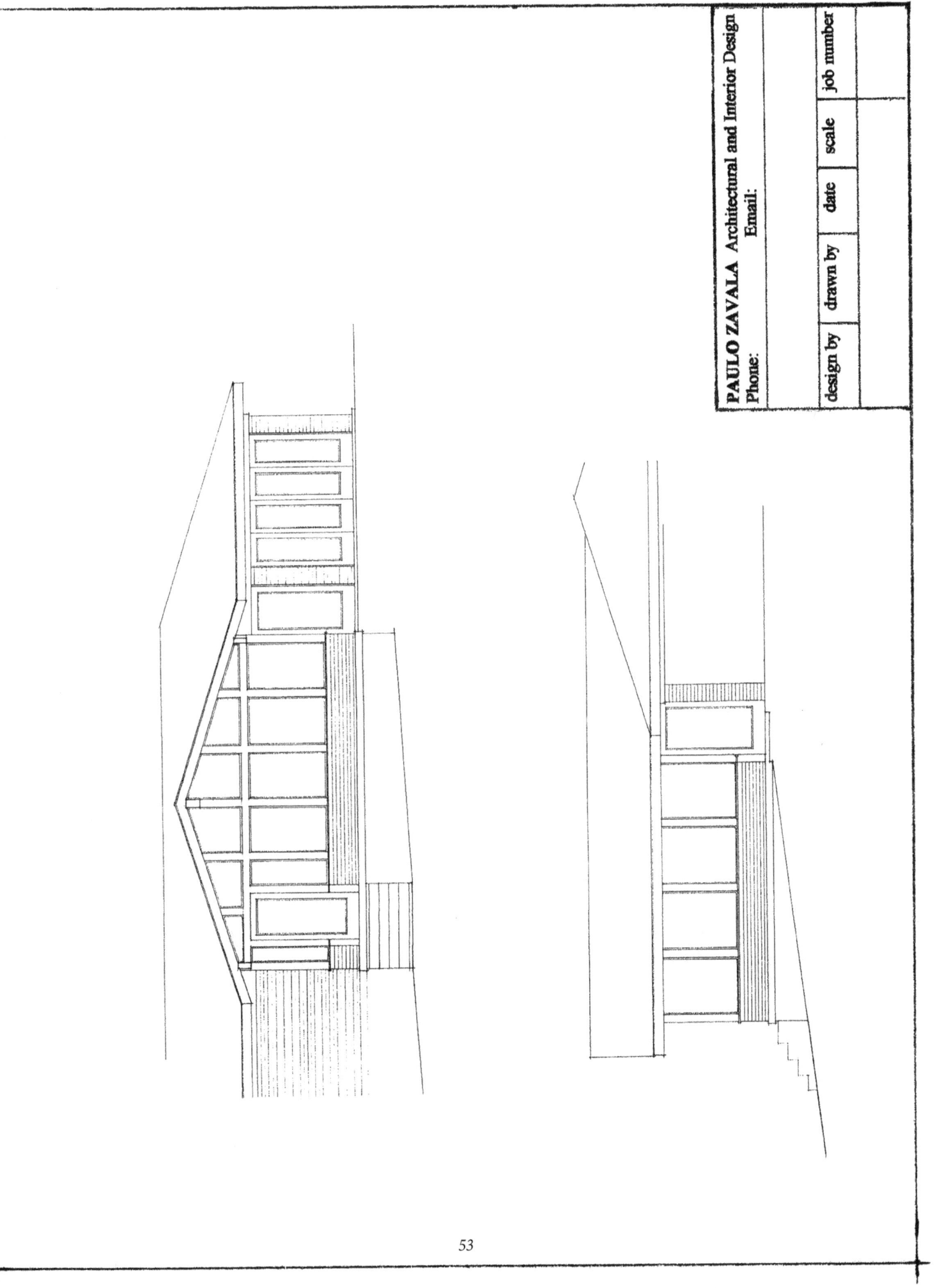

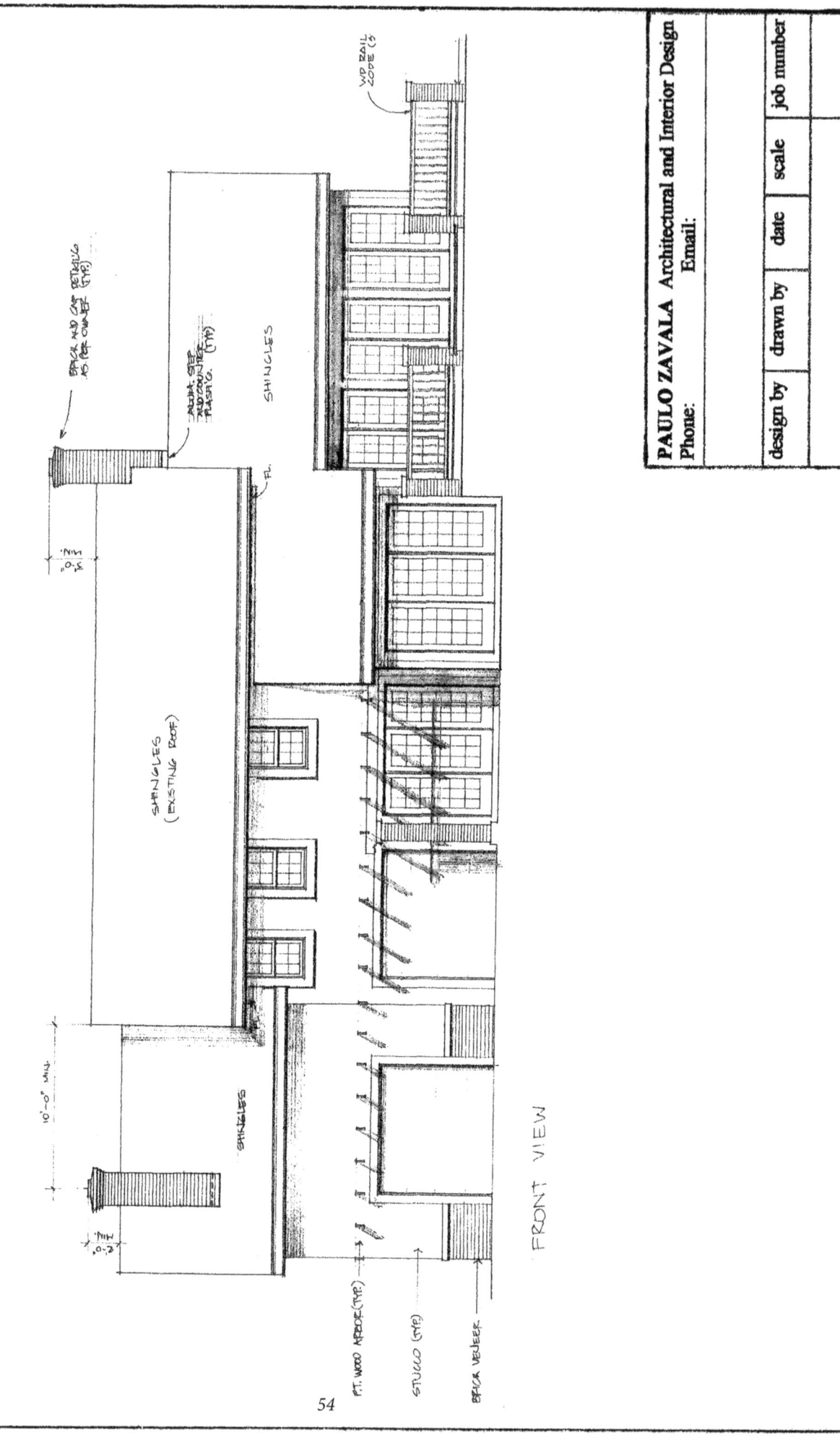

FRONT VIEW

PAULO ZAVALA Architectural and Interior Design
Phone:
Email:

design by	drawn by	date	scale	job number

FRONT ELEVATION

CHIMNEY AND FIREPLACE AS PER OWNER'S SPECS.

EXISTING TILA TILES ROOF

NEW ———— EXISTING ——— *

12
8

P.V.

F.F.

PAULO ZAVALA Architectural and Interior Design
Phone: Email:

design by	drawn by	date	scale	job number

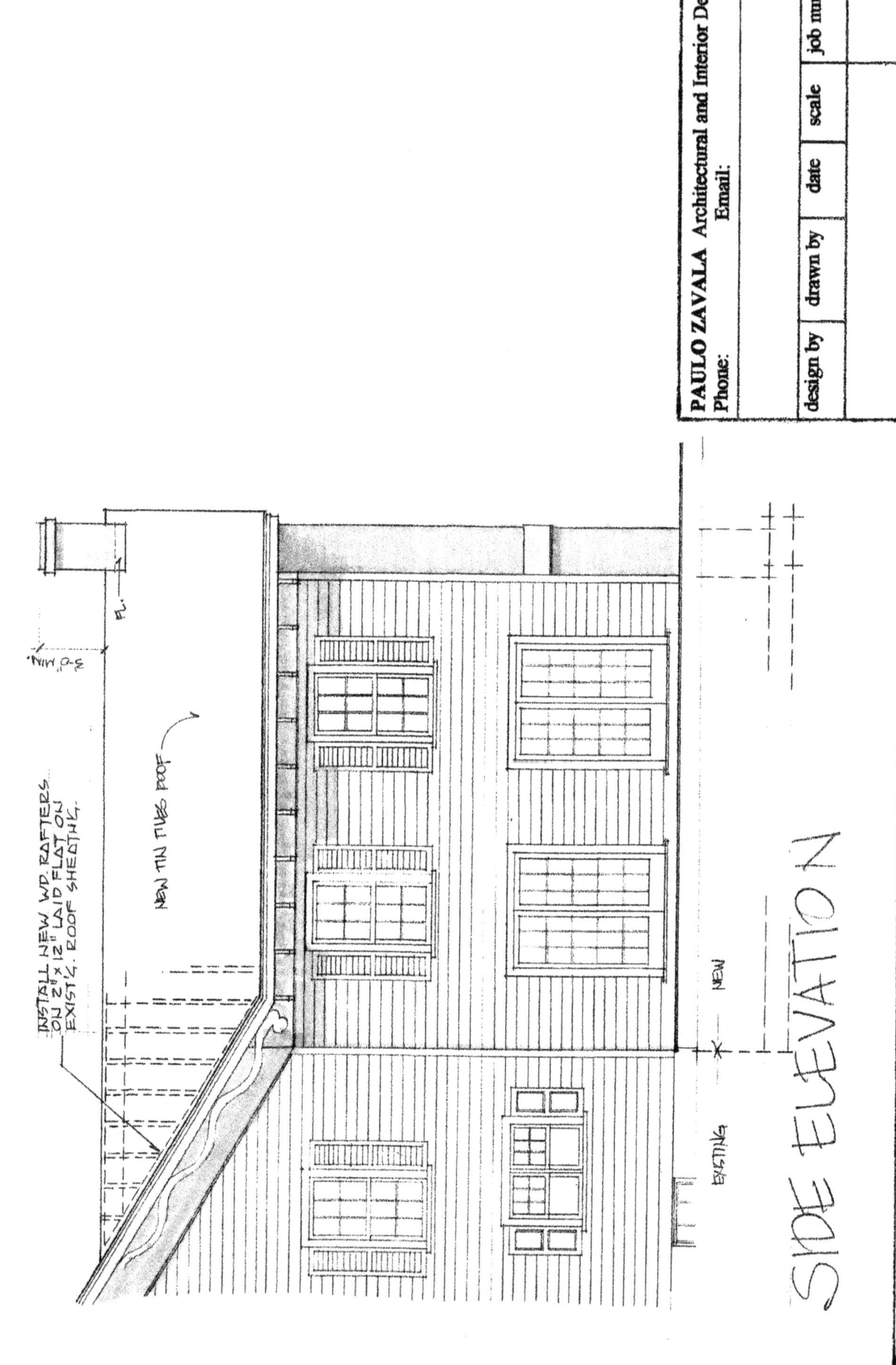

INSTALL NEW WD RAFTERS ON 2" x 12" LAID FLAT ON EXIST'G. ROOF SHEATING.

3'-0" MIN.

NEW TILE ROOF

SIDE ELEVATION

NEW

EXISTING

PAULO ZAVALA Architectural and Interior Design
Phone:
Email:

design by	drawn by	date	scale	job number

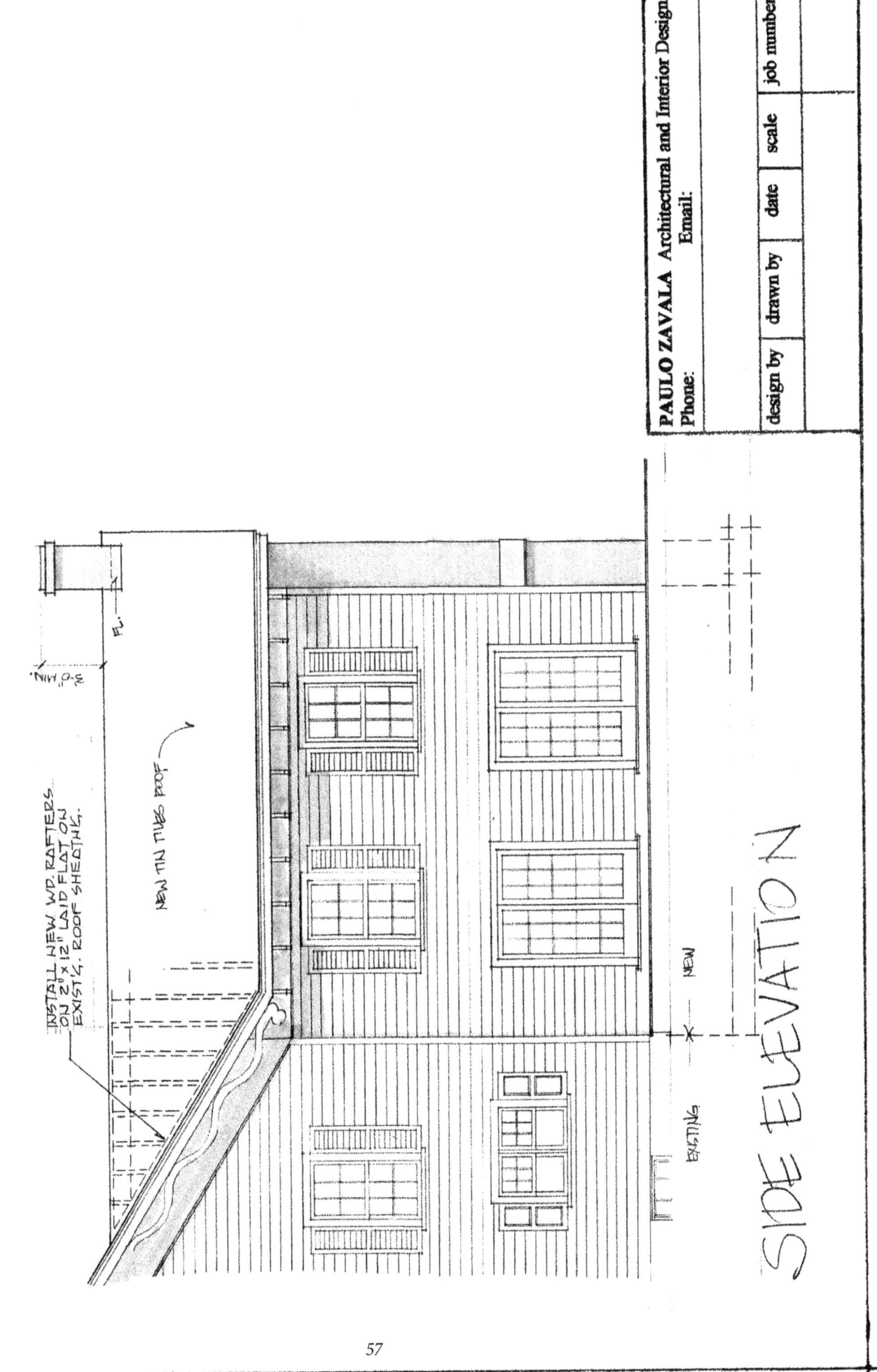

INSTALL NEW WD. RAFTERS ON 2"×12" LAID FLAT ON EXIST'G. ROOF SHEATH'G.

NEW TIN TILES ROOF

3'-0" MIN.

FL.

EXISTING ——×—— NEW

SIDE ELEVATION

PAULO ZAVALA Architectural and Interior Design
Phone: Email:

design by	drawn by	date	scale	job number

FRONT ELEVATION
SCALE 1/4" = 1'-0"

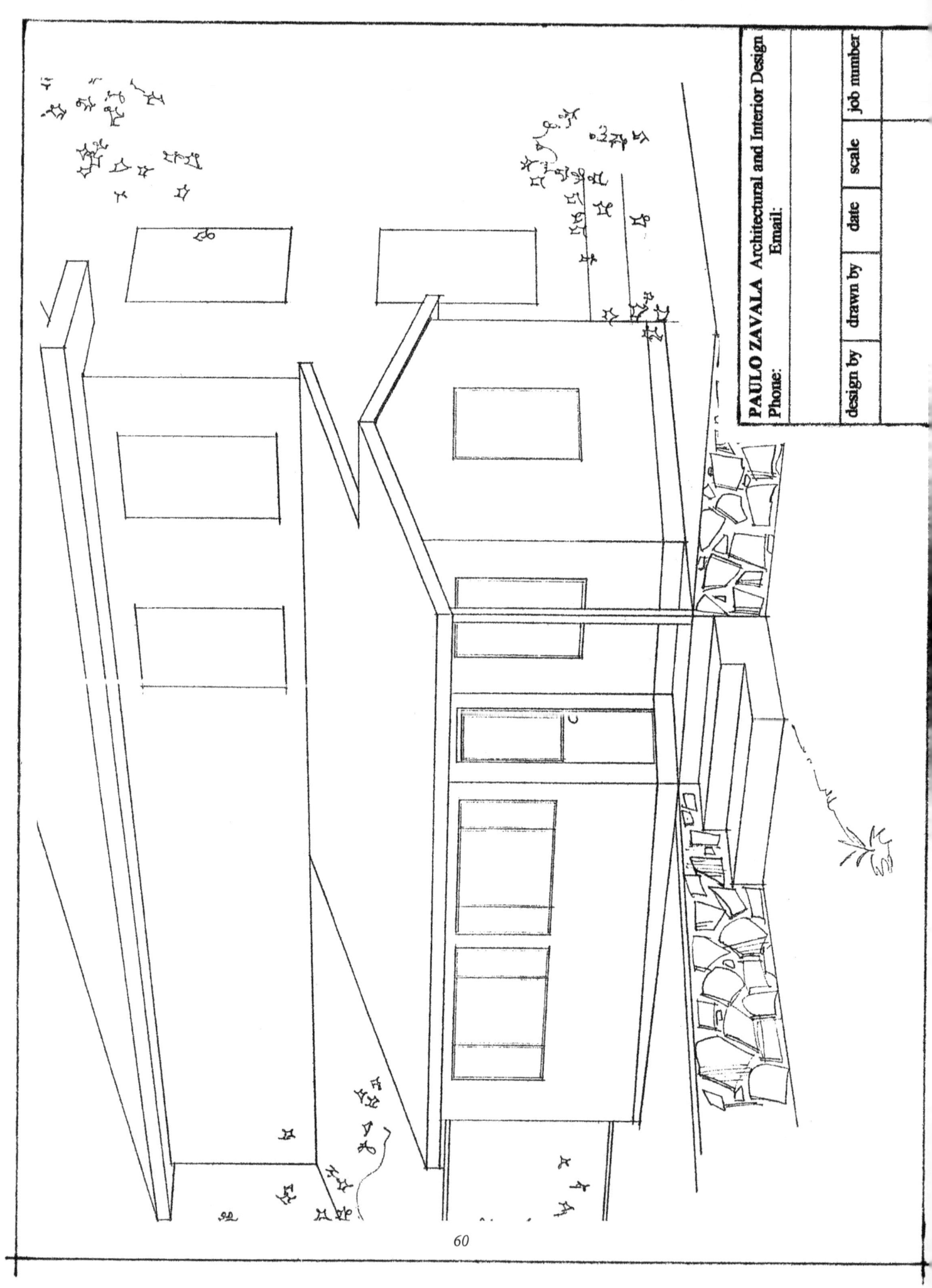

PAULO ZAVALA Architectural and Interior Design
Phone:
Email:

| design by | drawn by | date | scale | job number |

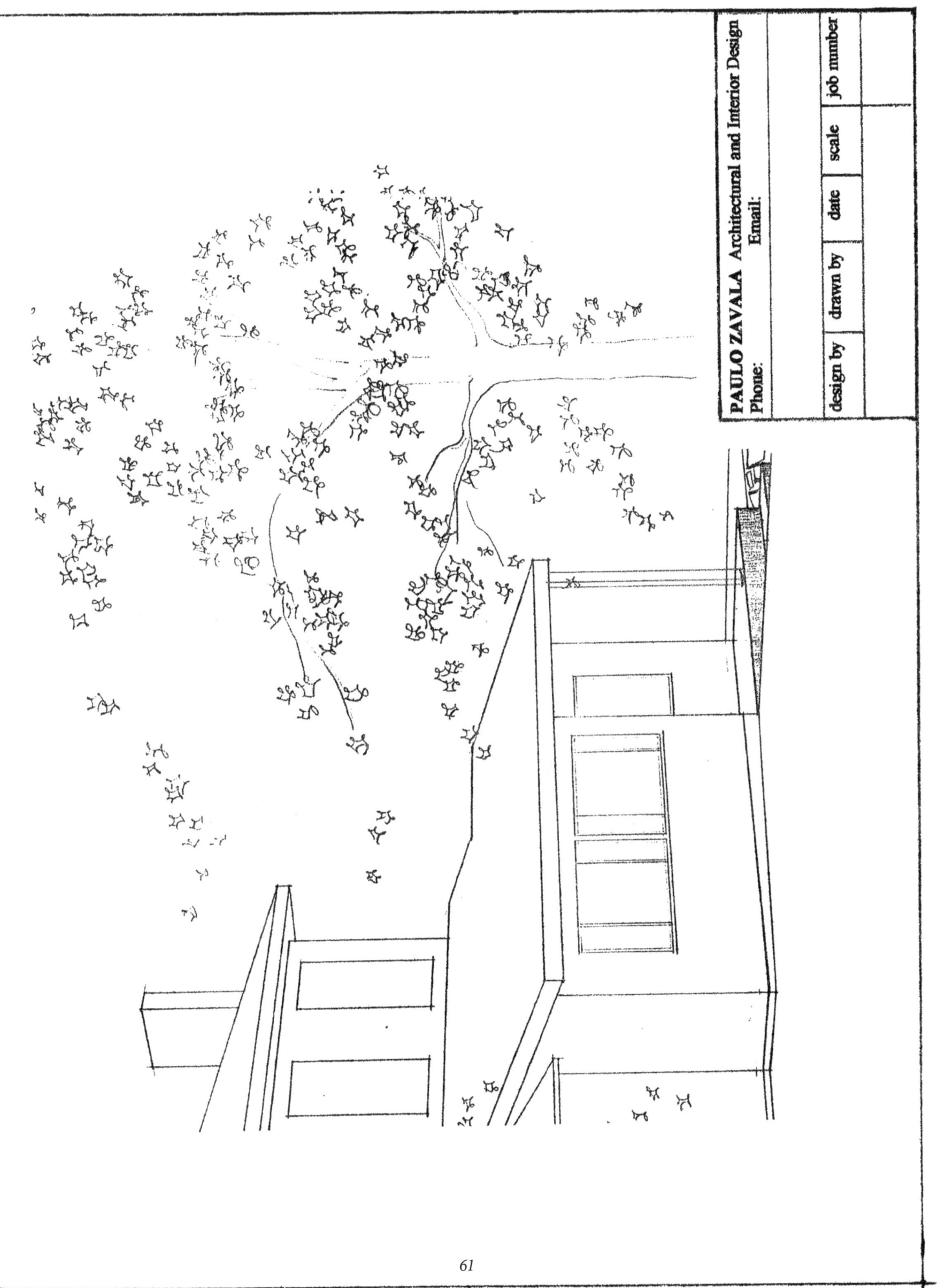

PAULO ZAVALA Architectural and Interior Design
Phone:
Email:

design by	drawn by	date	scale
			job number

PAULO ZAVALA Architectural and Interior Design
Phone: Email:

design by	drawn by	date	scale	job number

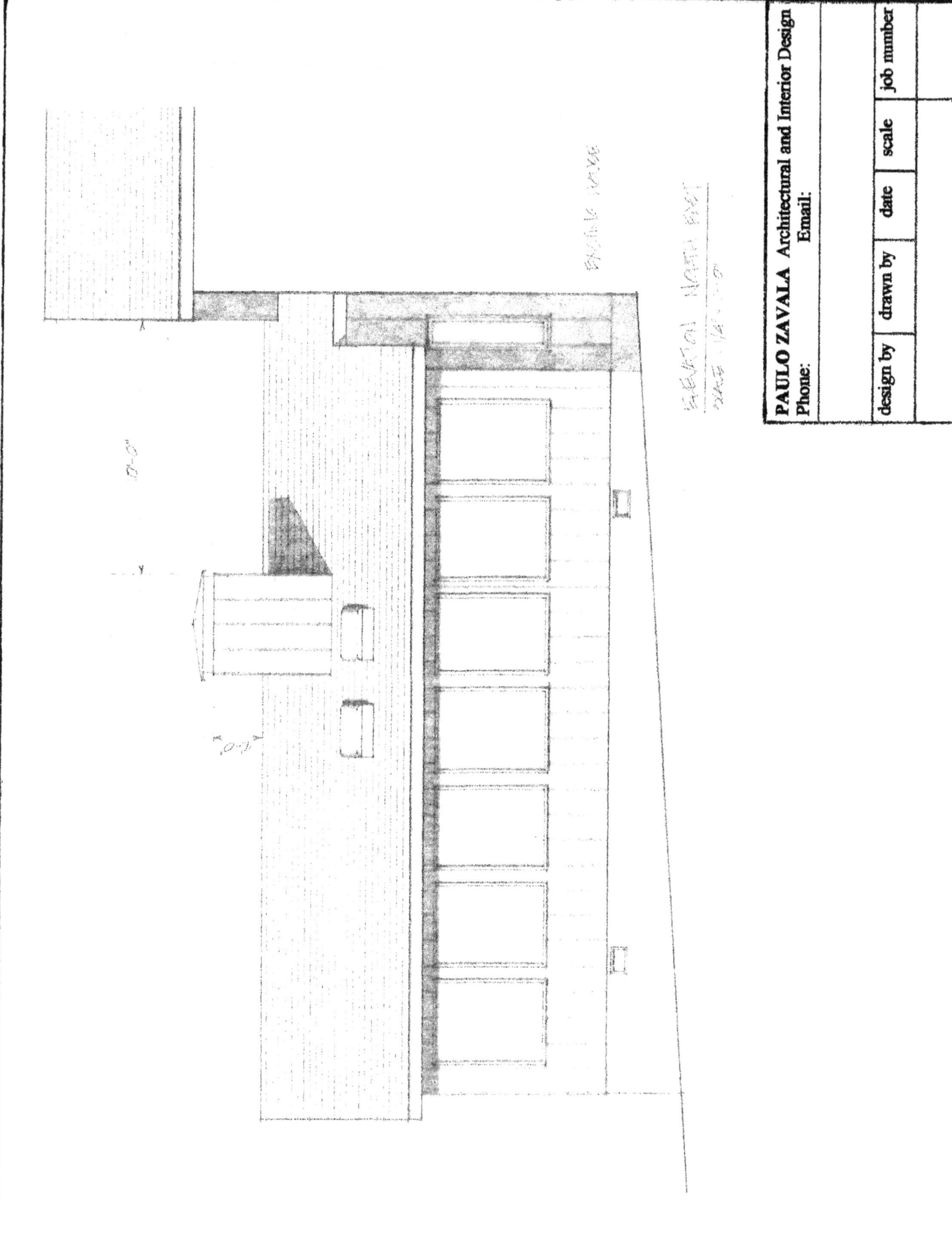

PAULO ZAVALA Architectural and Interior Design
Phone: Email:

design by	drawn by	date	scale	job number

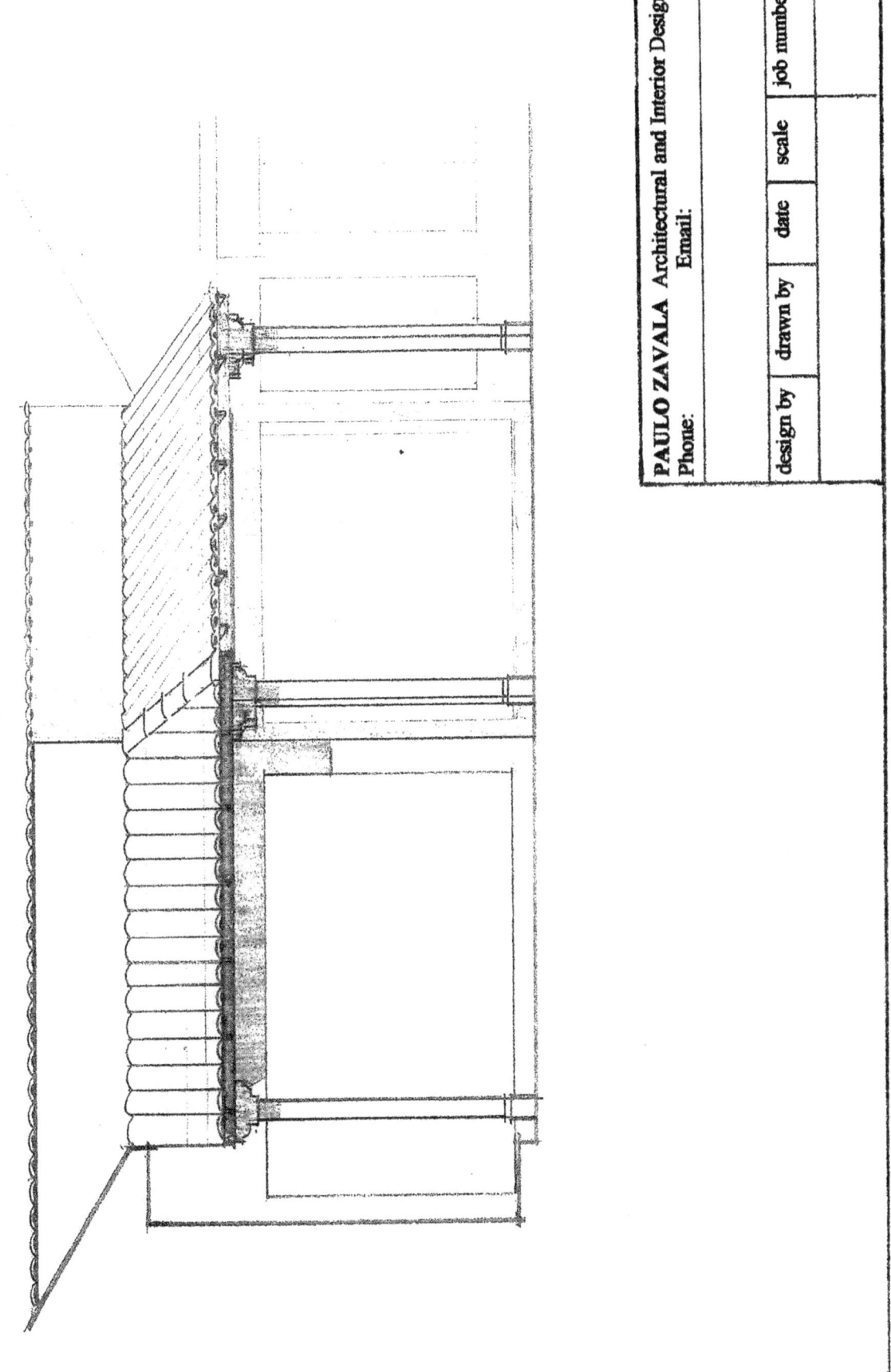

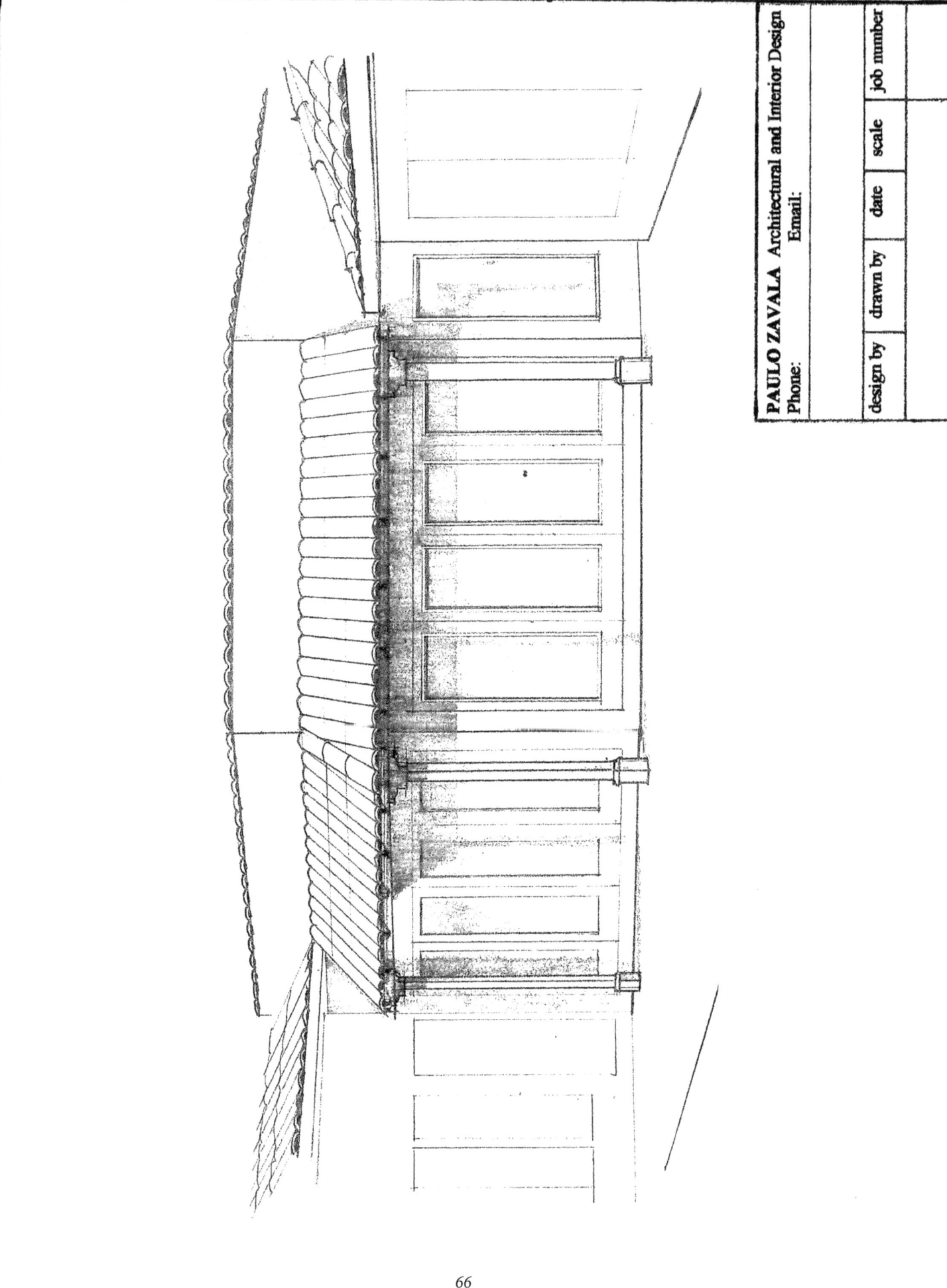

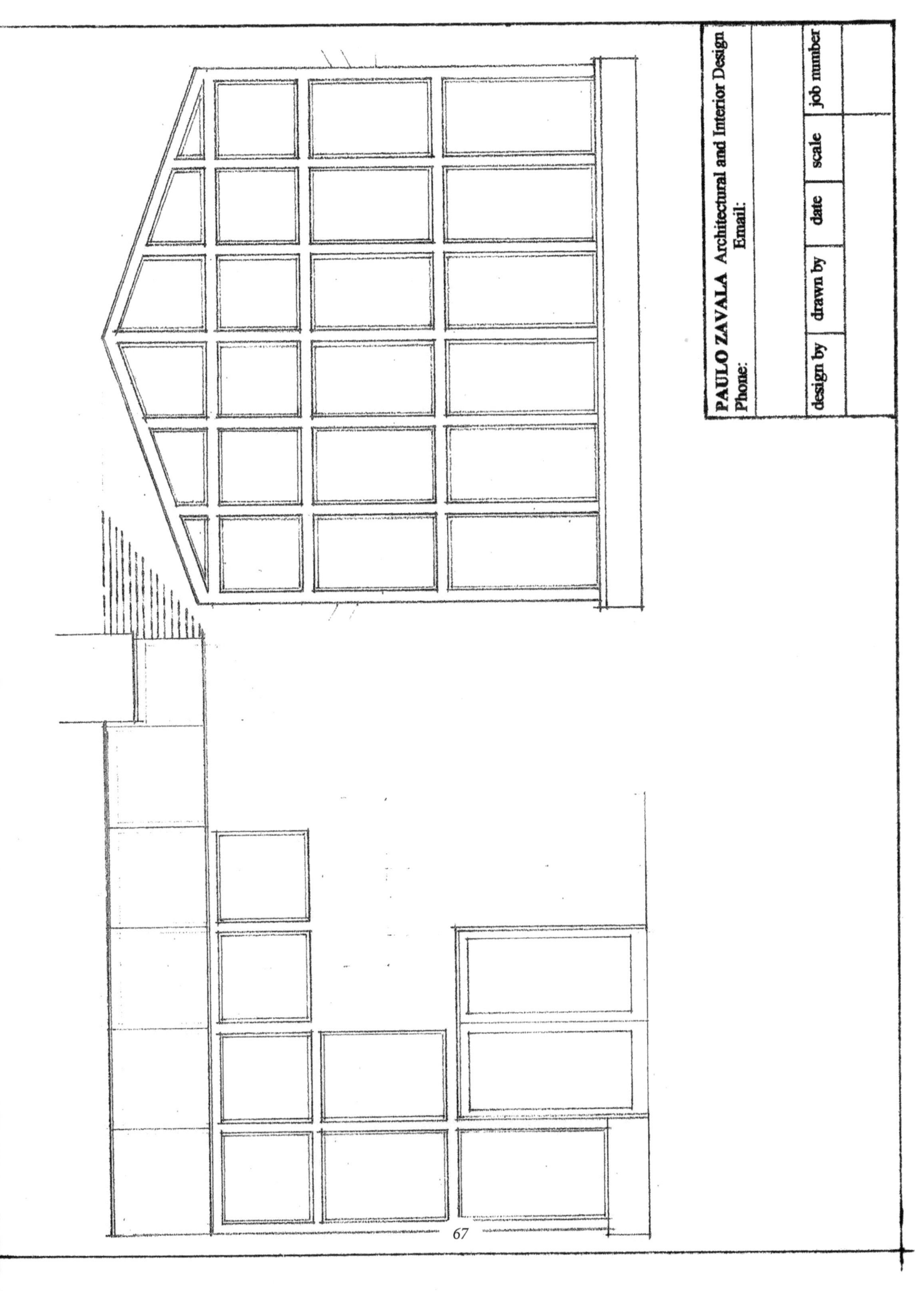

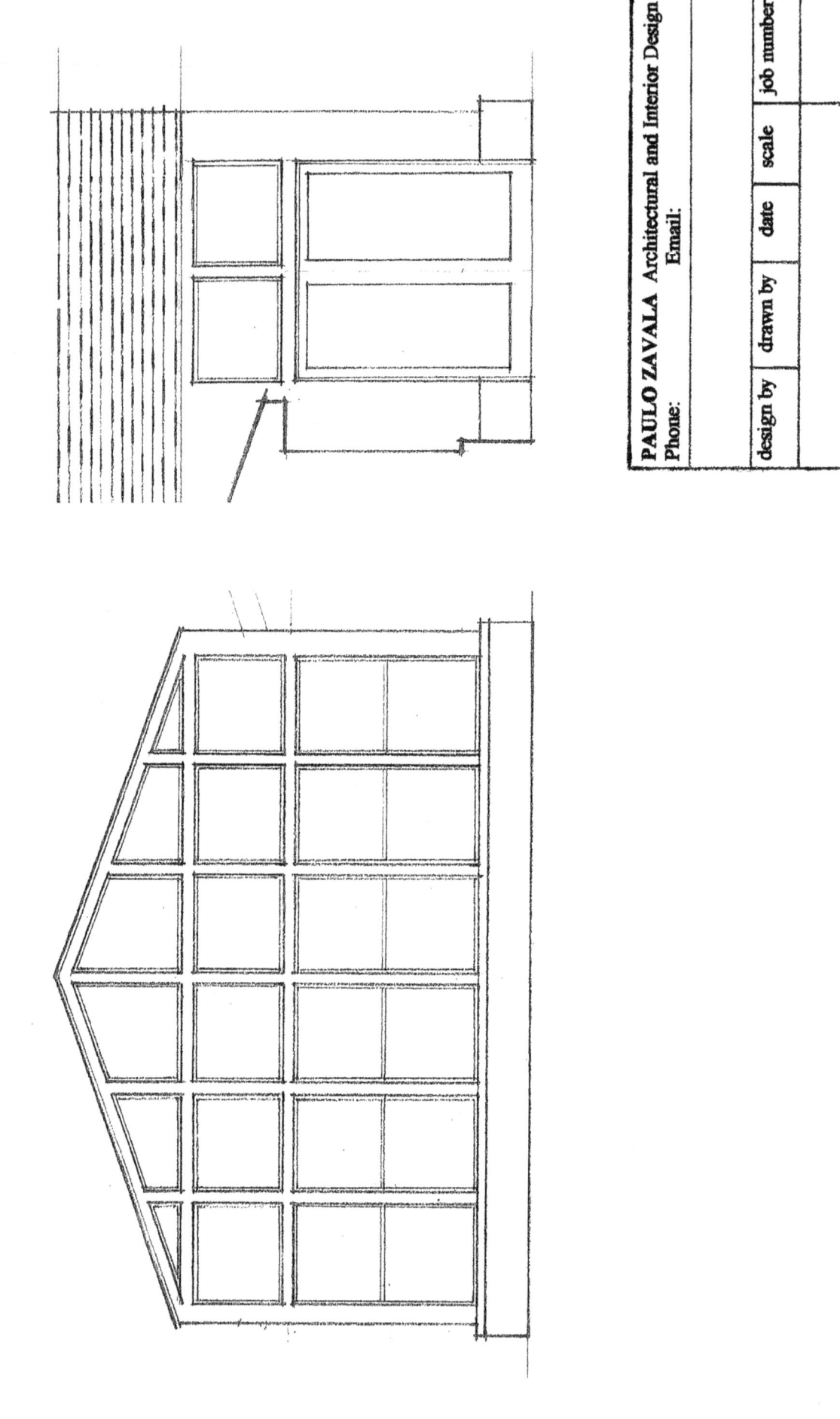

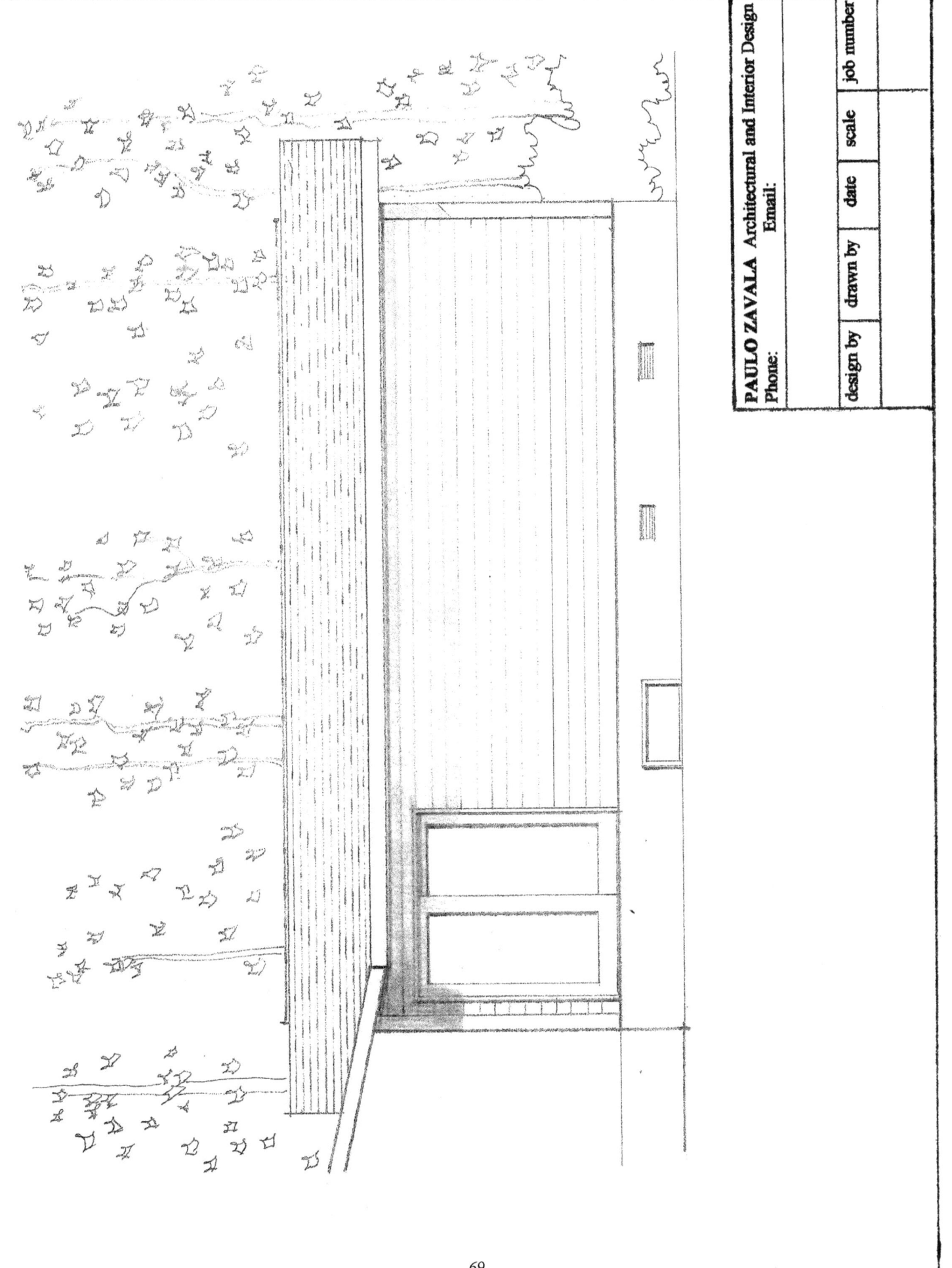

PAULO ZAVALA Architectural and Interior Design
Phone:
Email:

| design by | drawn by | date | scale | job number |

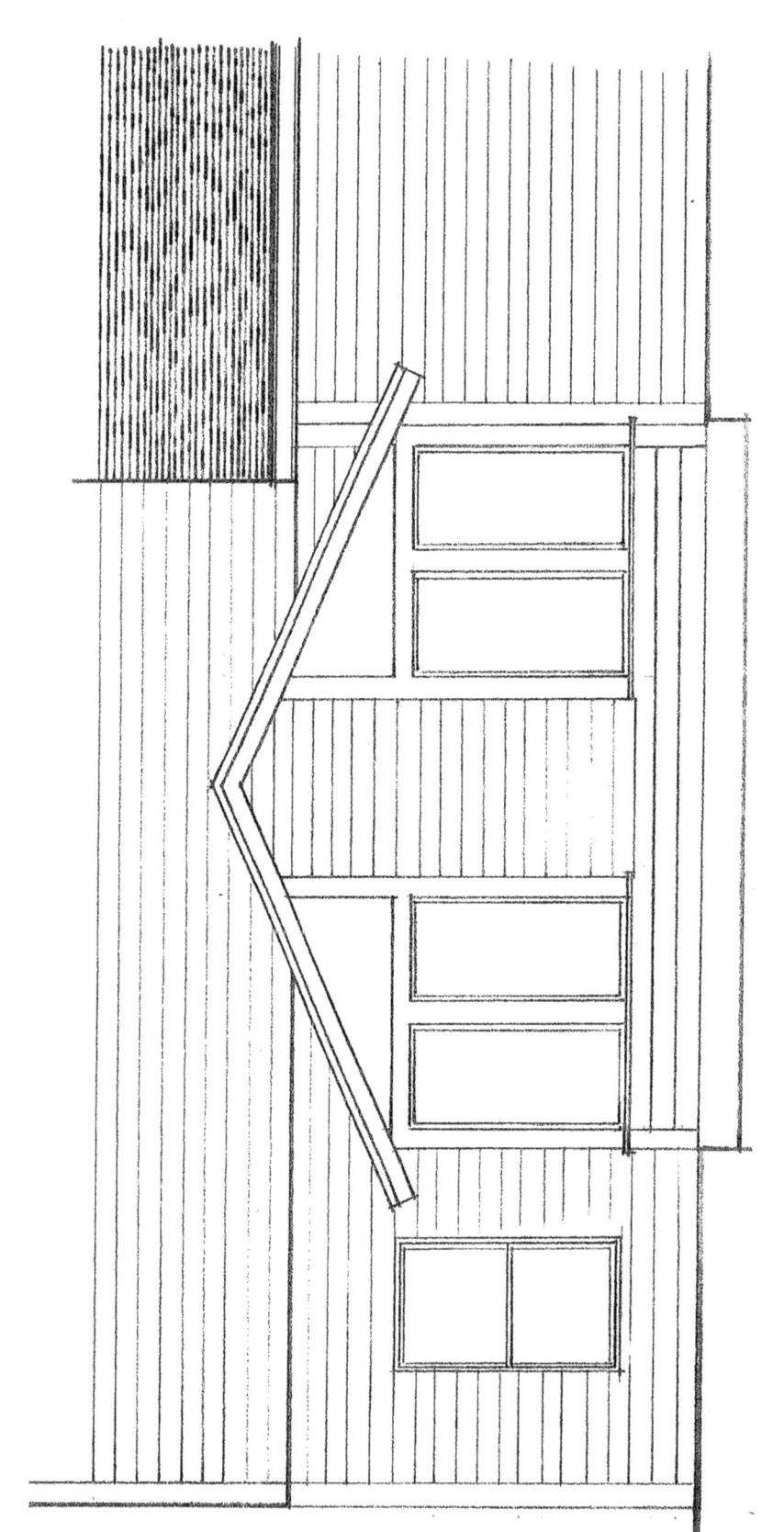

FRONT ELEVATION SCALE 1/4"=1'-0"

PAULO ZAVALA Architectural and Interior Design
Phone: Email:

design by	drawn by	date	scale	job number

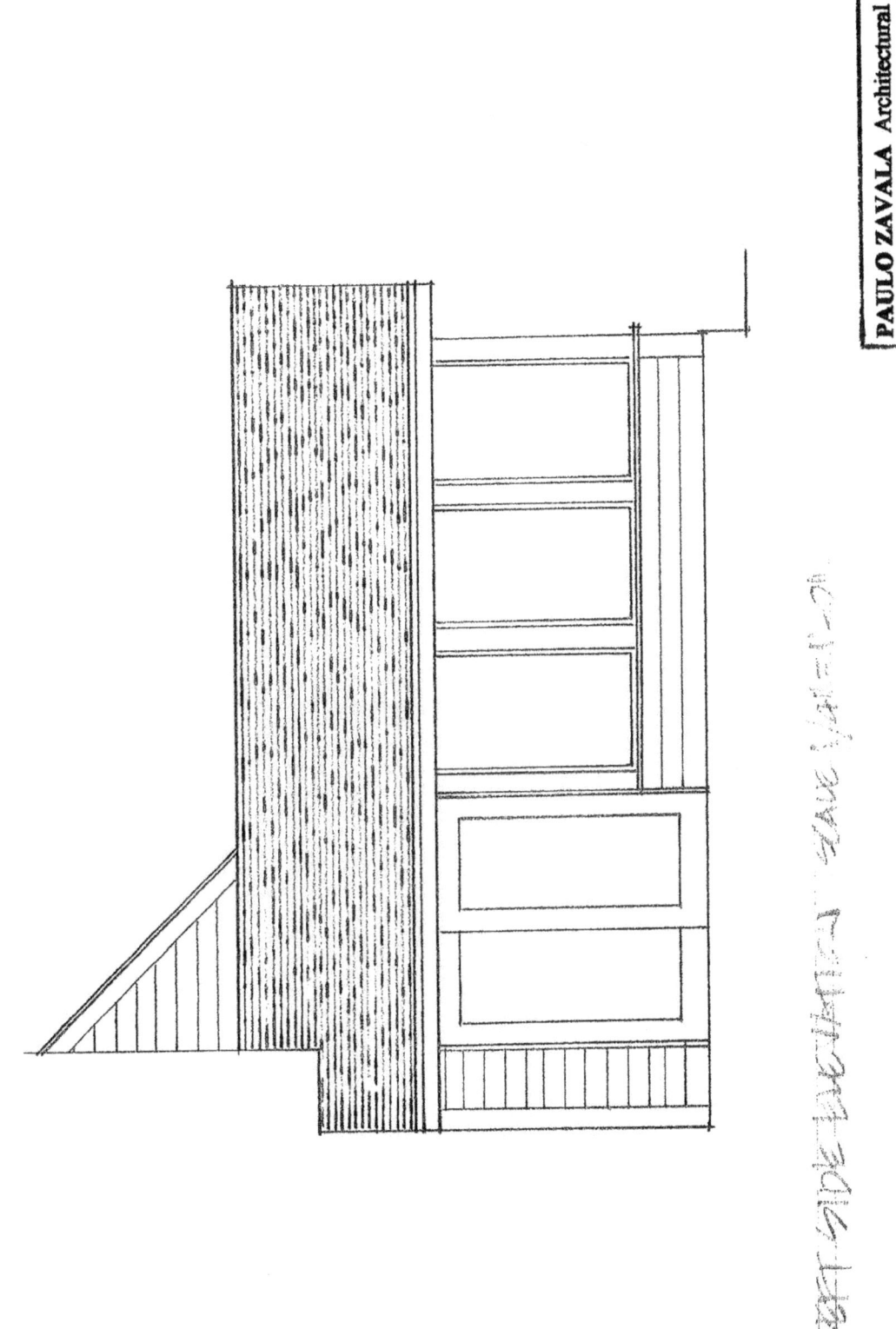

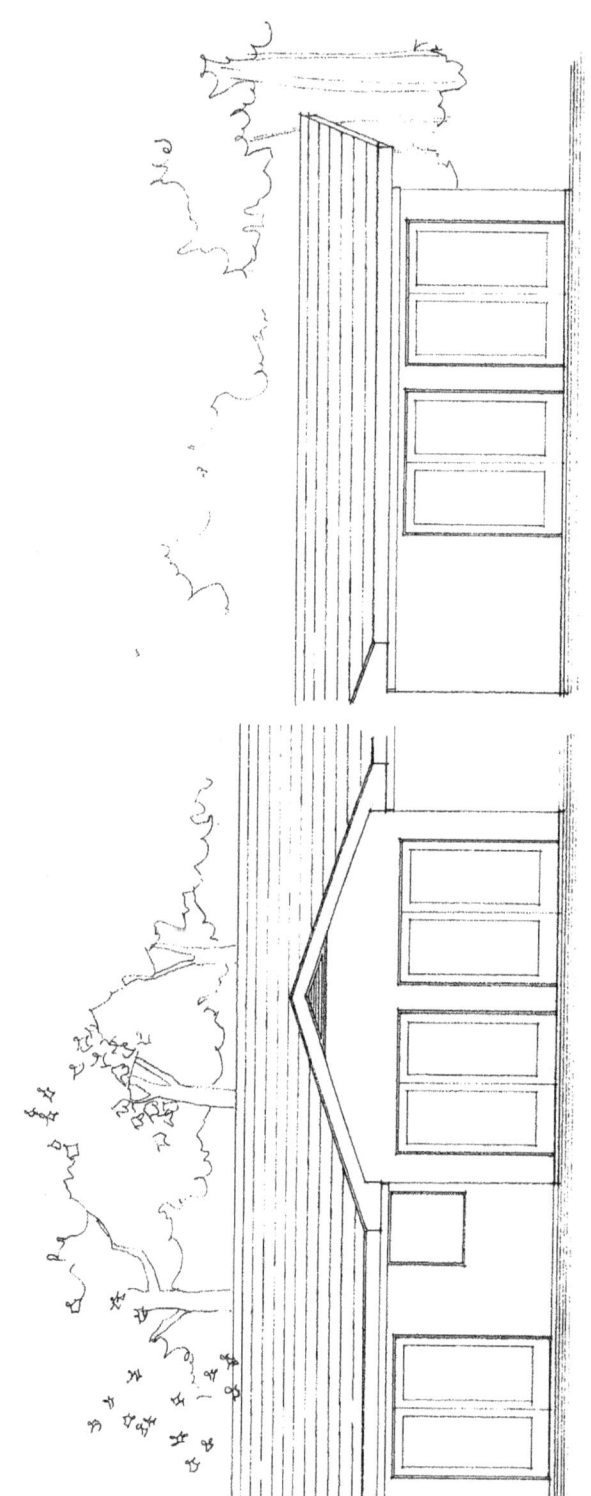

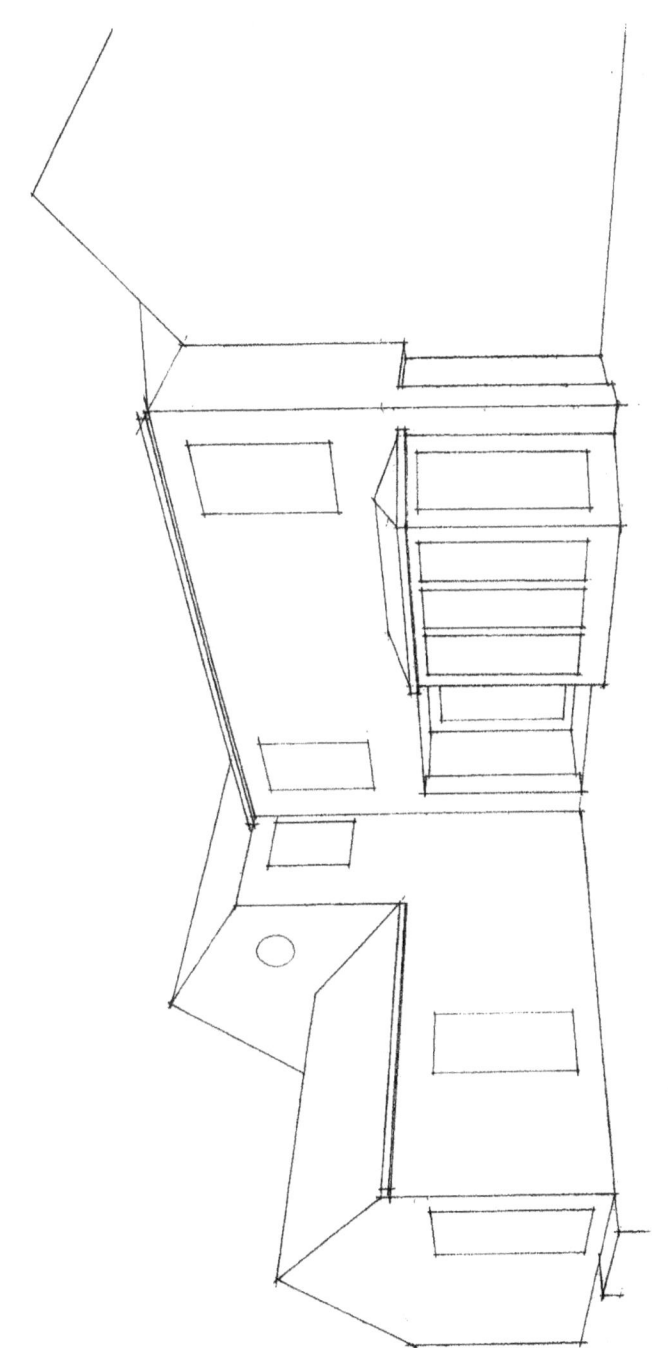

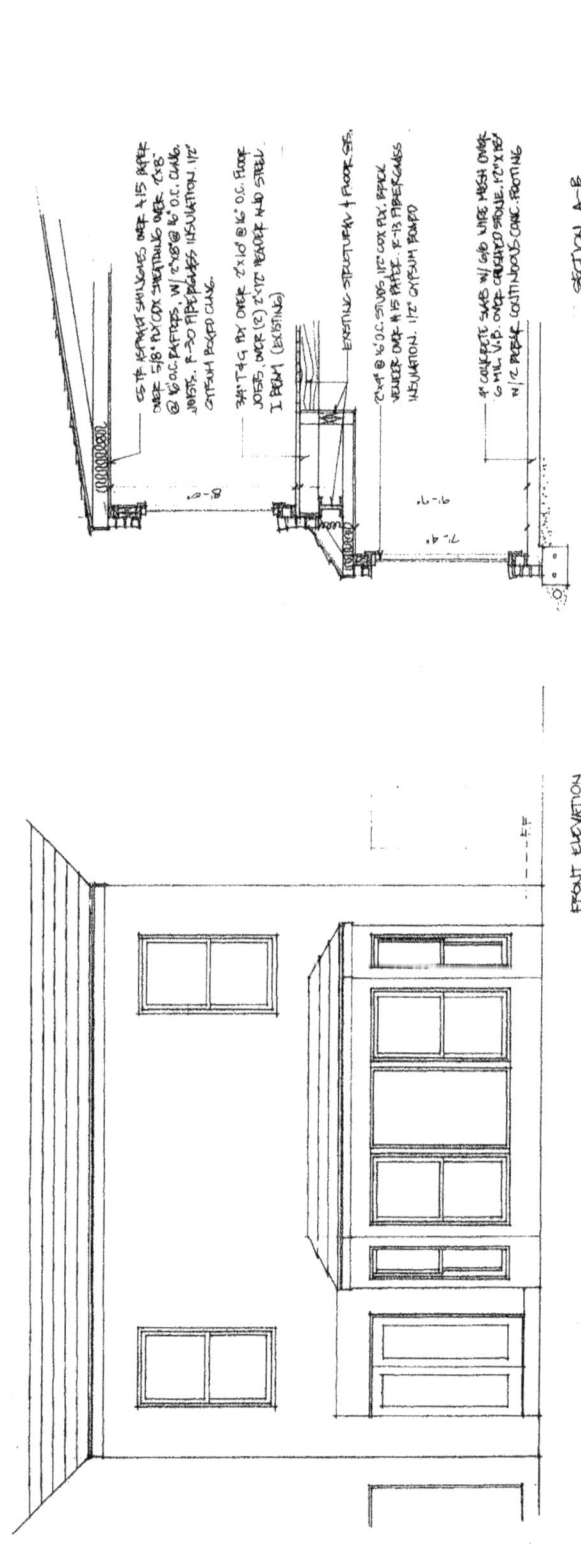

SECTION A-B

FRONT ELEVATION

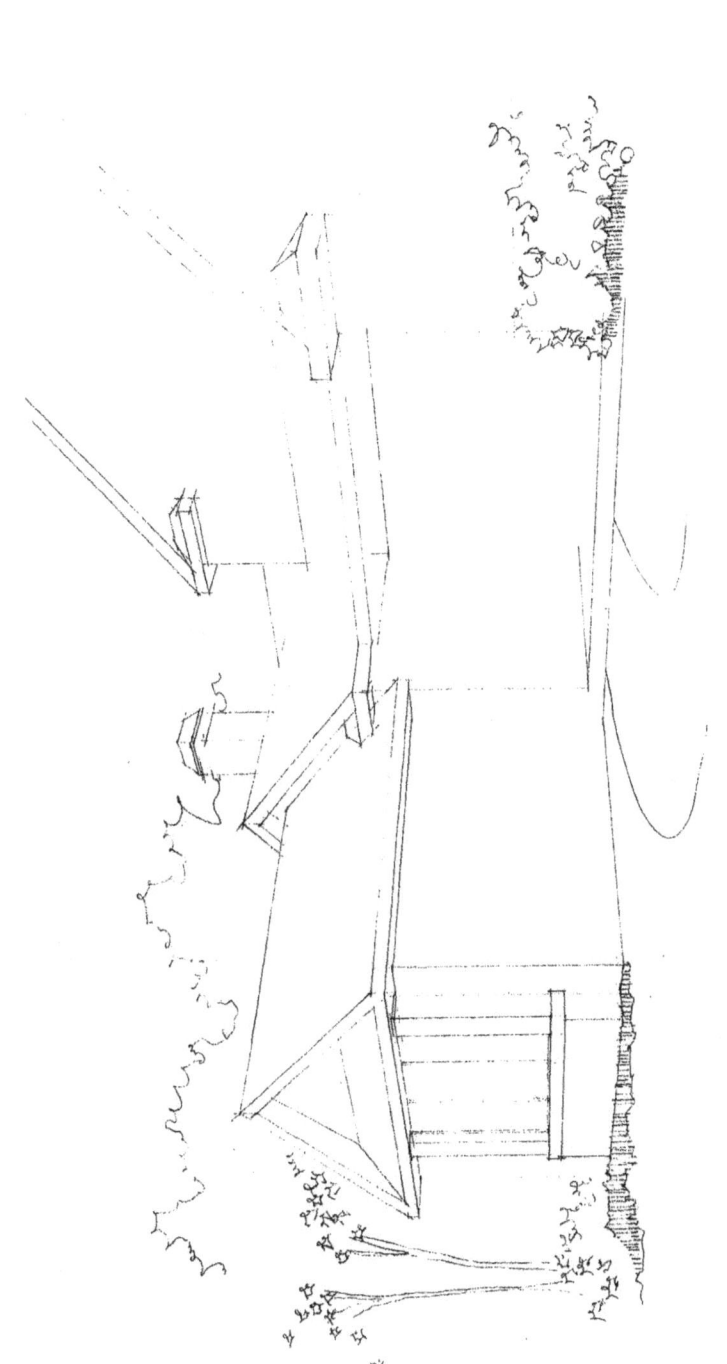

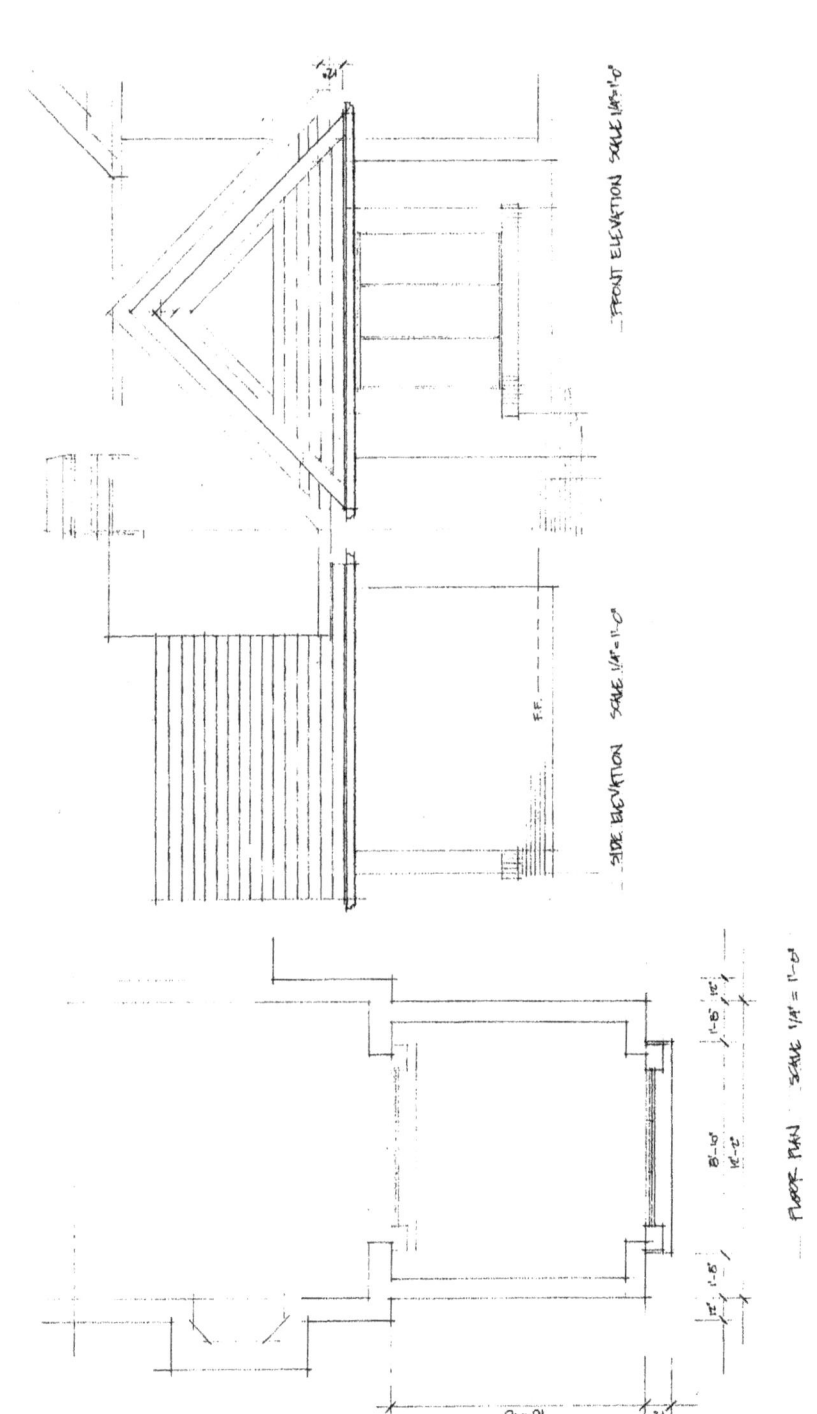

FRONT ELEVATION SCALE 1/4"=1'-0"

SIDE ELEVATION SCALE 1/4"=1'-0"

F.F.

FLOOR PLAN SCALE 1/4" = 1'-0"

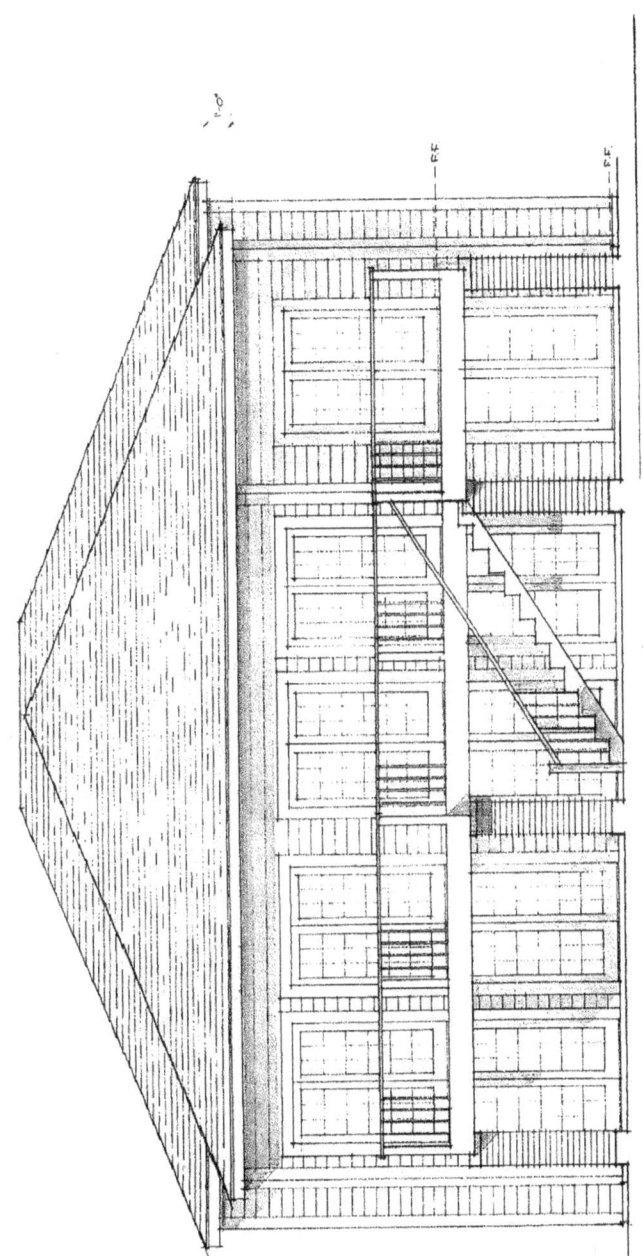

PAULO ZAVALA Architectural and Interior Design
Phone:
Email:

design by	drawn by	date	scale	job number

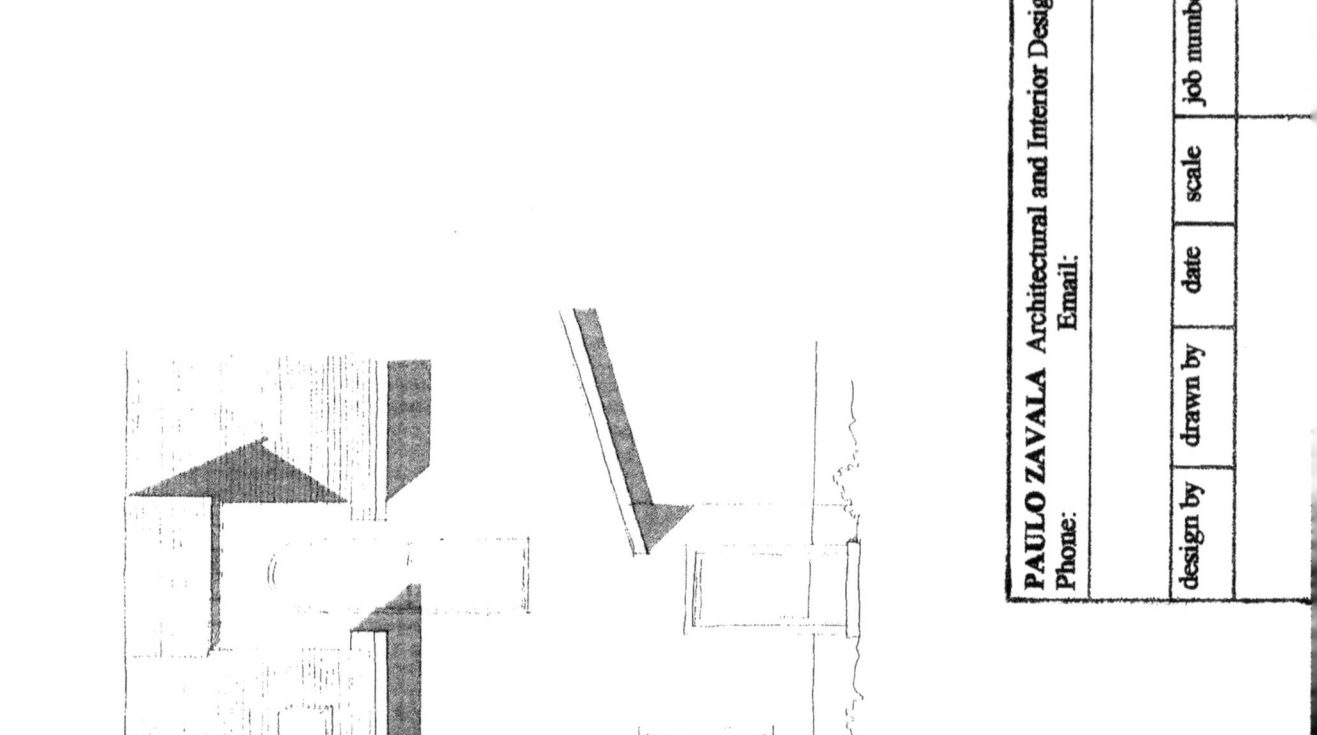

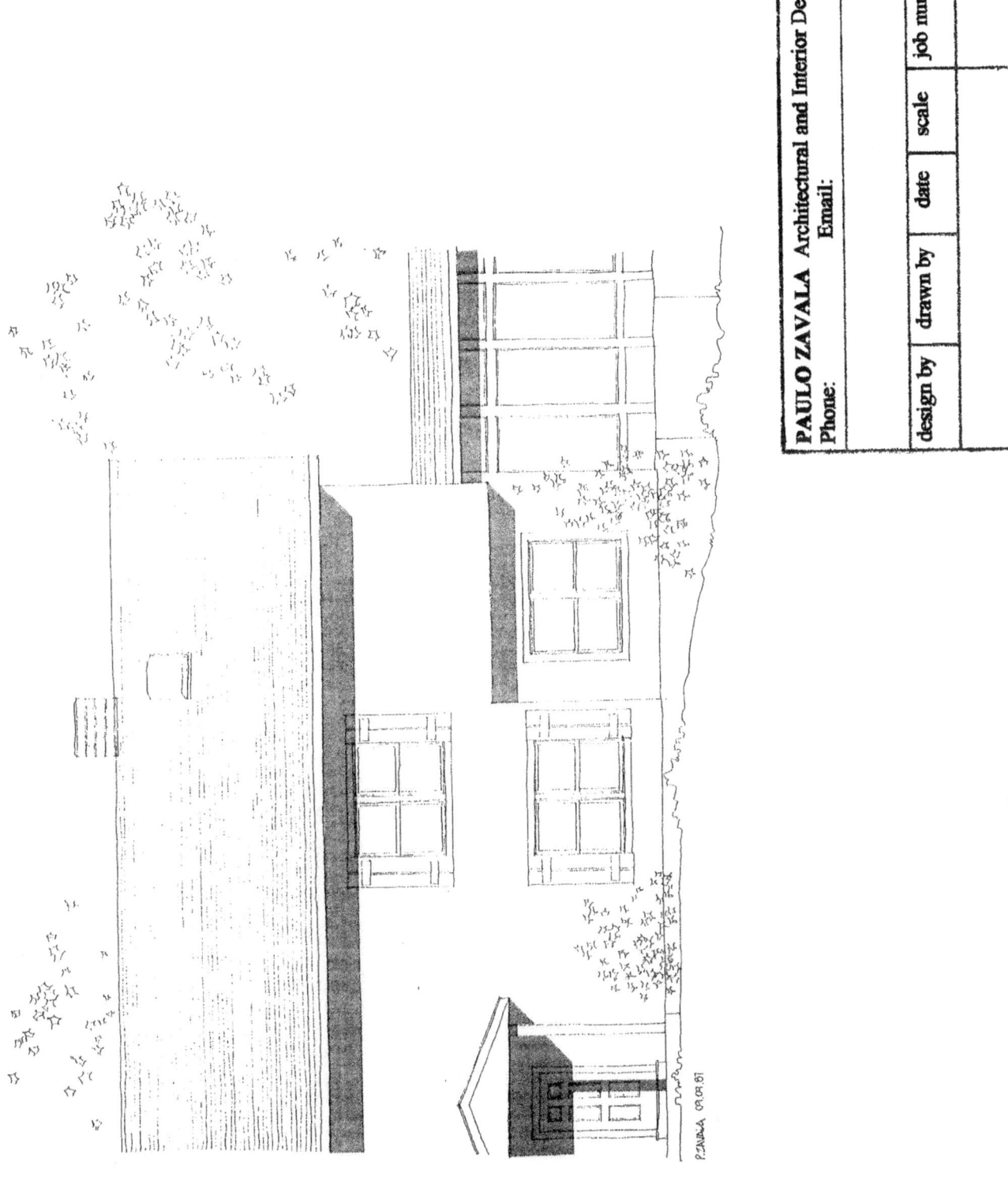

P.ZAVALA 09.09.81

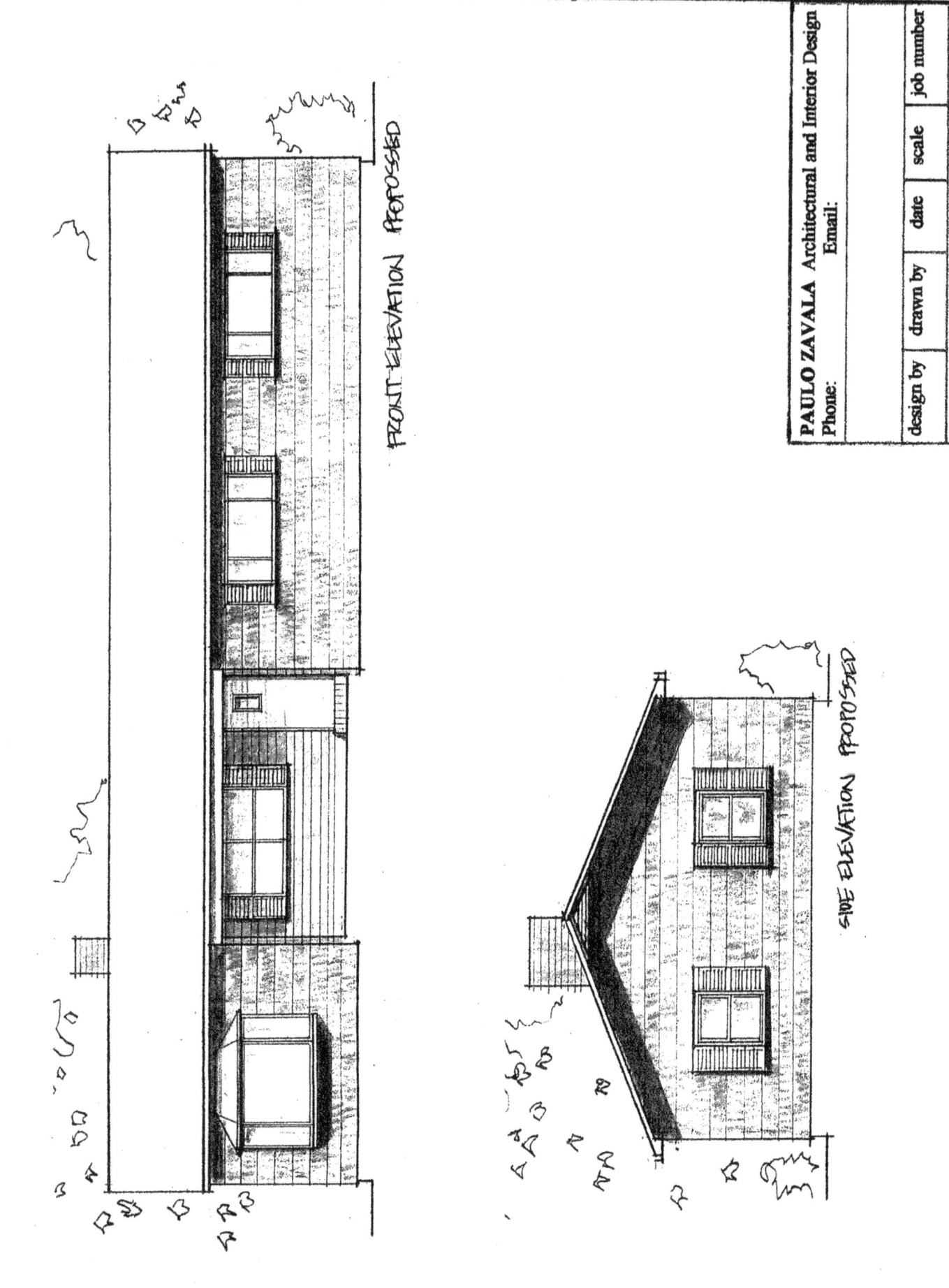

FRONT ELEVATION PROPOSSED

SIDE ELEVATION PROPOSSED

PAULO ZAVALA Architectural and Interior Design
Phone:
Email:

design by	drawn by	date	scale	job number

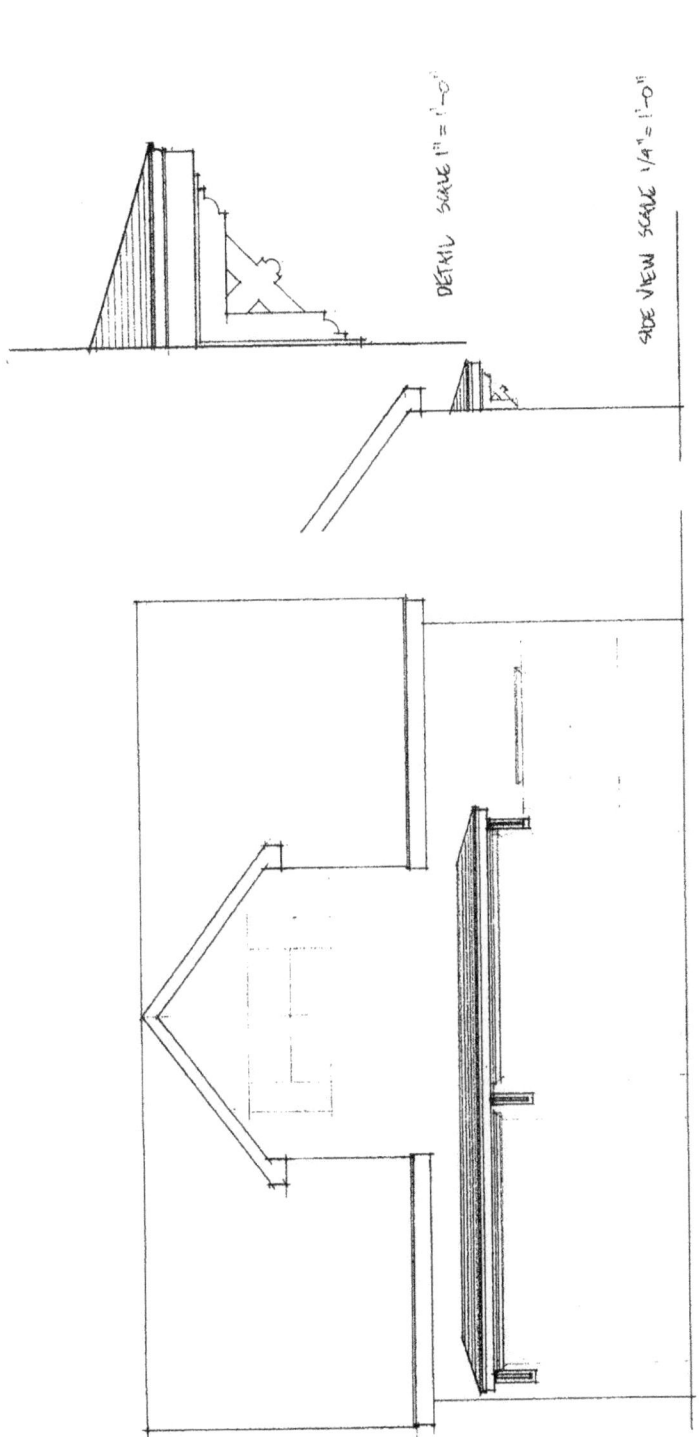

DETAIL SCALE 1" = 1'-0"

SIDE VIEW SCALE 1/4" = 1'-0"

ELEVATION SCALE 1/4" = 1'-0"

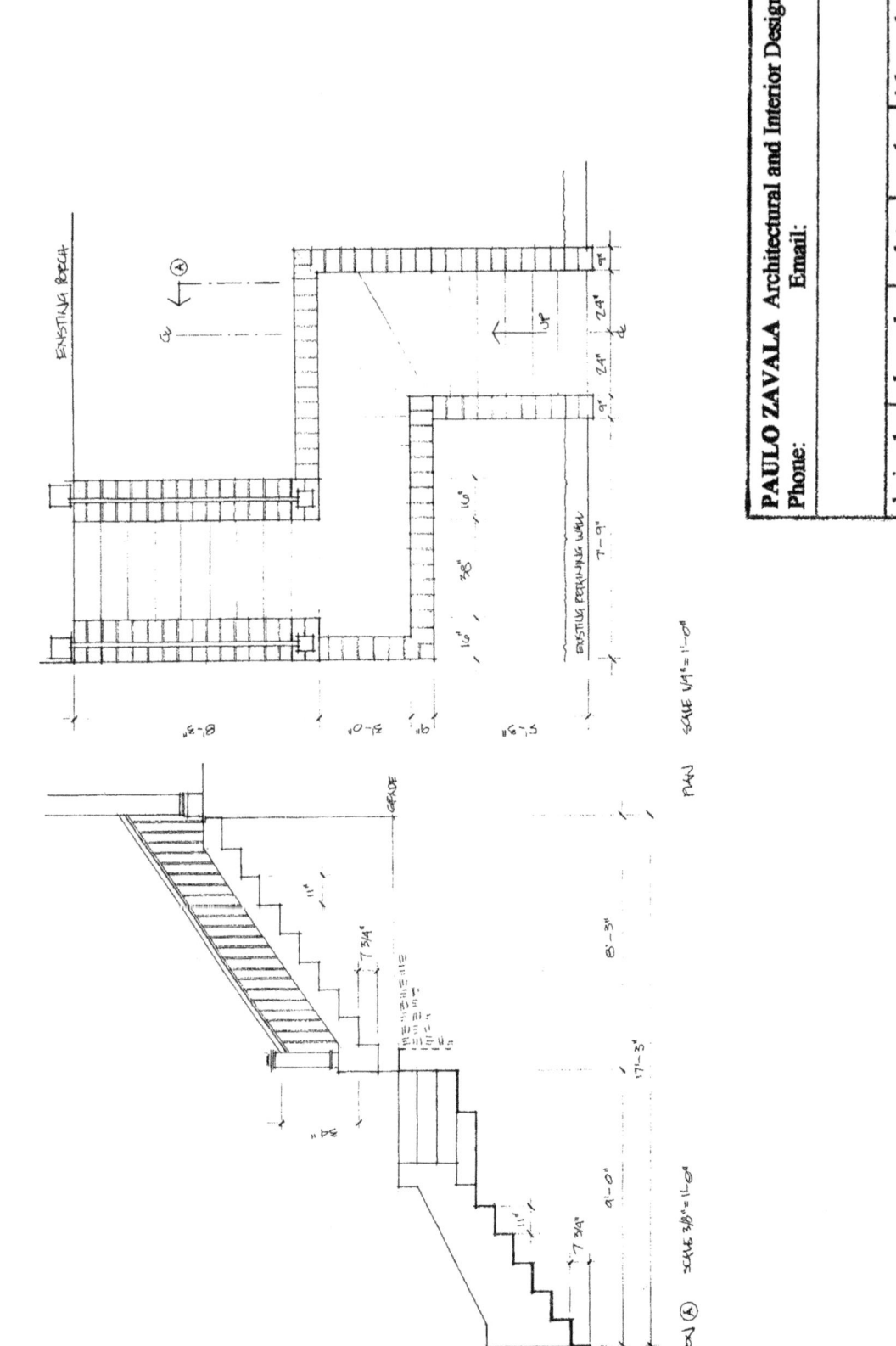

PLAN   SCALE 1/4"=1'-0"

SECTION A   SCALE 3/8"=1'-0"

PAULO ZAVALA Architectural and Interior Design
Phone:
Email:

design by	drawn by	date	scale	job number

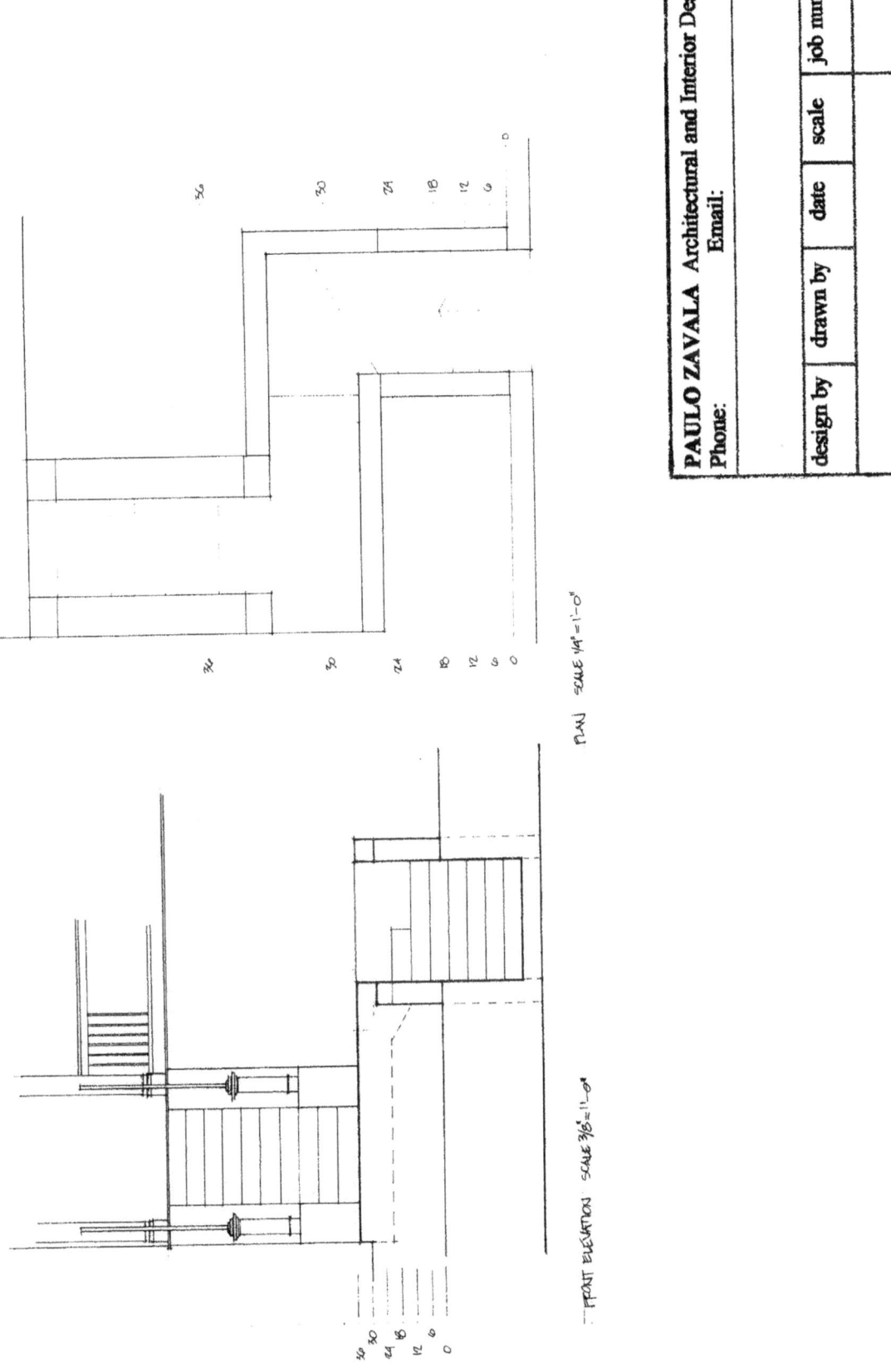

PLAN SCALE 1/4" = 1'-0"

FRONT ELEVATION SCALE 3/8" = 1'-0"

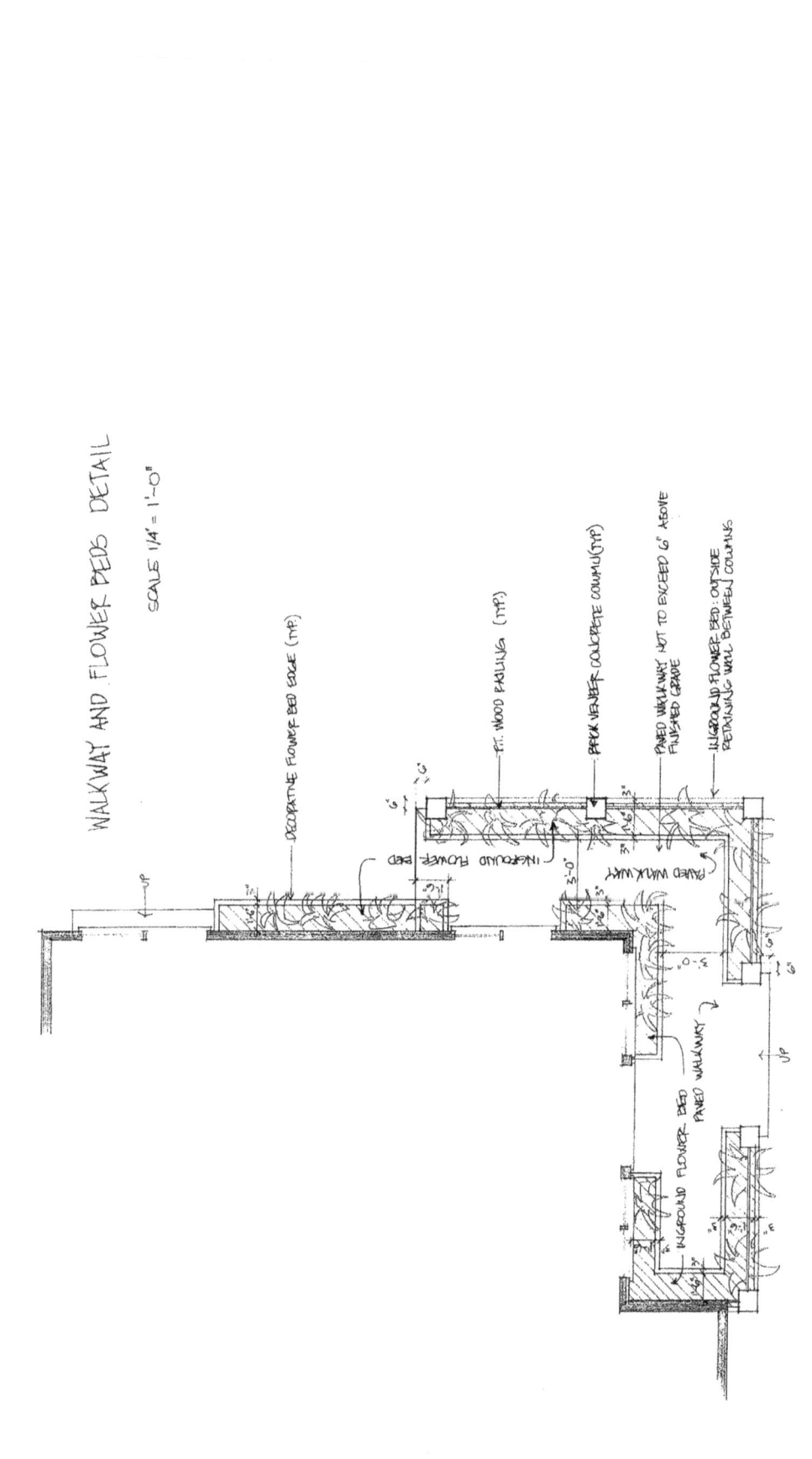

WALKWAY AND FLOWER BEDS DETAIL

SCALE 1/4" = 1'-0"

DECORATIVE FLOWER BED EDGE (TYP.)

PT. WOOD RAILING (TYP.)

BRICK VENEER CONCRETE COLUMN (TYP)

PAVED WALKWAY NOT TO EXCEED 6" ABOVE FINISHED GRADE

INGROUND FLOWER BED OUTSIDE RETAINING WALL BETWEEN COLUMNS

INGROUND FLOWER BED

PAVED WALKWAY

INGROUND FLOWER BED

PAVED WALKWAY

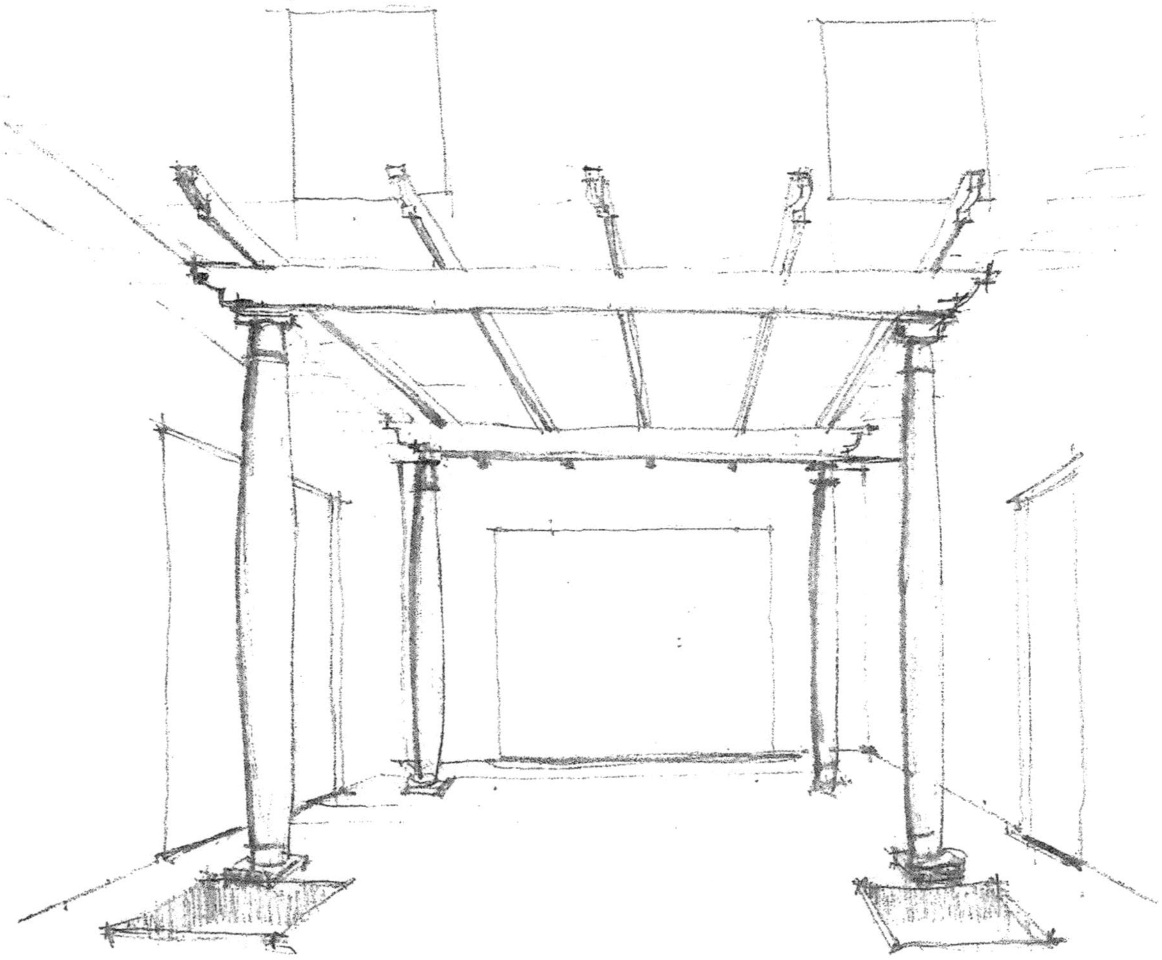

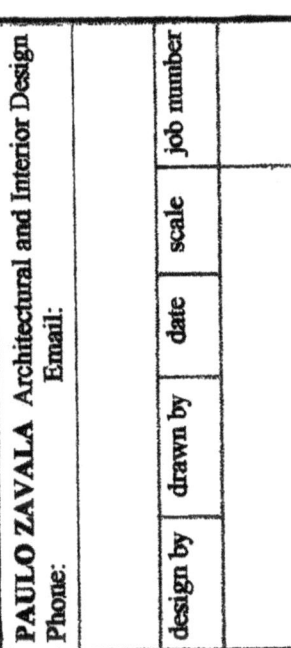

PAULO ZAVALA Architectural and Interior Design
Phone:
Email:

design by	drawn by	date	scale	job number

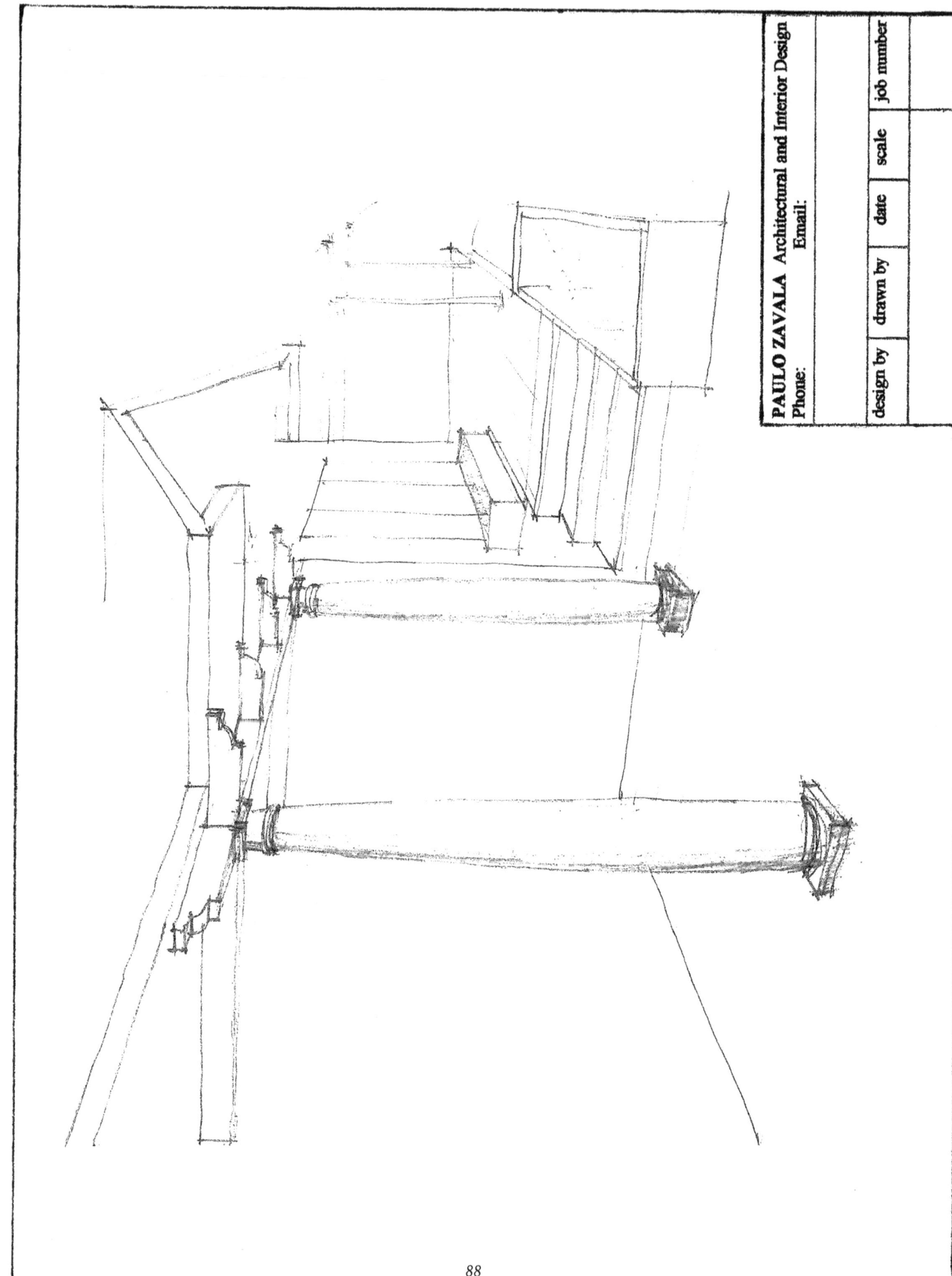

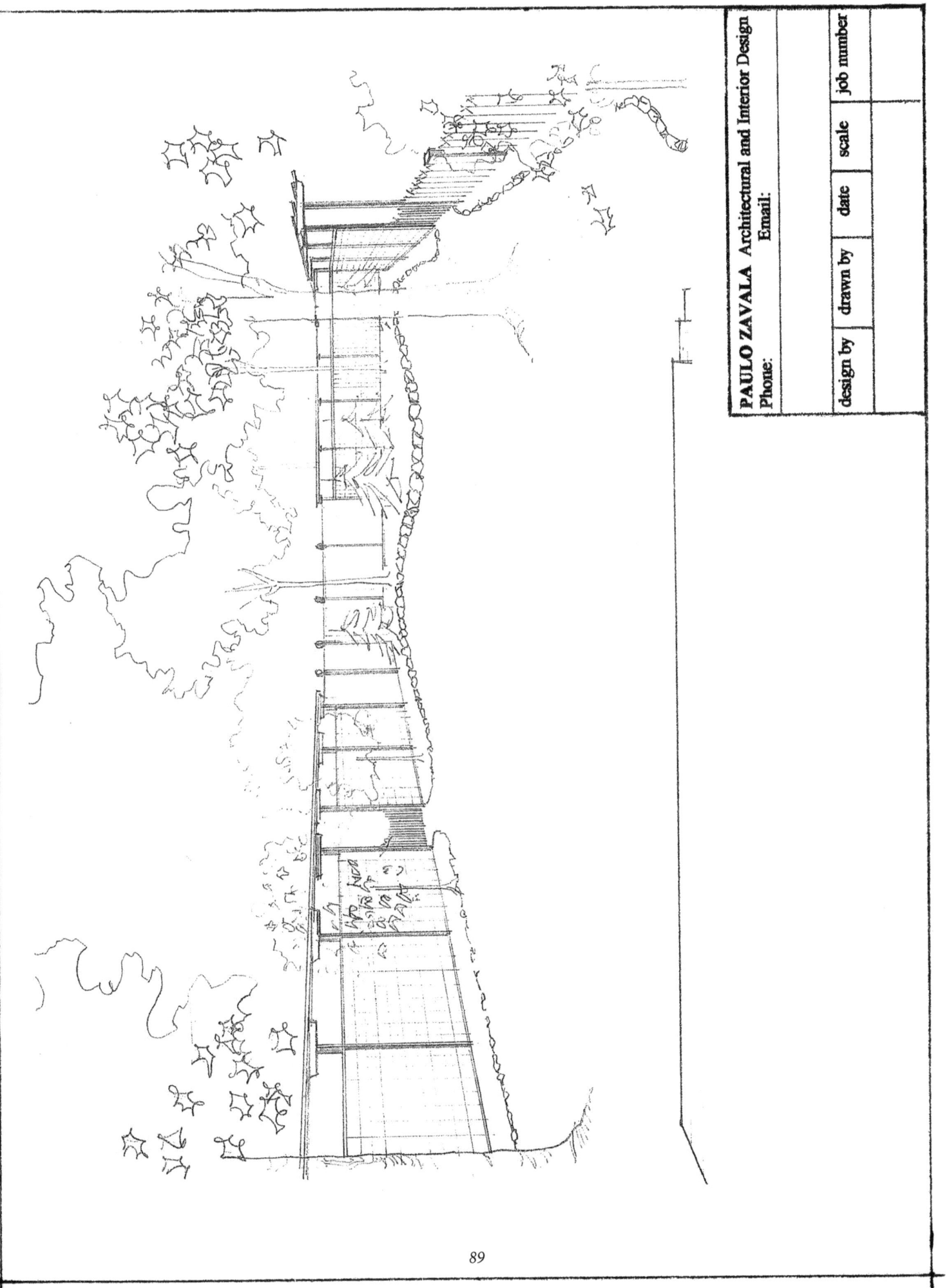

PAULO ZAVALA Architectural and Interior Design
Phone:
Email:

design by	drawn by	date	scale	job number

FRONT ELEVATION

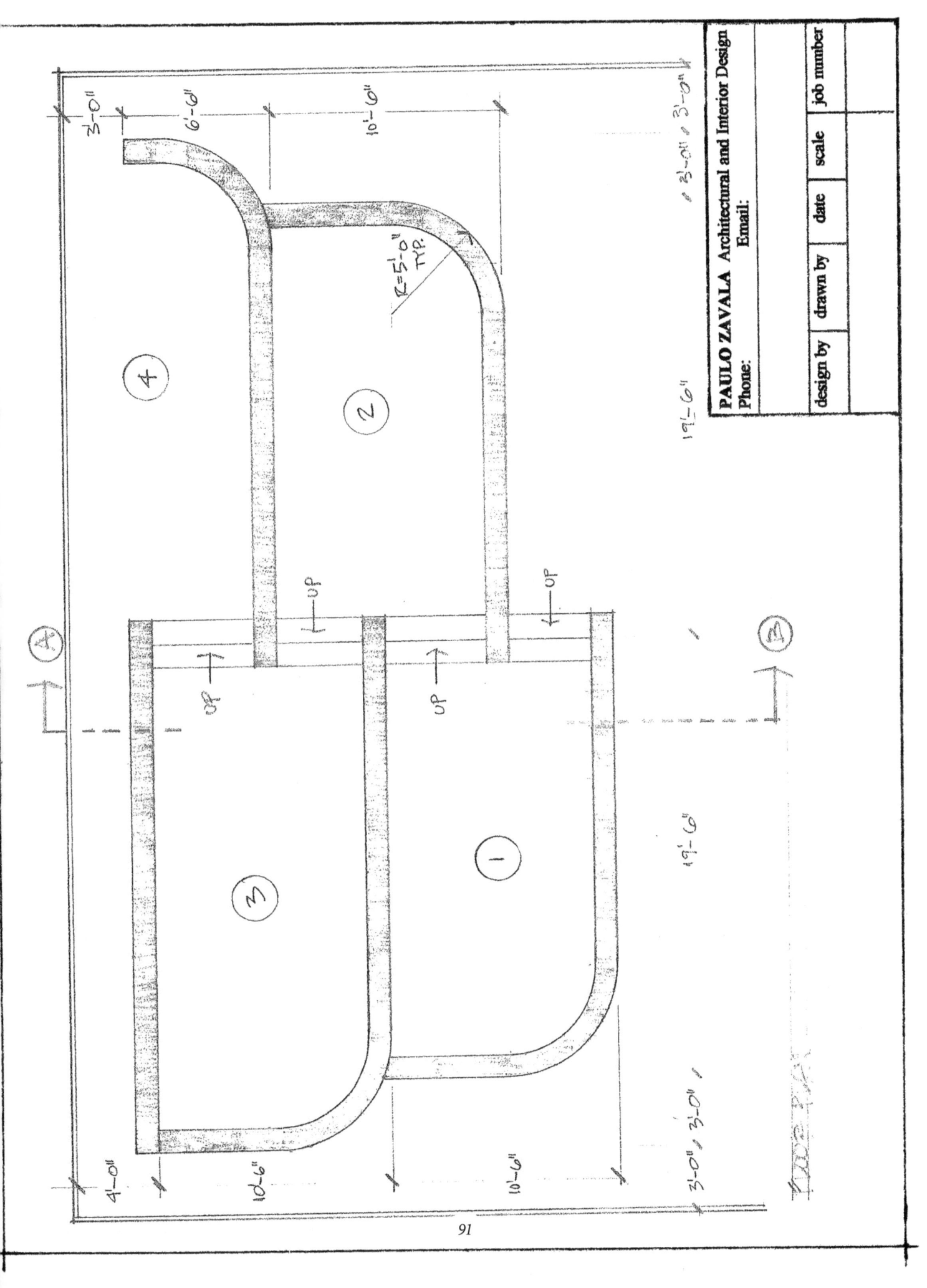

NOTE: PANELS TO BE PLACE INWARDS ON EITHER

SECTION Ⓐ - Ⓑ

PAULO ZAVALA Architectural and Interior Design
Phone:
Email:

design by	drawn by	date	scale	job number

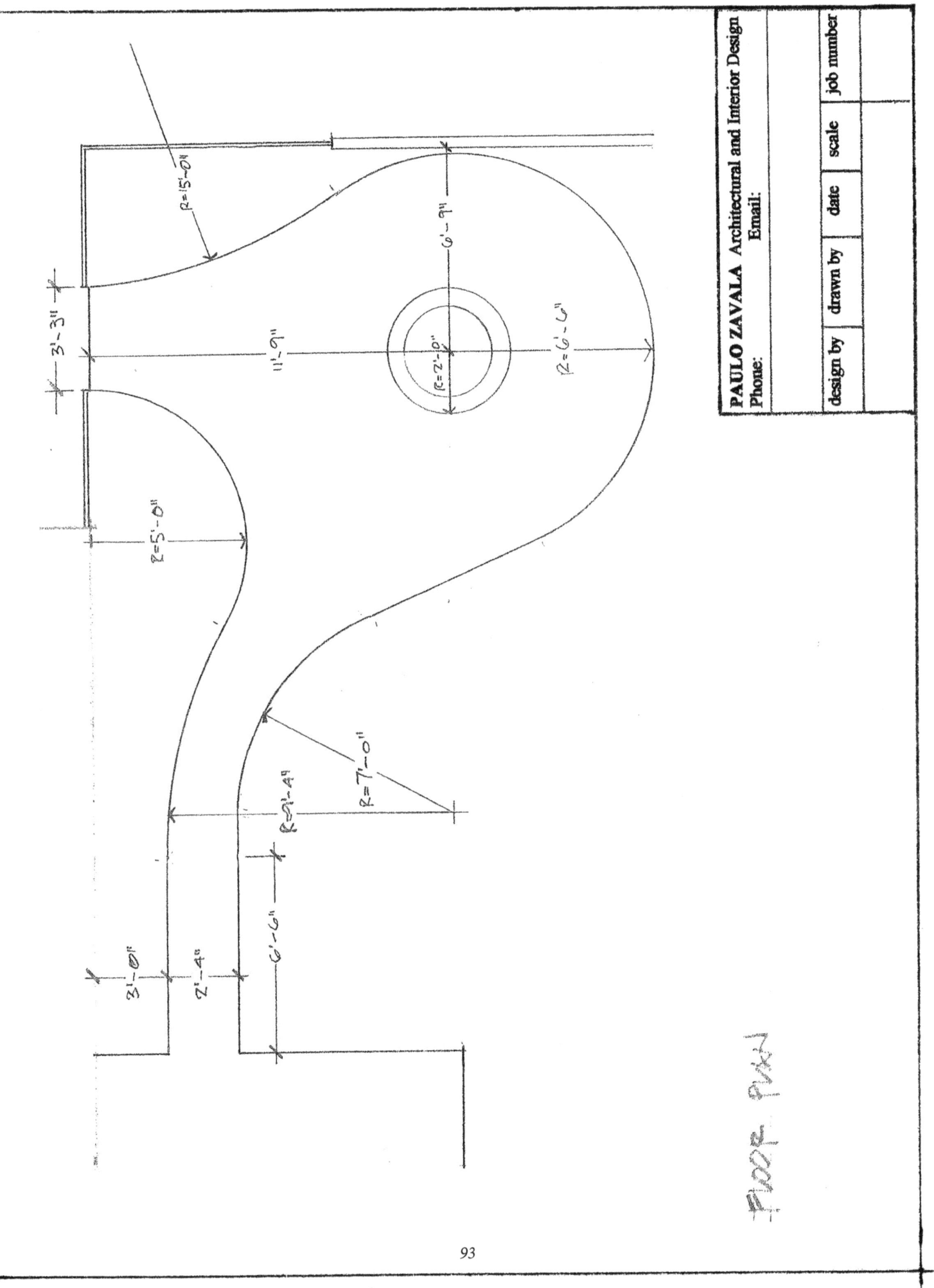

R=15'-0"

3'-3"

R=5'-0"

11'-9"

R=2'-0"

6'-9"

R=6'-0"

R=7'-0"

R=2'-4"

3'-0"

2'-4"

6'-6"

FLOOR PLAN

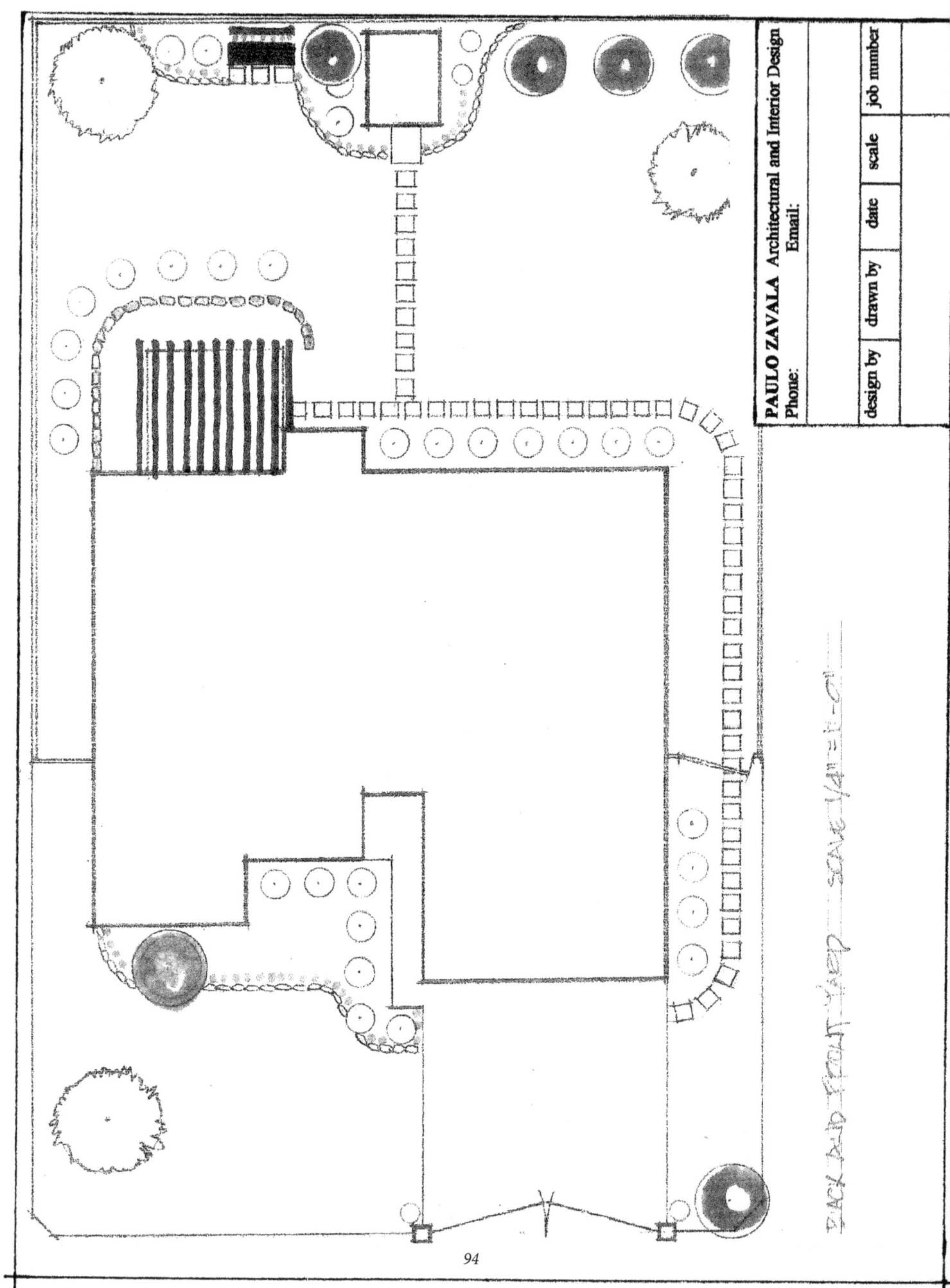

PAULO ZAVALA Architectural and Interior Design
Phone: Email:

job number

scale

date

drawn by

design by

94

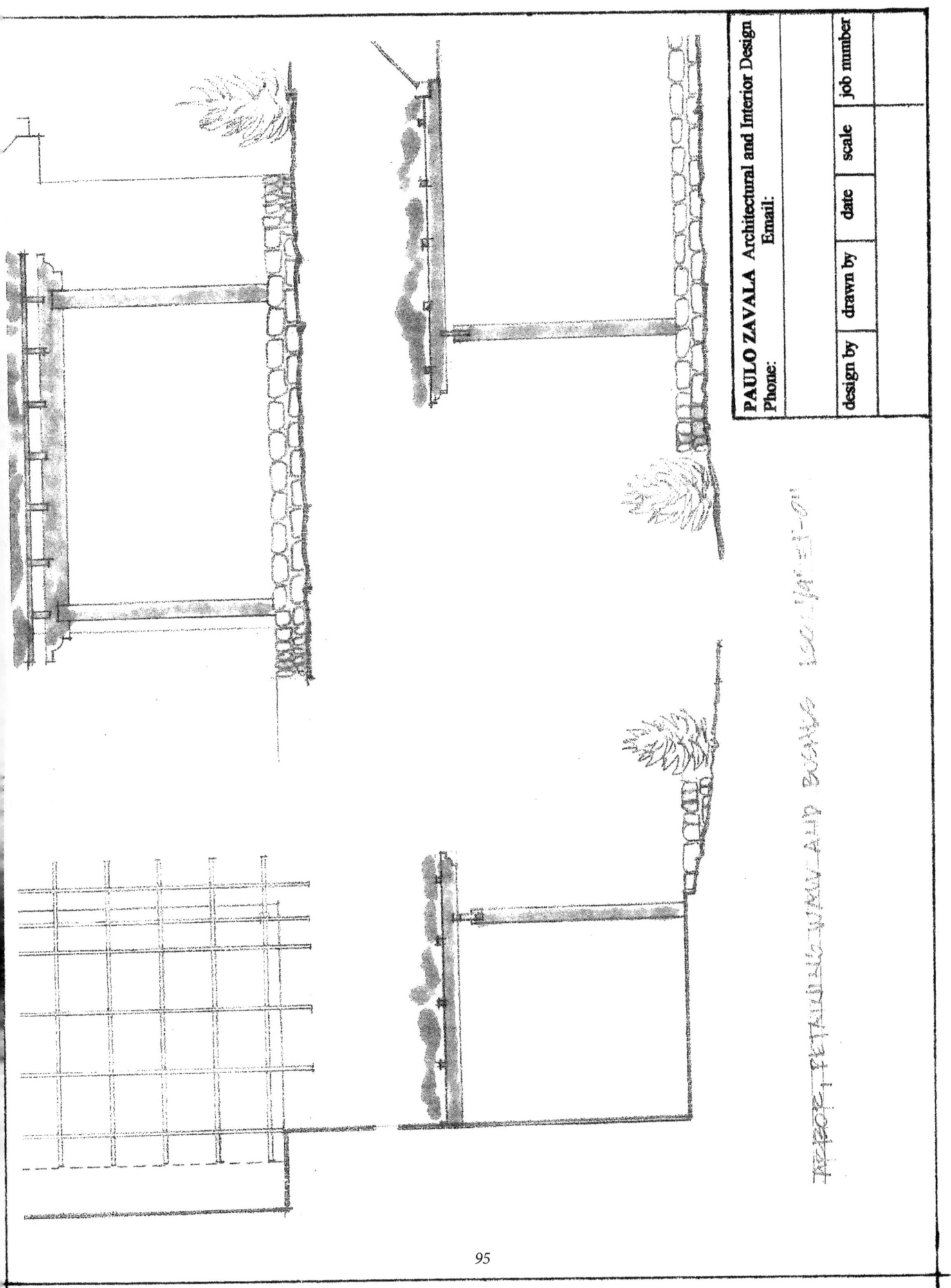

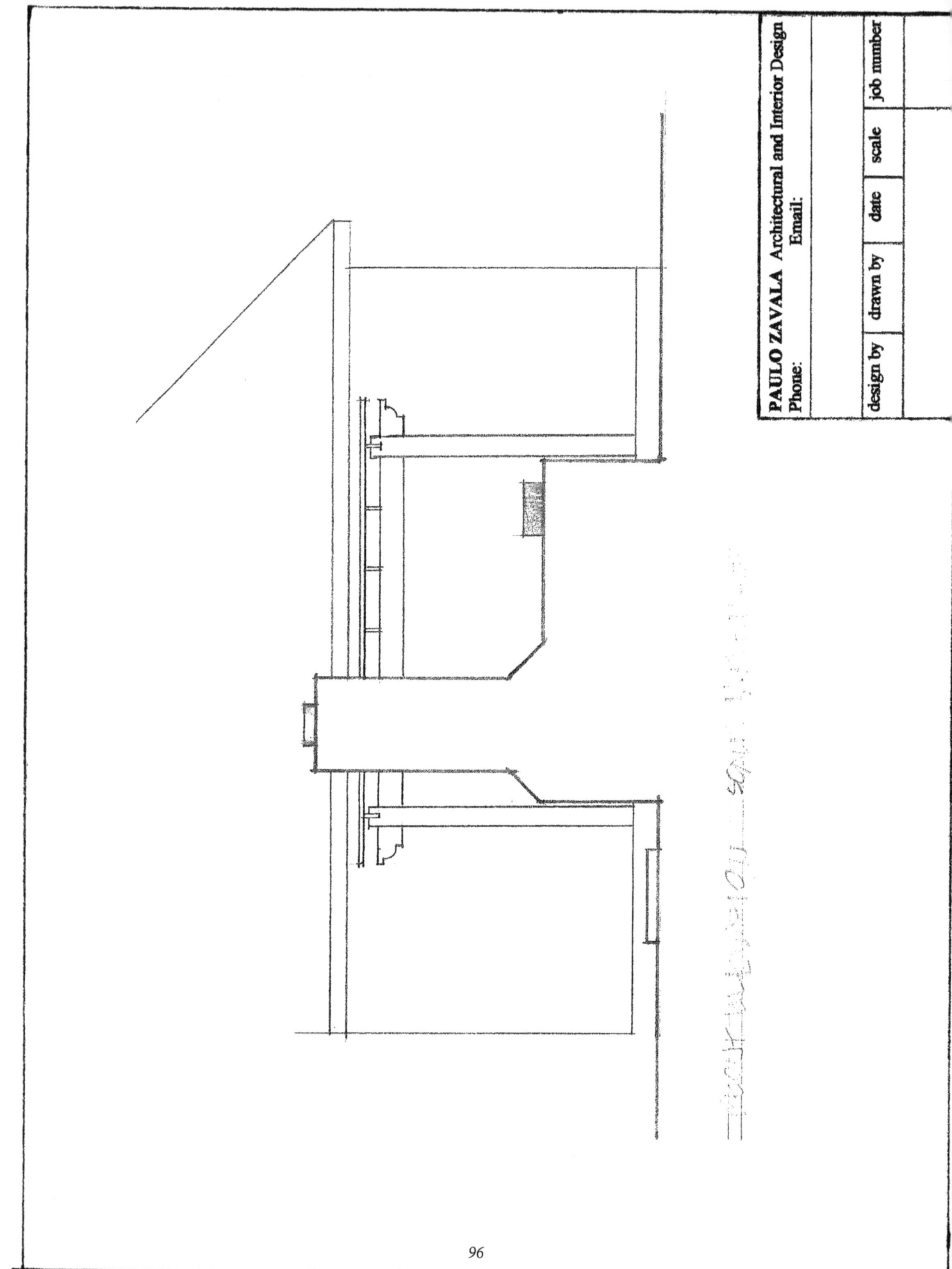

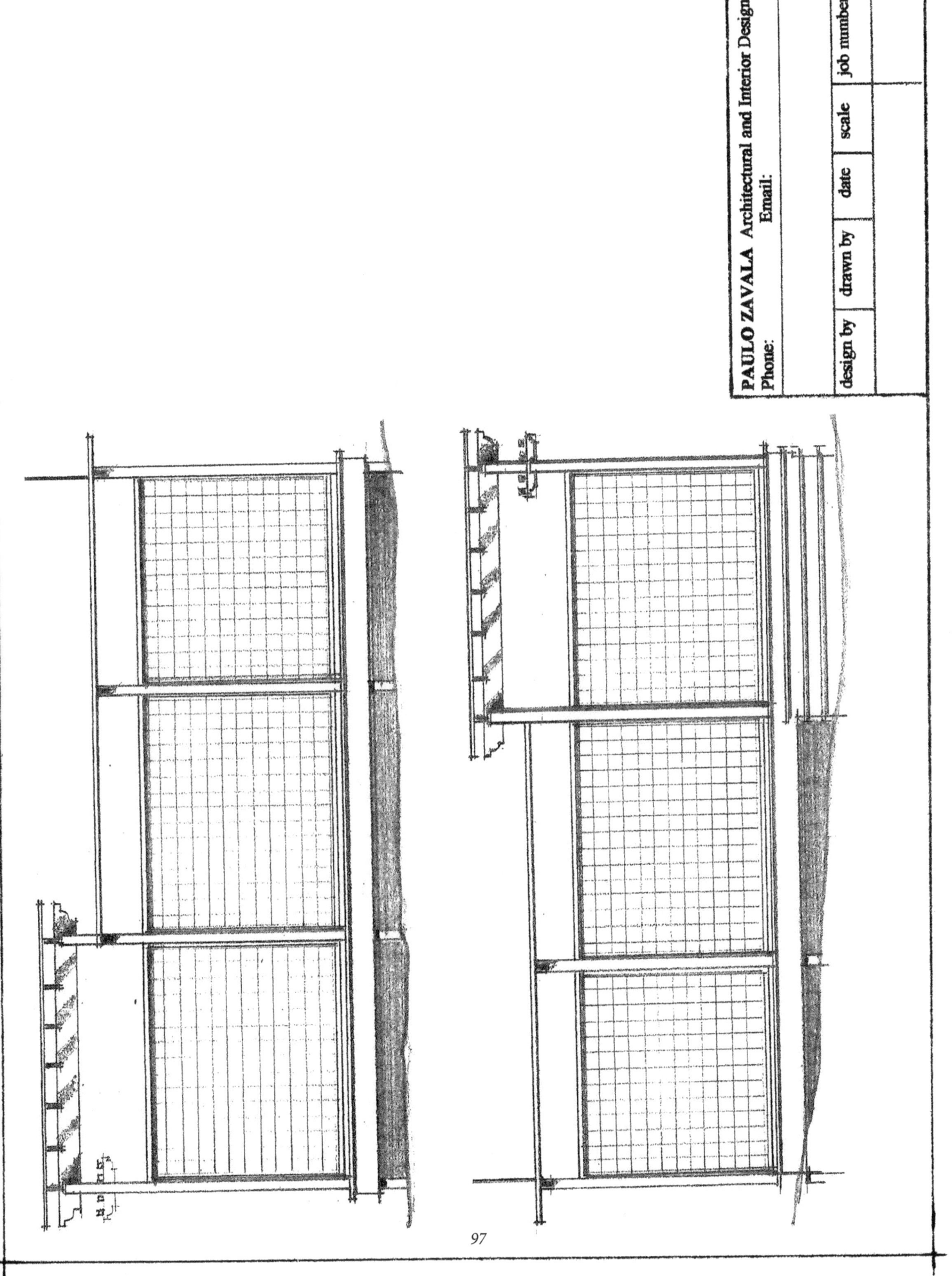

PAULO ZAVALA Architectural and Interior Design
Phone:
Email:

design by	drawn by	date	scale	job number

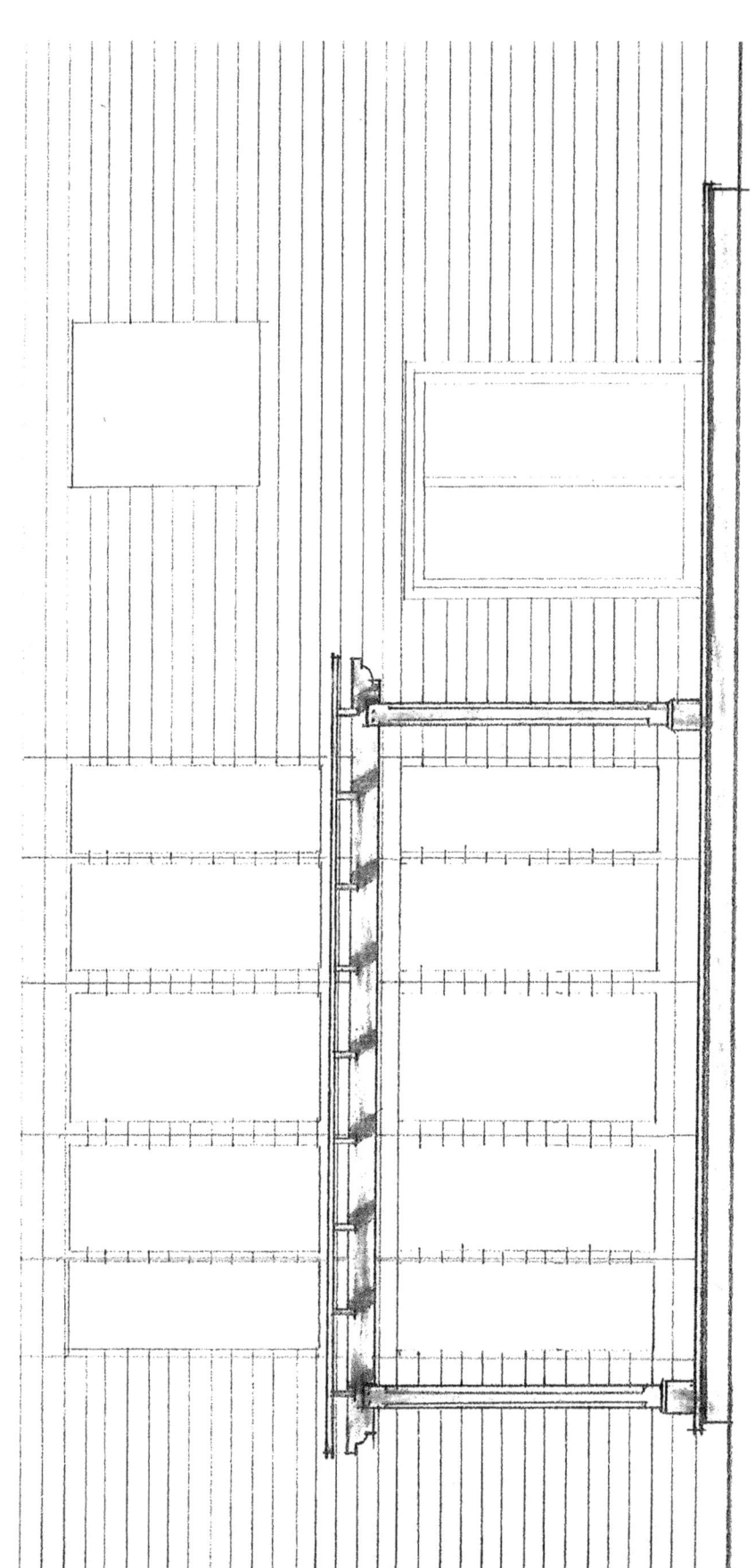

FRONT ELEVATION SCALE 1/4" = 1'-0"

PAULO ZAVALA Architectural and Interior Design
Phone: Email:

design by	drawn by	date	scale	job number

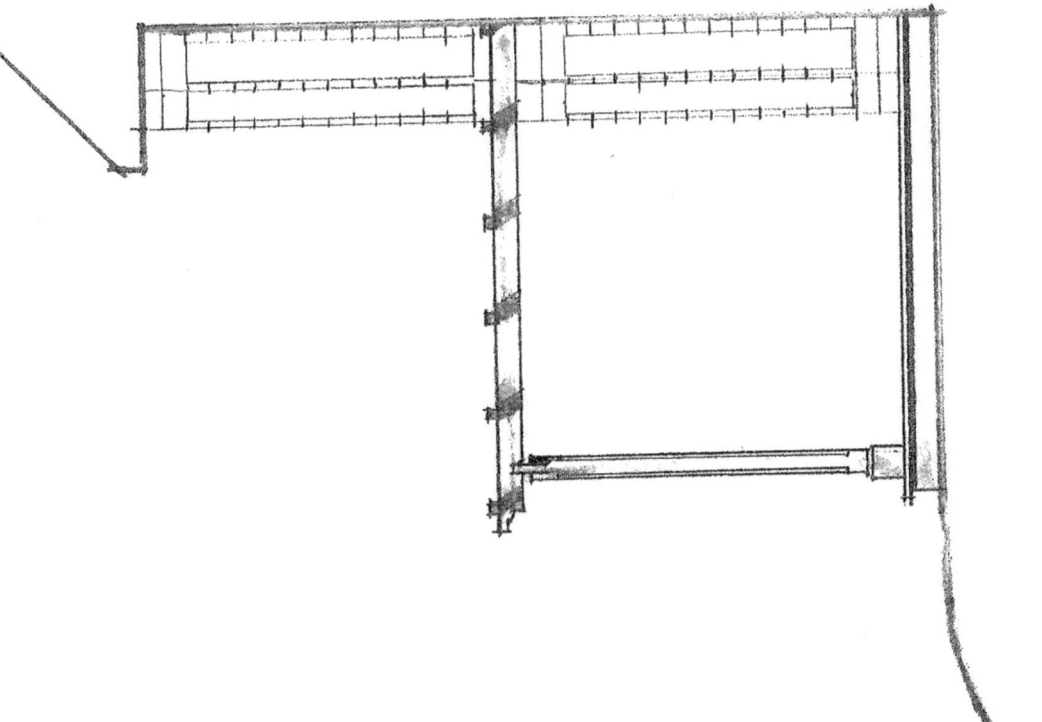

RIGHT SIDE ELEVATION   SCALE 1/4" = 1'-0"

PAULO ZAVALA Architectural and Interior Design
Phone: Email:

design by	drawn by	date	scale	job number

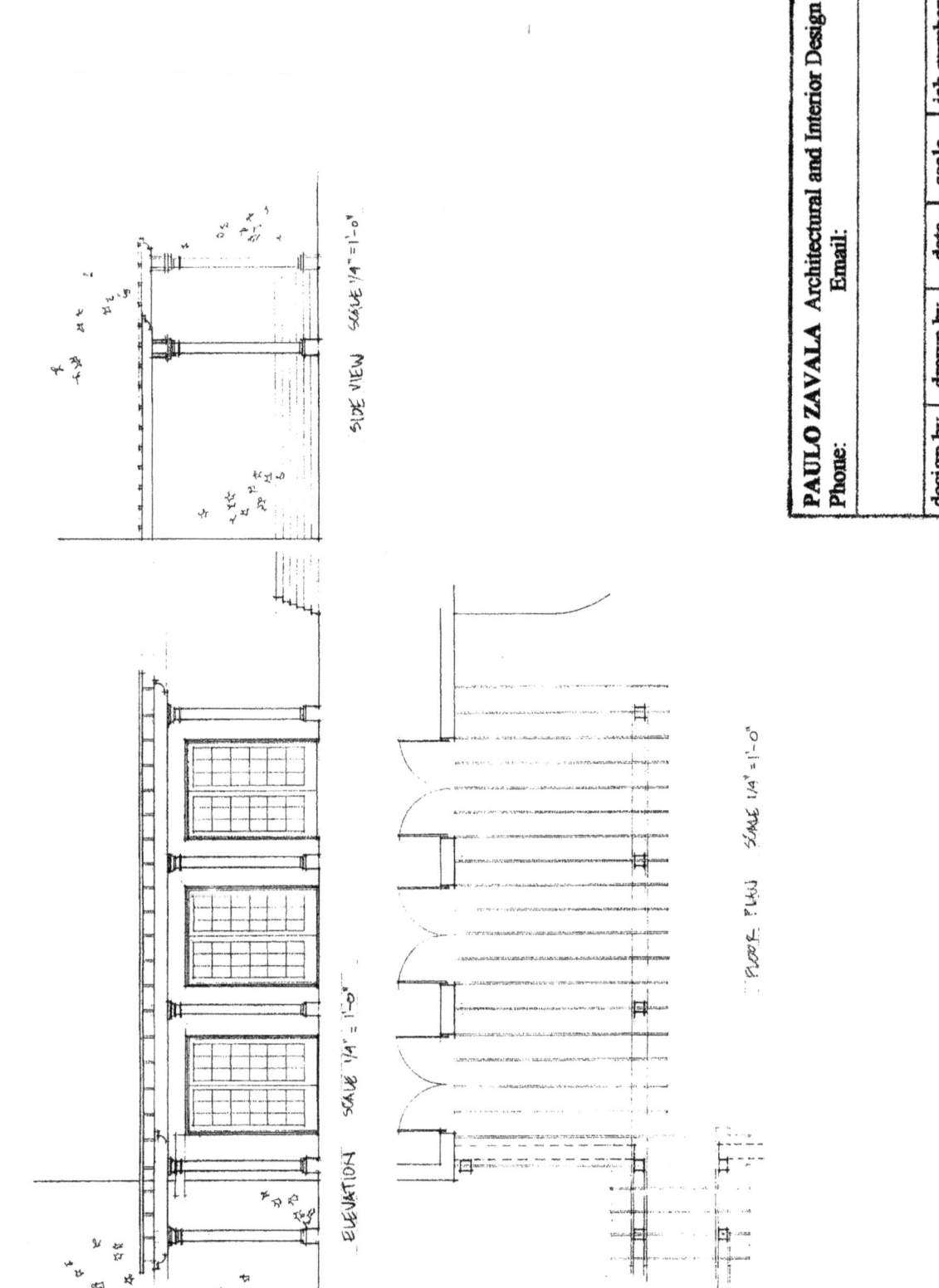

SIDE VIEW SCALE 1/4" = 1'-0"

ELEVATION SCALE 1/4" = 1'-0"

FLOOR PLAN SCALE 1/4" = 1'-0"

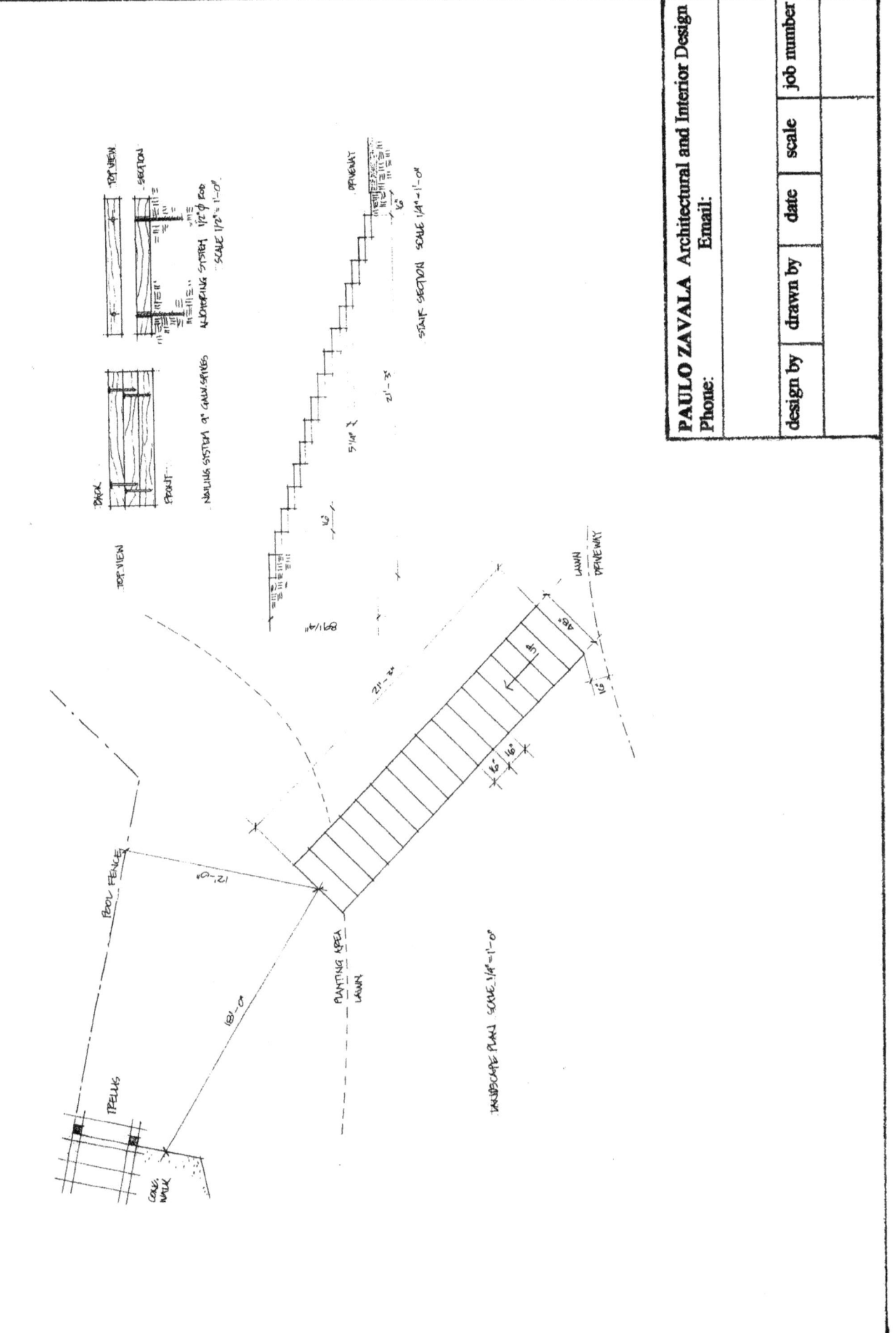

TOP VIEW

SECTION

ALTERNATING SYSTEM 1/2"Ø BOO

SCALE 1/2" = 1'-0"

BACK

FRONT

NAILING SYSTEM OF GALV. SCREWS

TOP VIEW

DRIVEWAY

STAIR SECTION SCALE 1/4"=1'-0"

21'-3"

LAWN
DRIVEWAY

POOL FENCE

PLANTING AREA
LAWN

TRELLIS

CONC. WALK

LANDSCAPE PLAN SCALE 1/4"=1'-0"

PAULO ZAVALA Architectural and Interior Design

Phone:

Email:

job number

scale

date

drawn by

design by

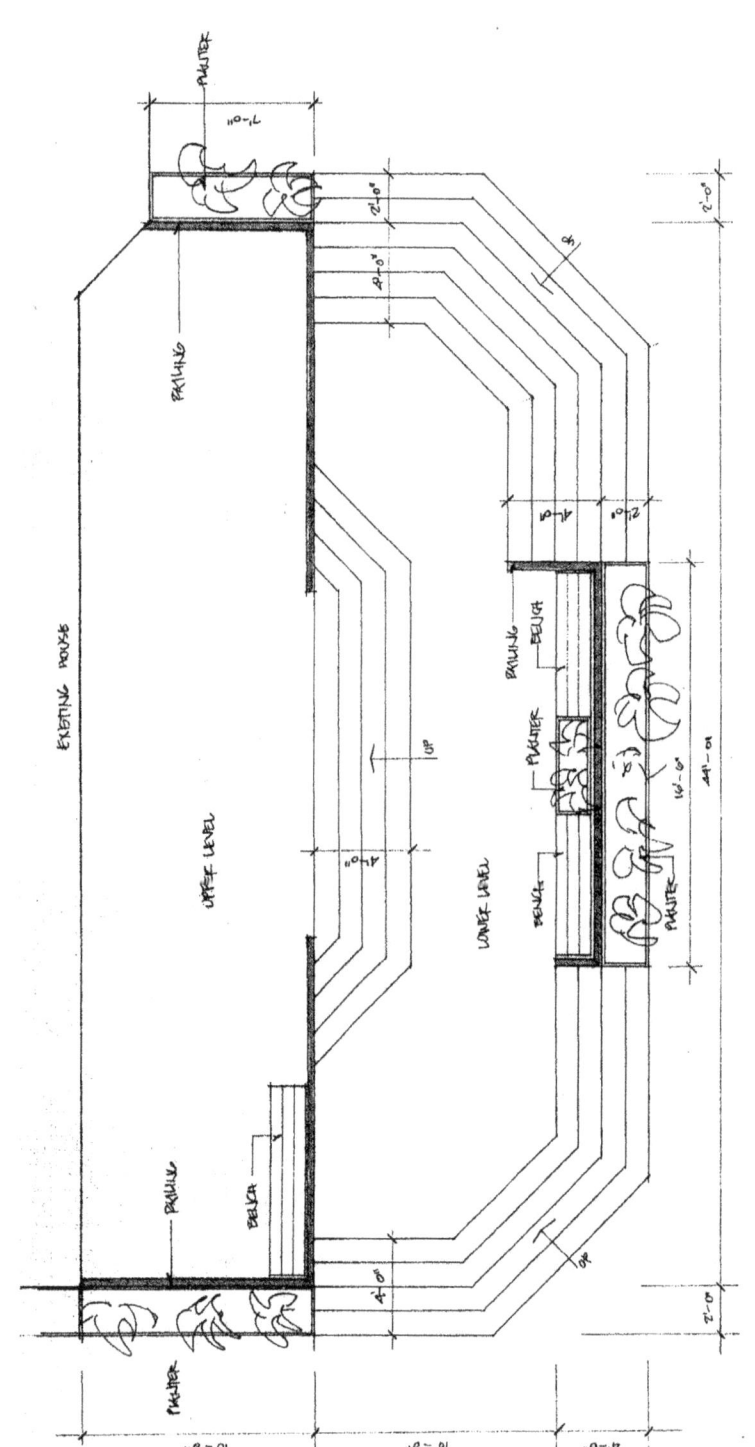

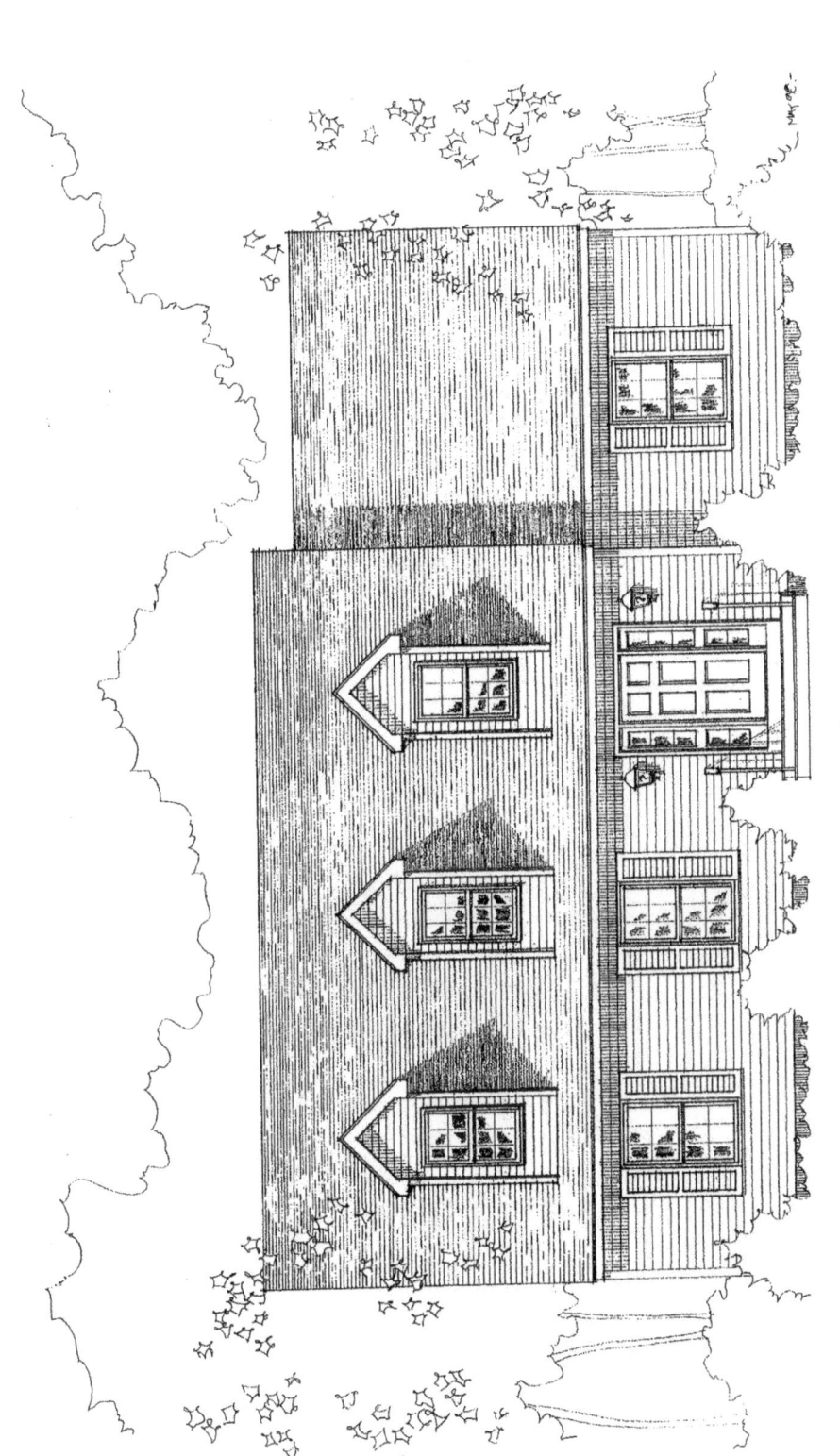

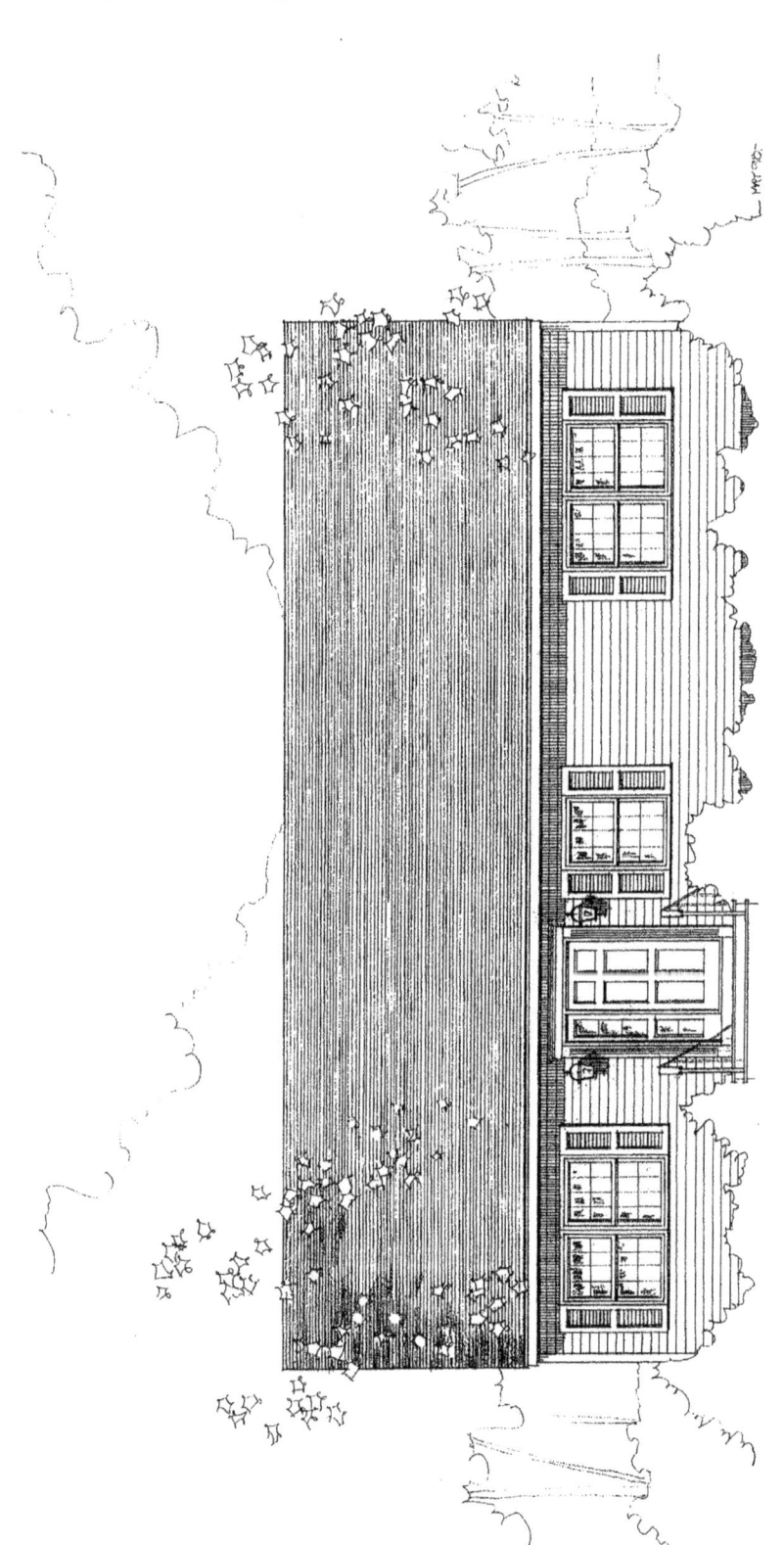

PAULO ZAVALA Architectural and Interior Design

Phone:

Email:

design by	drawn by	date	scale	job number

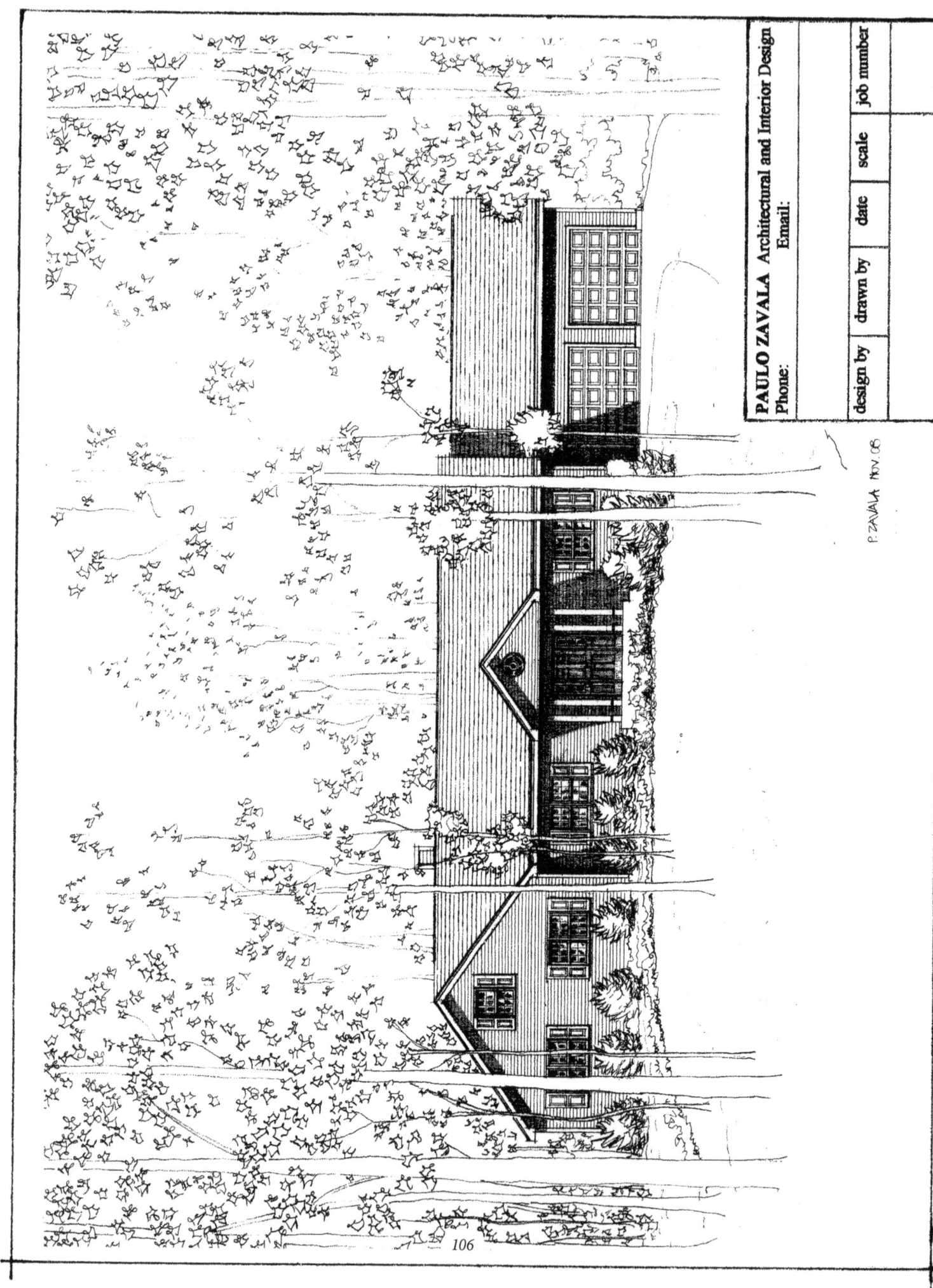

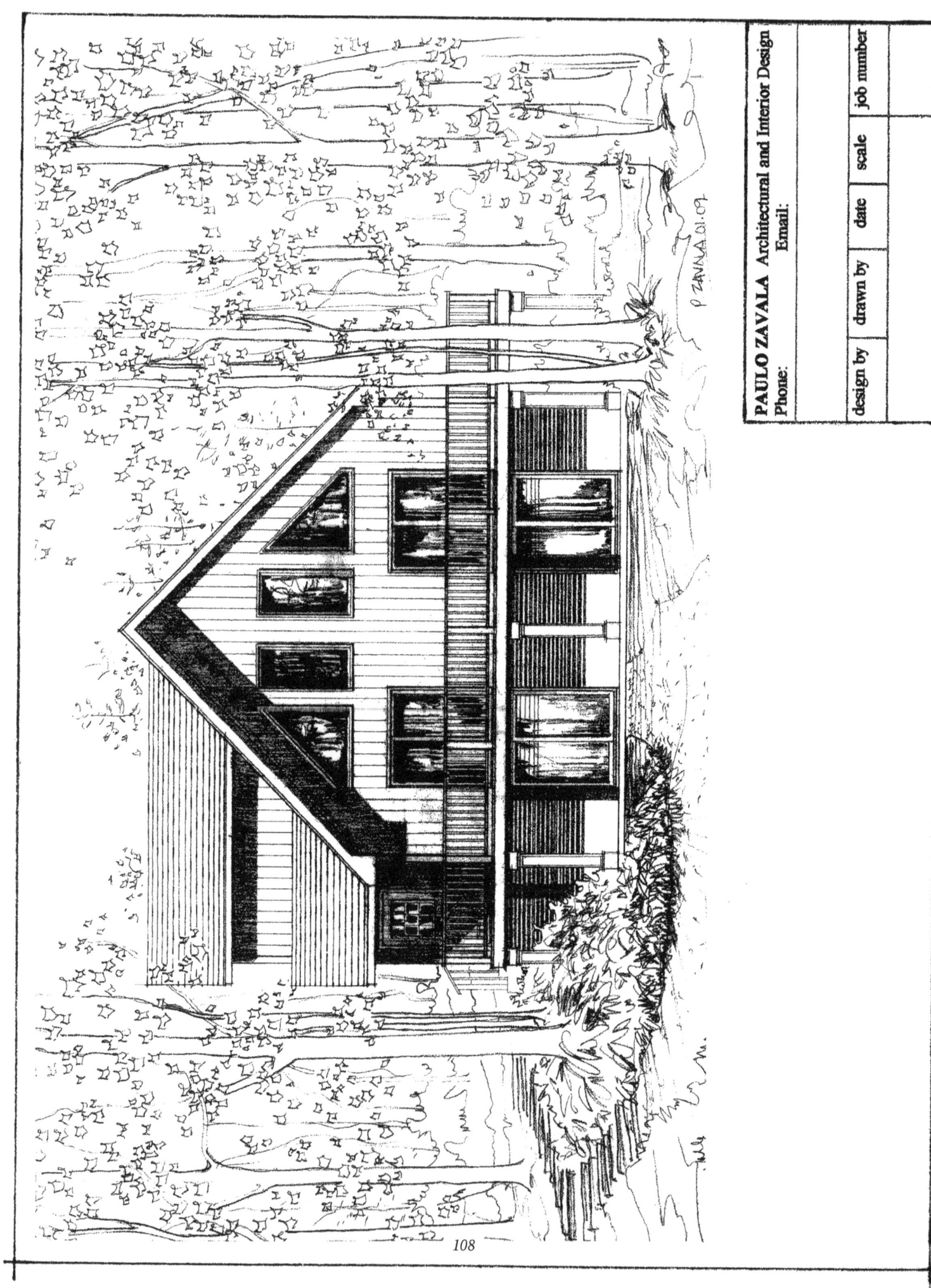

P. ZAVALA 01.07

PAULO ZAVALA **Architectural and Interior Design**
Phone:
Email:

design by	drawn by	date	scale	job number

P.ZAVALA 11.08

PAULO ZAVALA Architectural and Interior Design
Phone:
Email:

design by	drawn by	date	scale	job number

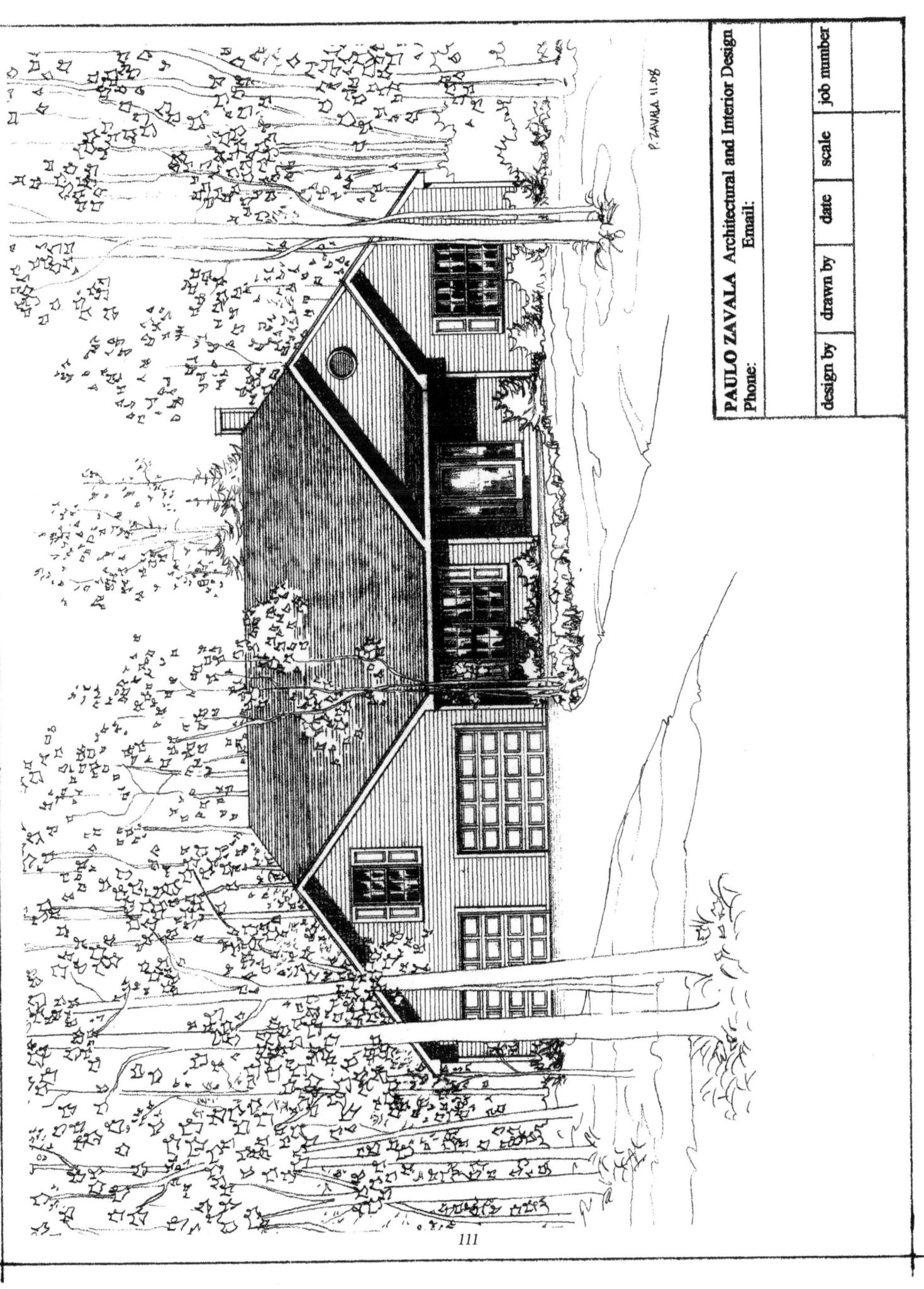

PAULO ZAVALA Architectural and Interior Design
Phone:
Email:

design by	drawn by	date	scale	job number

P. ZAVALA 11.08

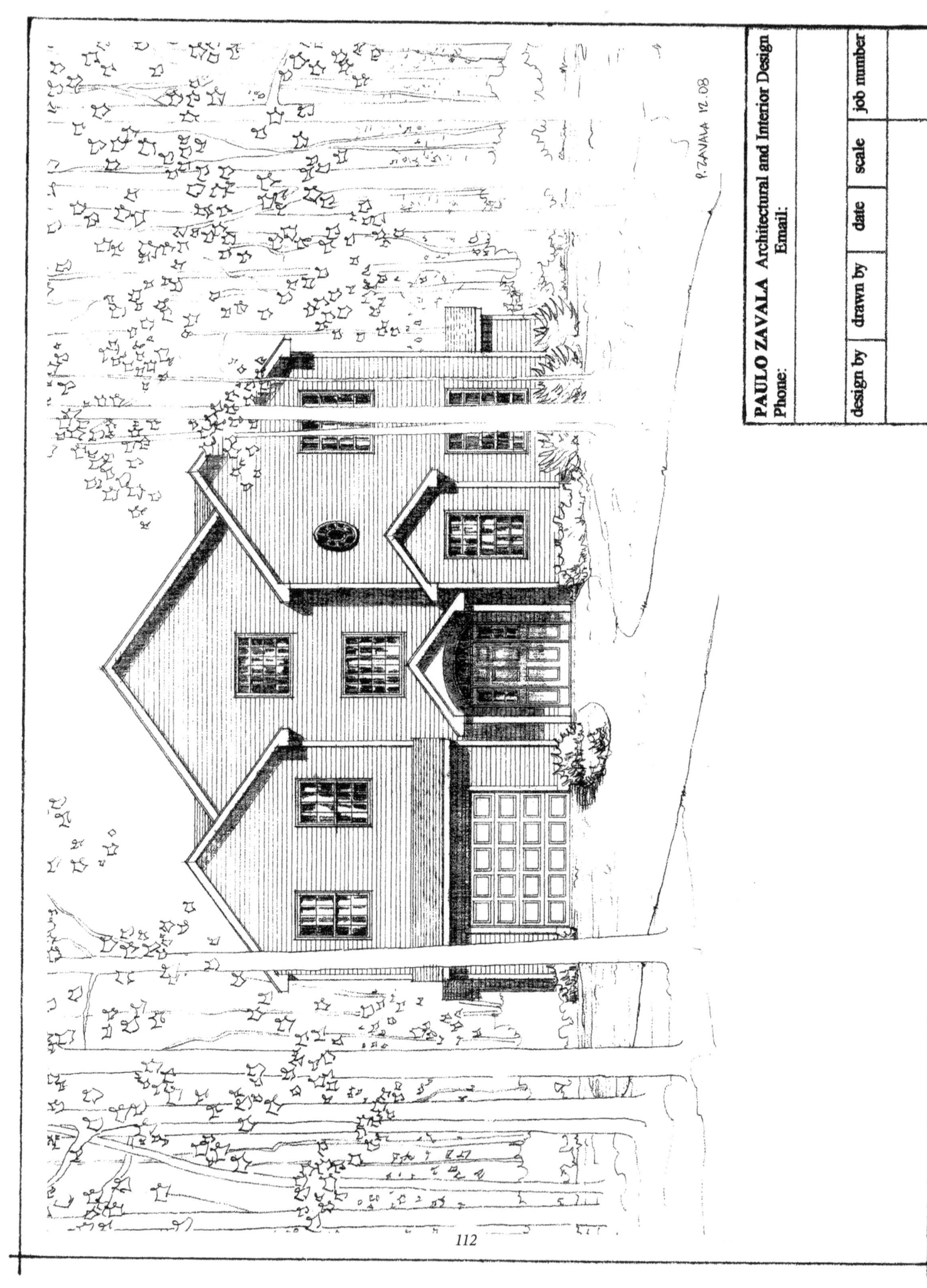

P. ZAVALA 12.08

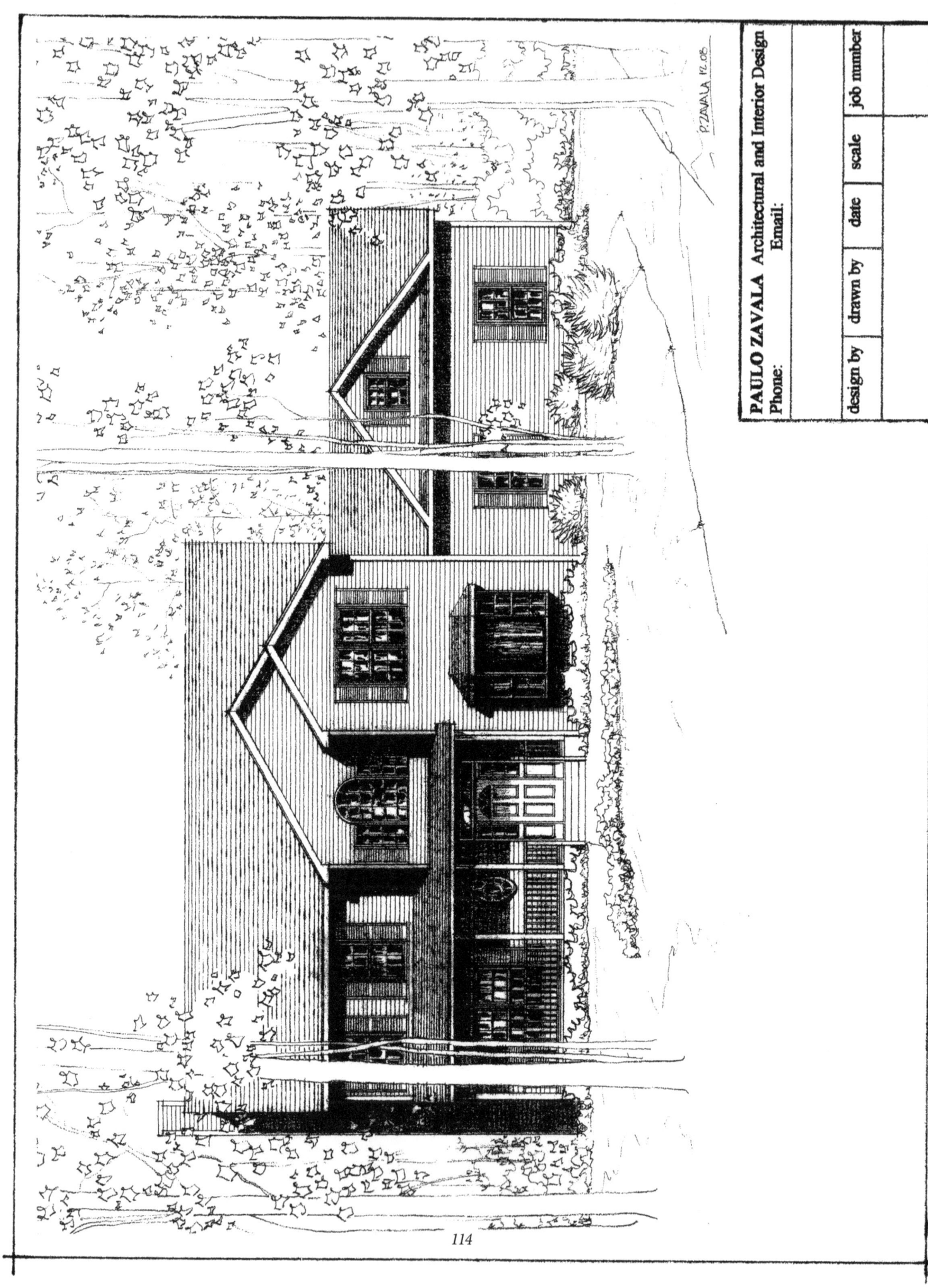

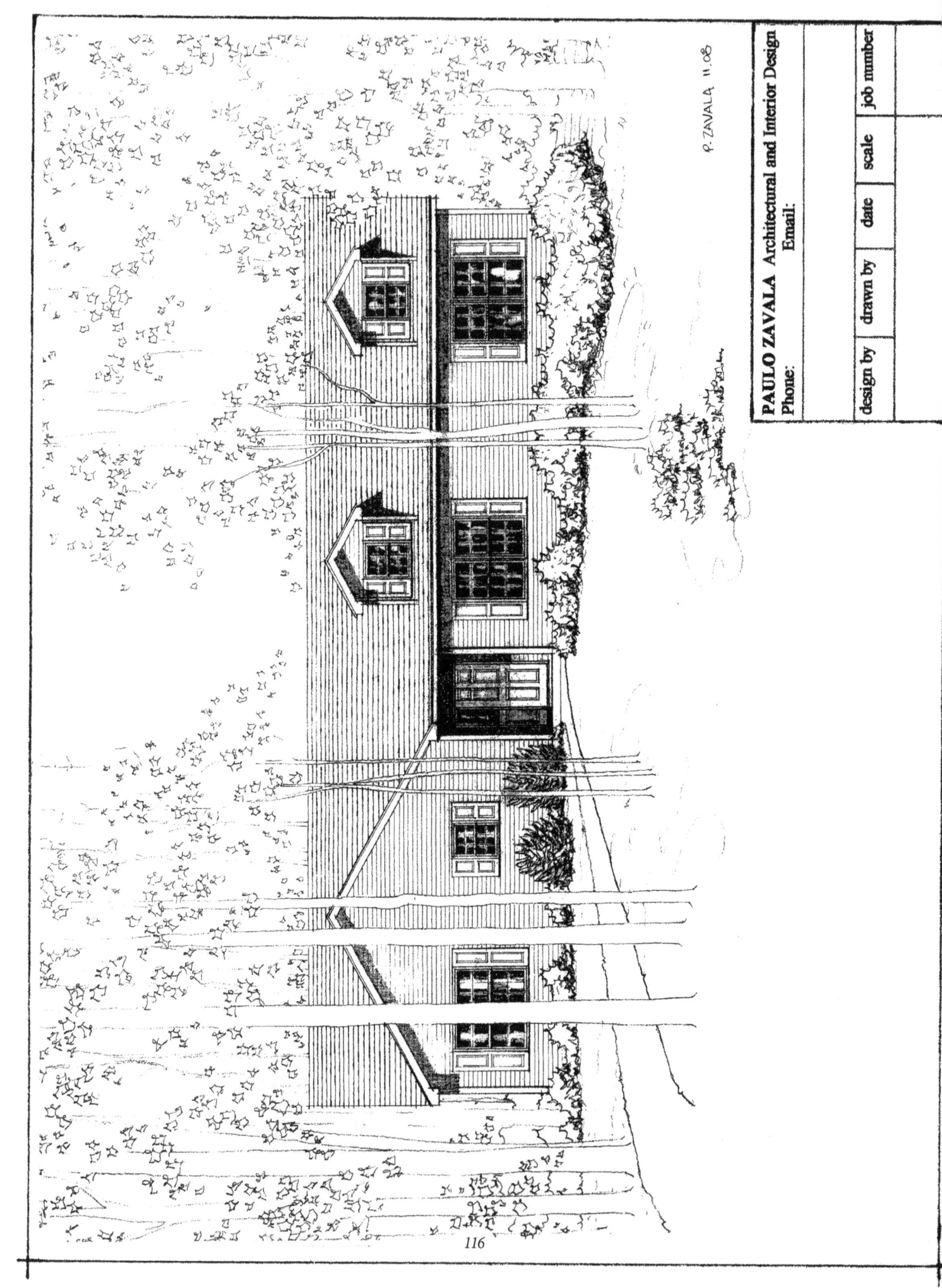

PAULO ZAVALA Architectural and Interior Design
Phone:
Email:

design by	drawn by	date	scale	job number

P. ZAVALA 11.08

PAULO ZAVALA **Architectural and Interior Design**
Phone: Email:

design by	drawn by	date	scale	job number

P. ZAVALA 01.09

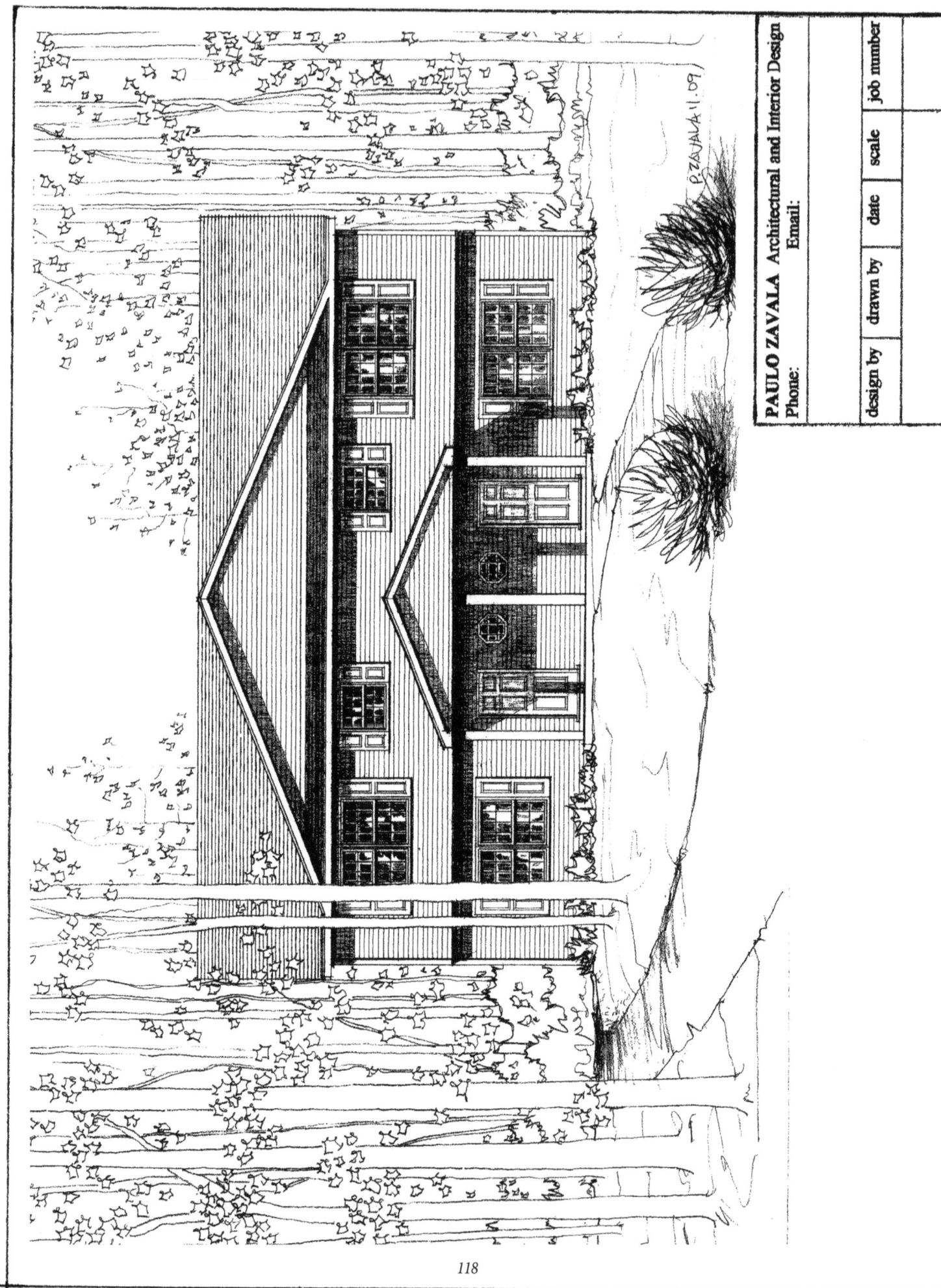

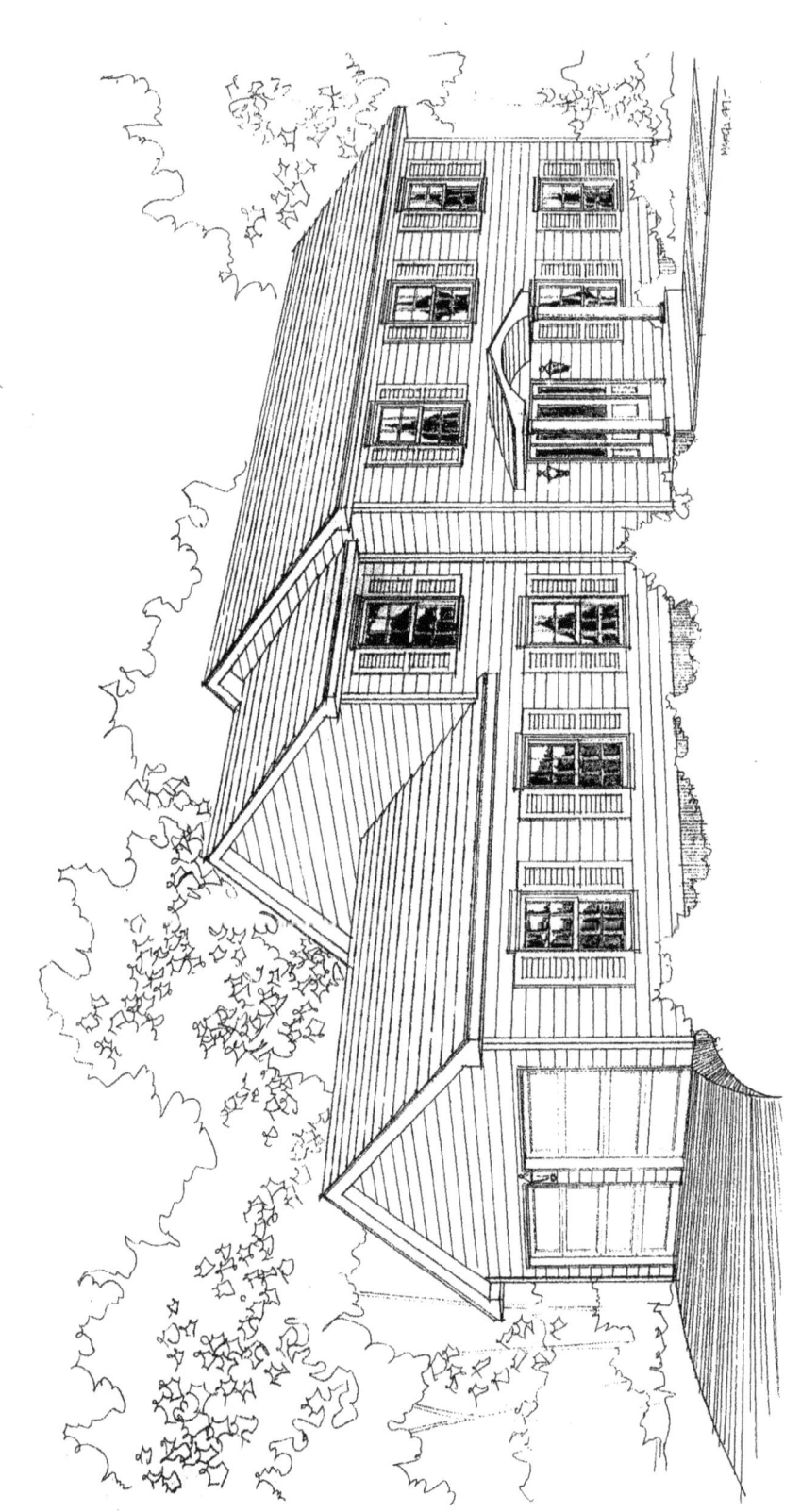

PAULO ZAVALA Architectural and Interior Design

Phone:

Email:

design by	drawn by	date	scale	job number

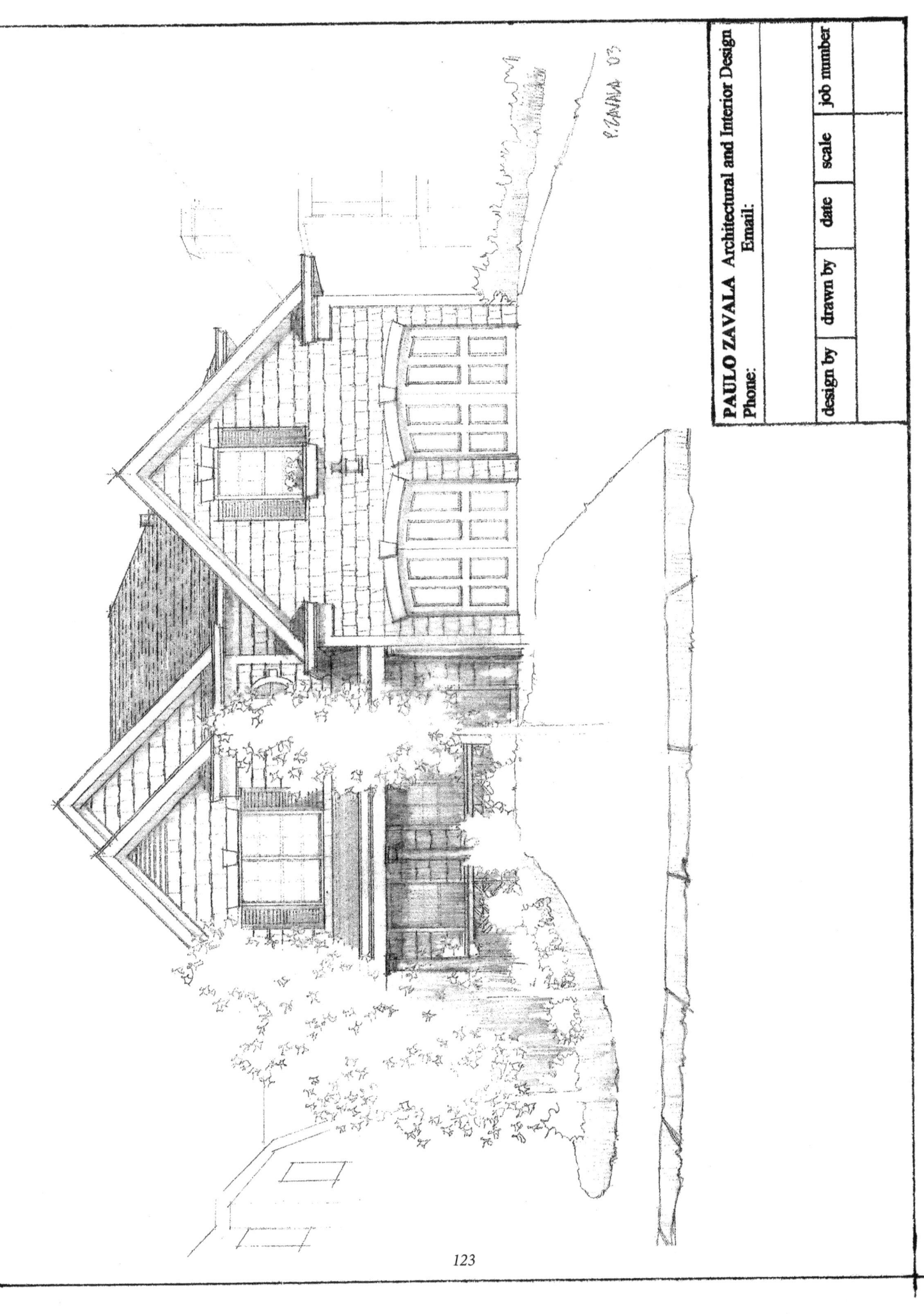

PAULO ZAVALA Architectural and Interior Design
Phone:
Email:

design by	drawn by	date	scale	job number

P. ZAVALA 05.03

PAULO ZAVALA Architectural and Interior Design
Phone:
Email:

design by	drawn by	date	scale	job number

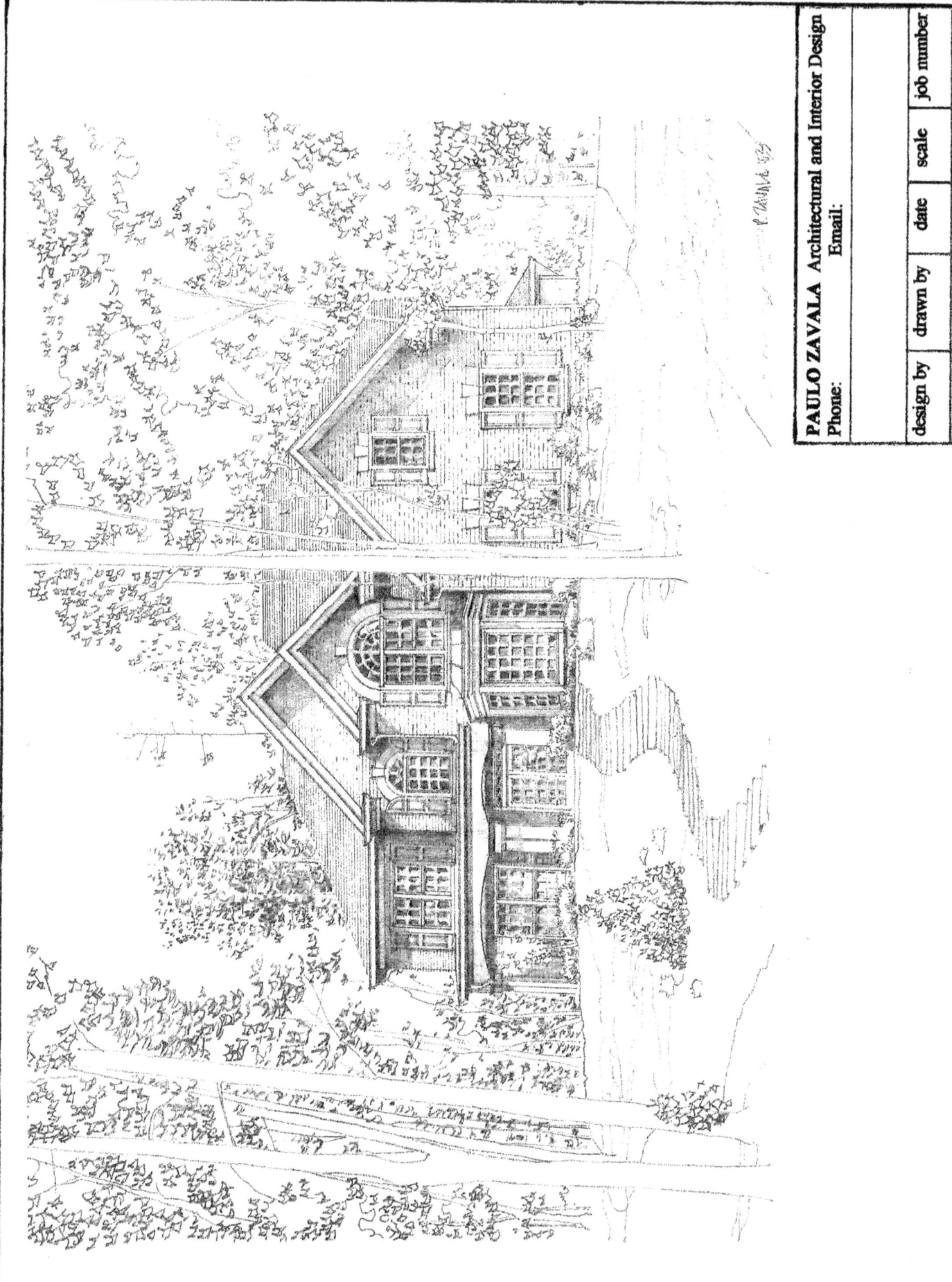

PAULO ZAVALA Architectural and Interior Design
Phone:
Email:

design by	drawn by	date	scale	job number

P. ZAVALA 4.10

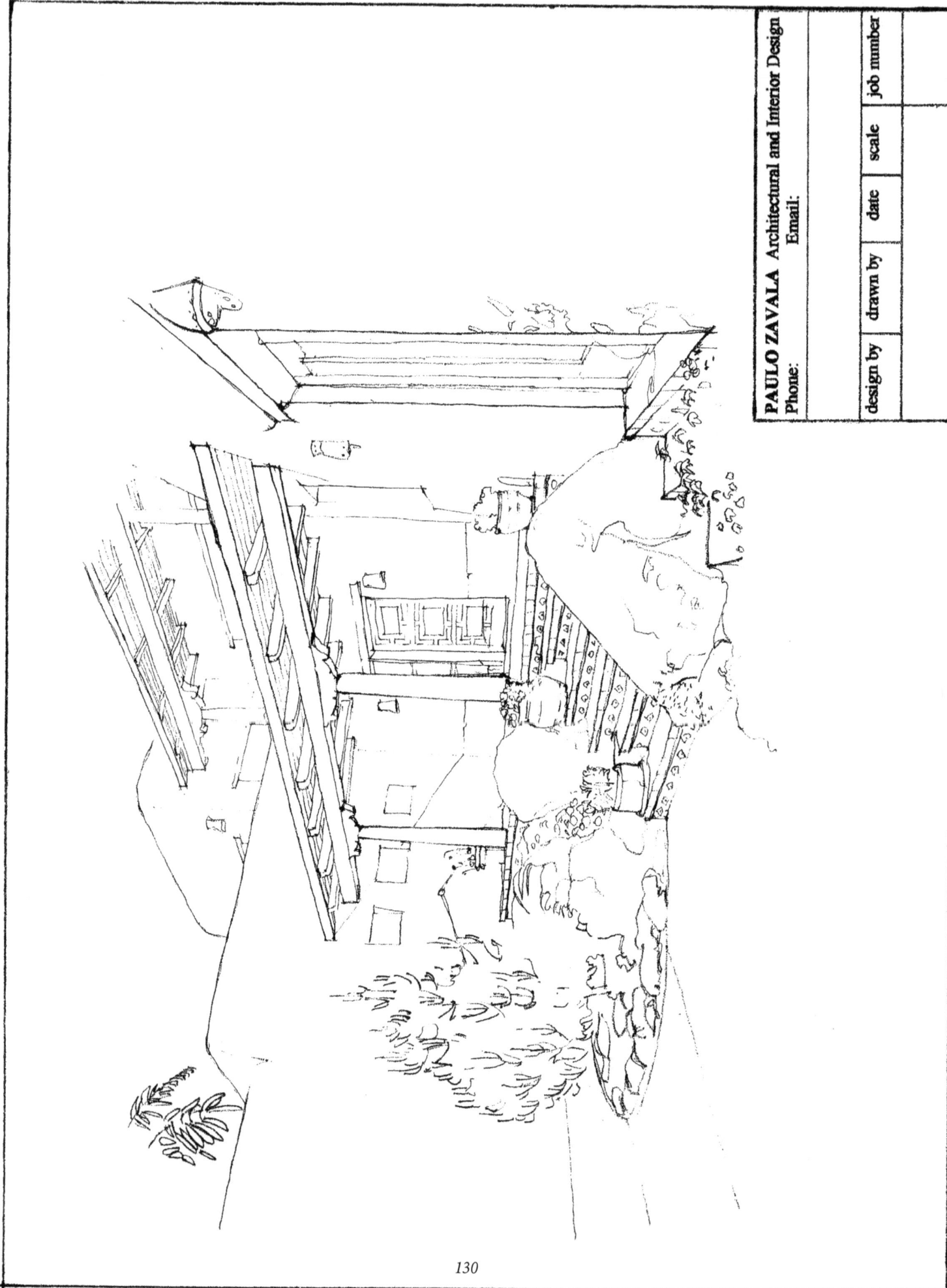

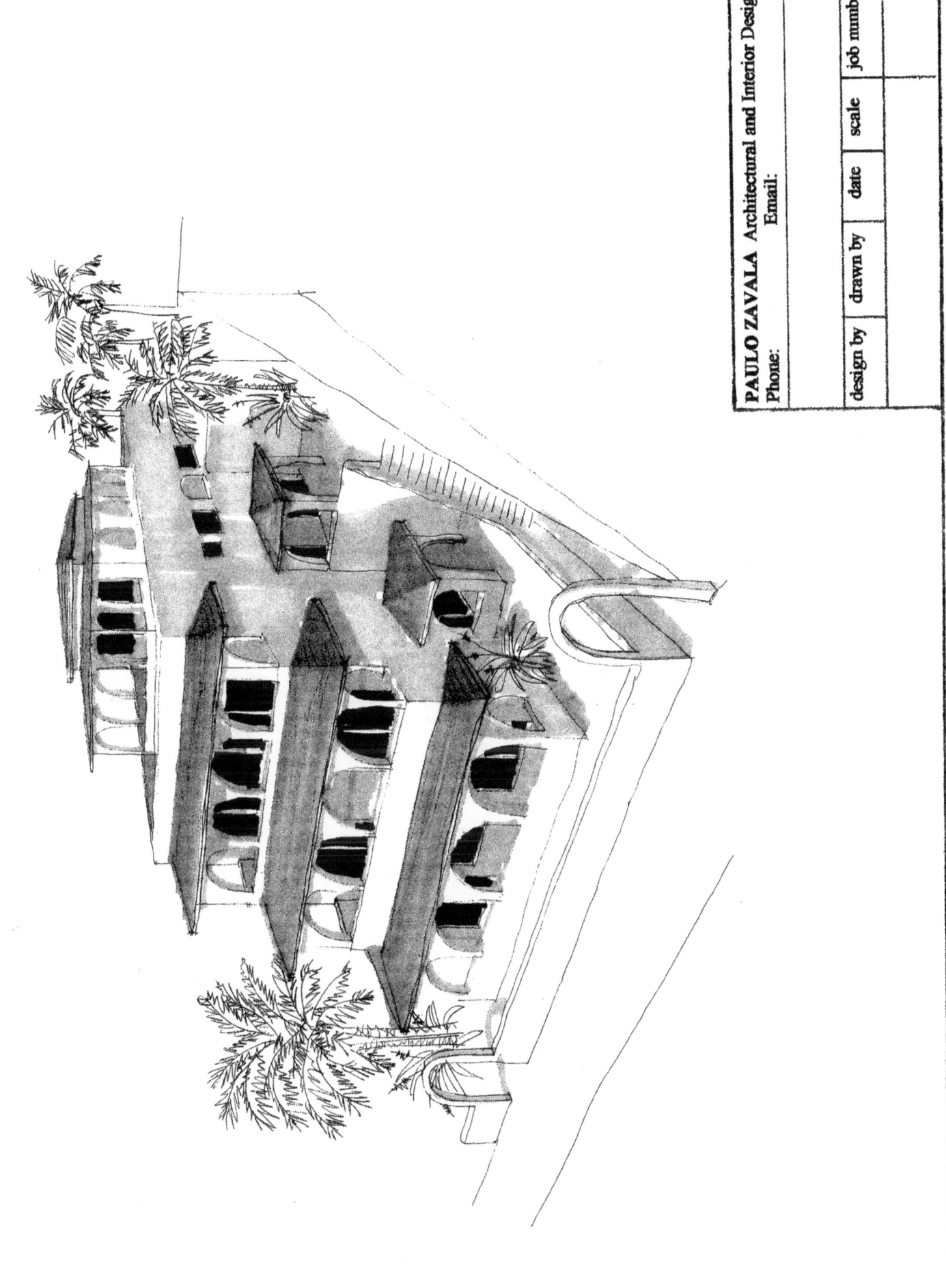

PAULO ZAVALA Architectural and Interior Design
Phone:
Email:

design by	drawn by	date	scale	job number

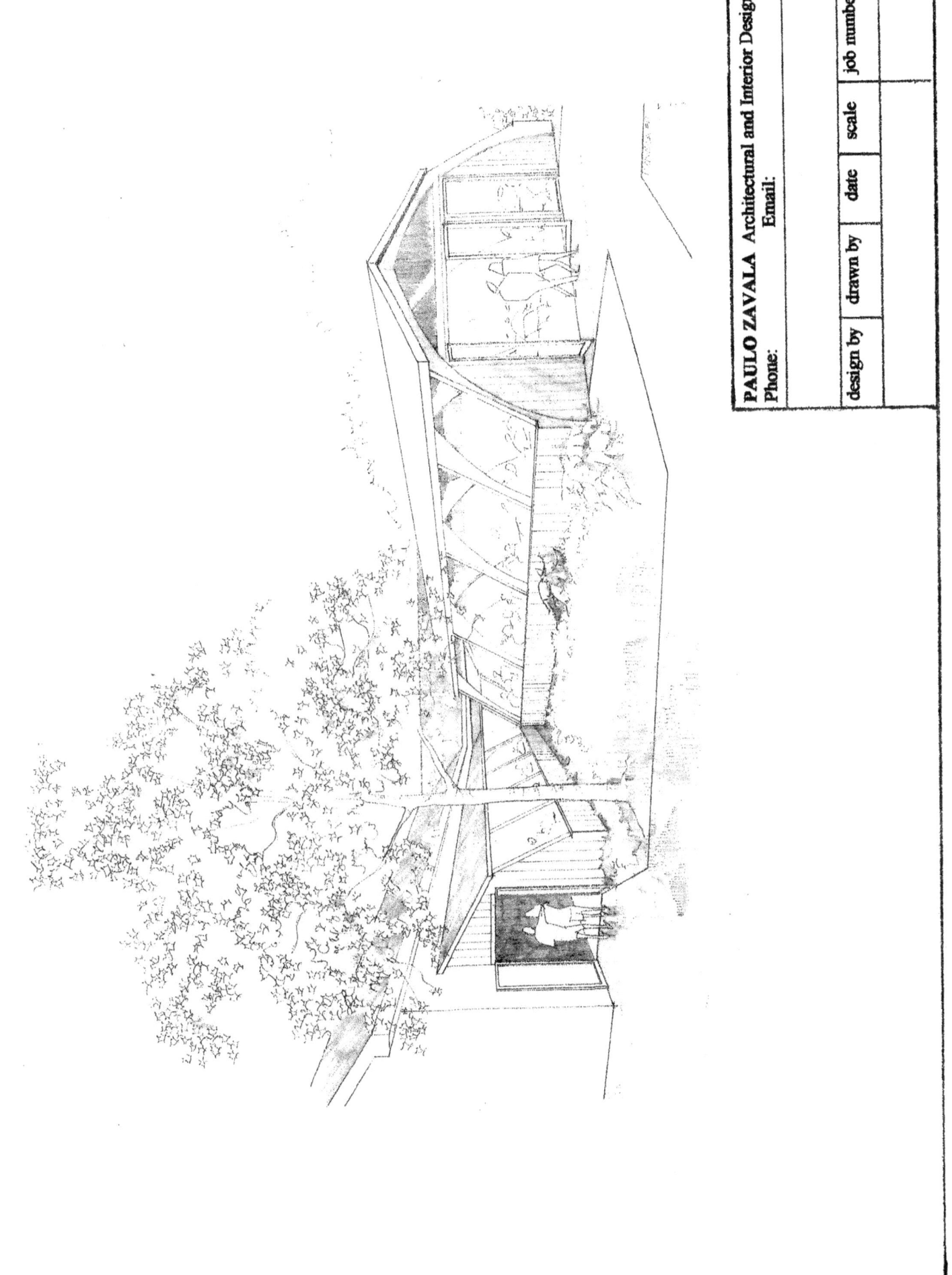

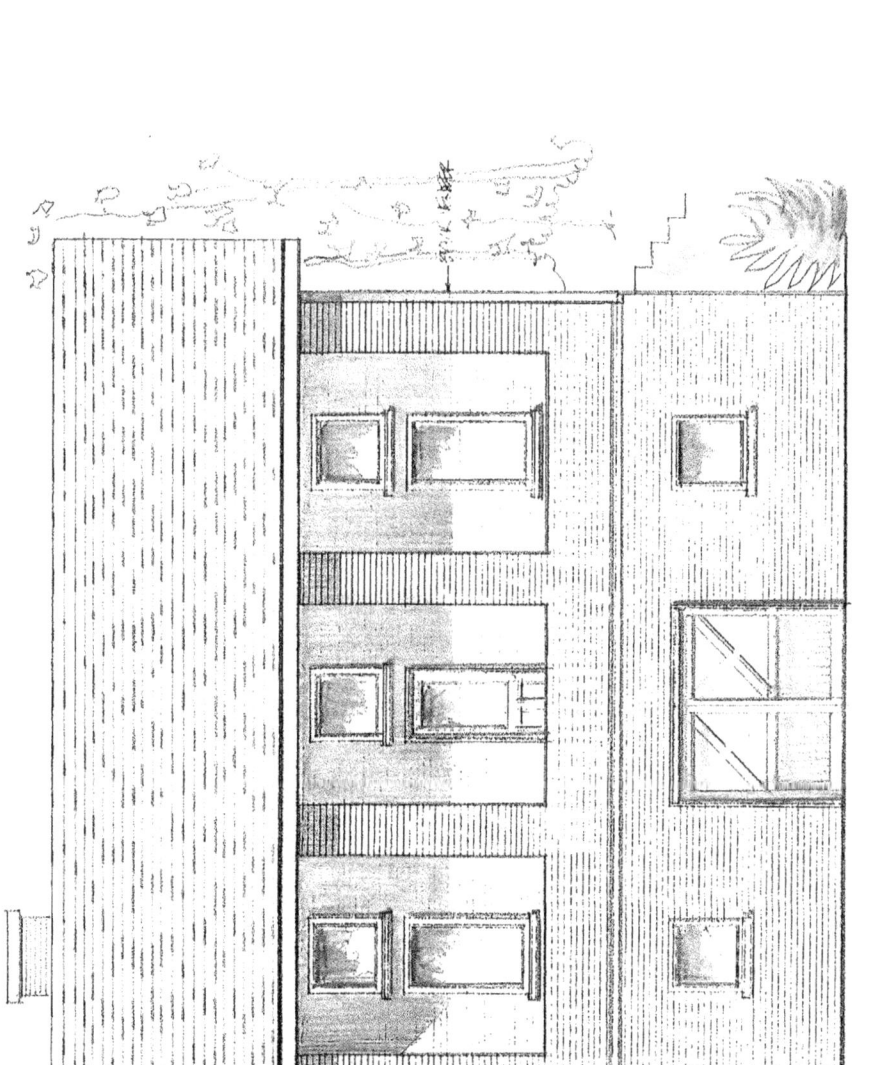

FRONT ELEVATION

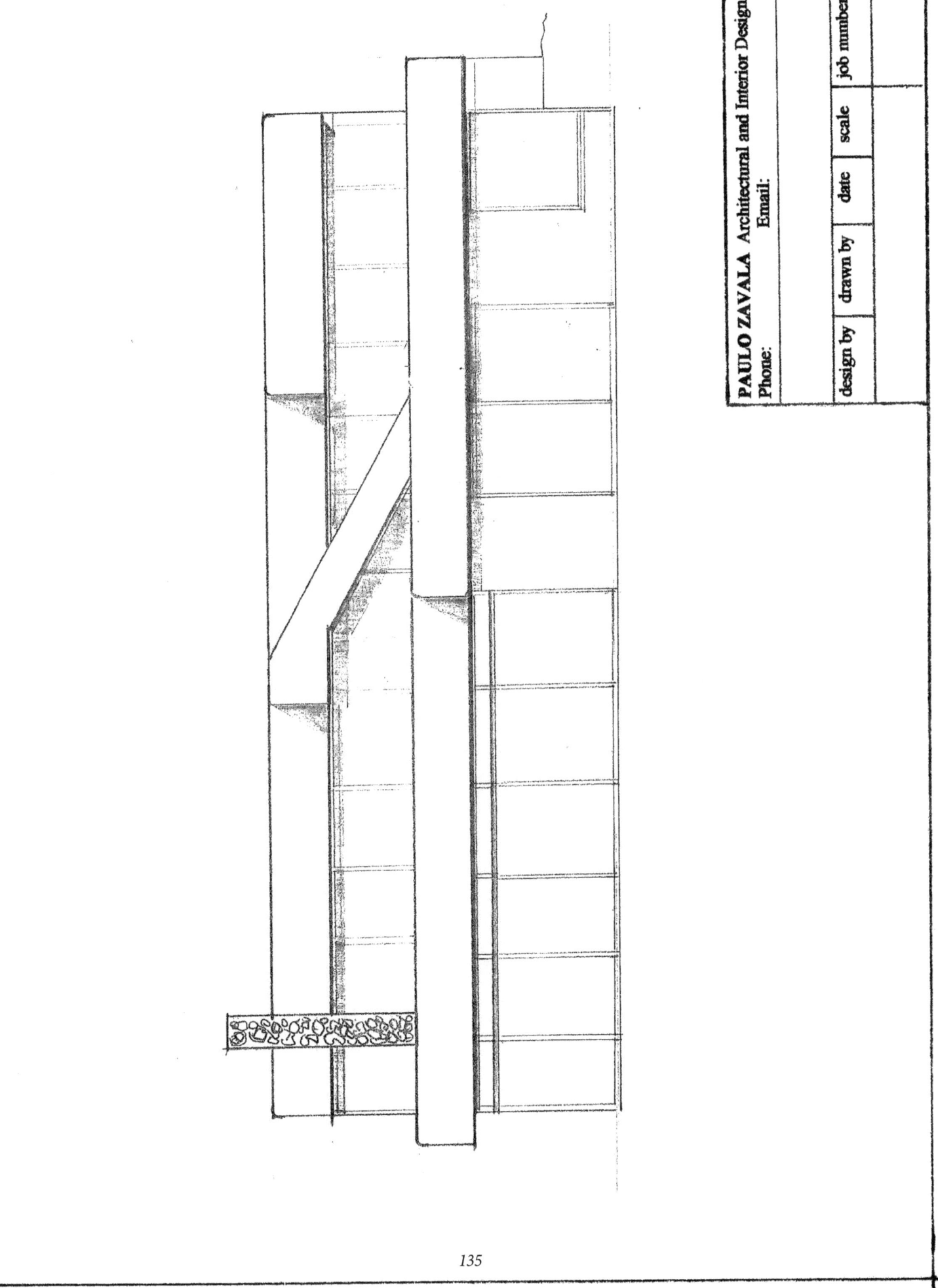

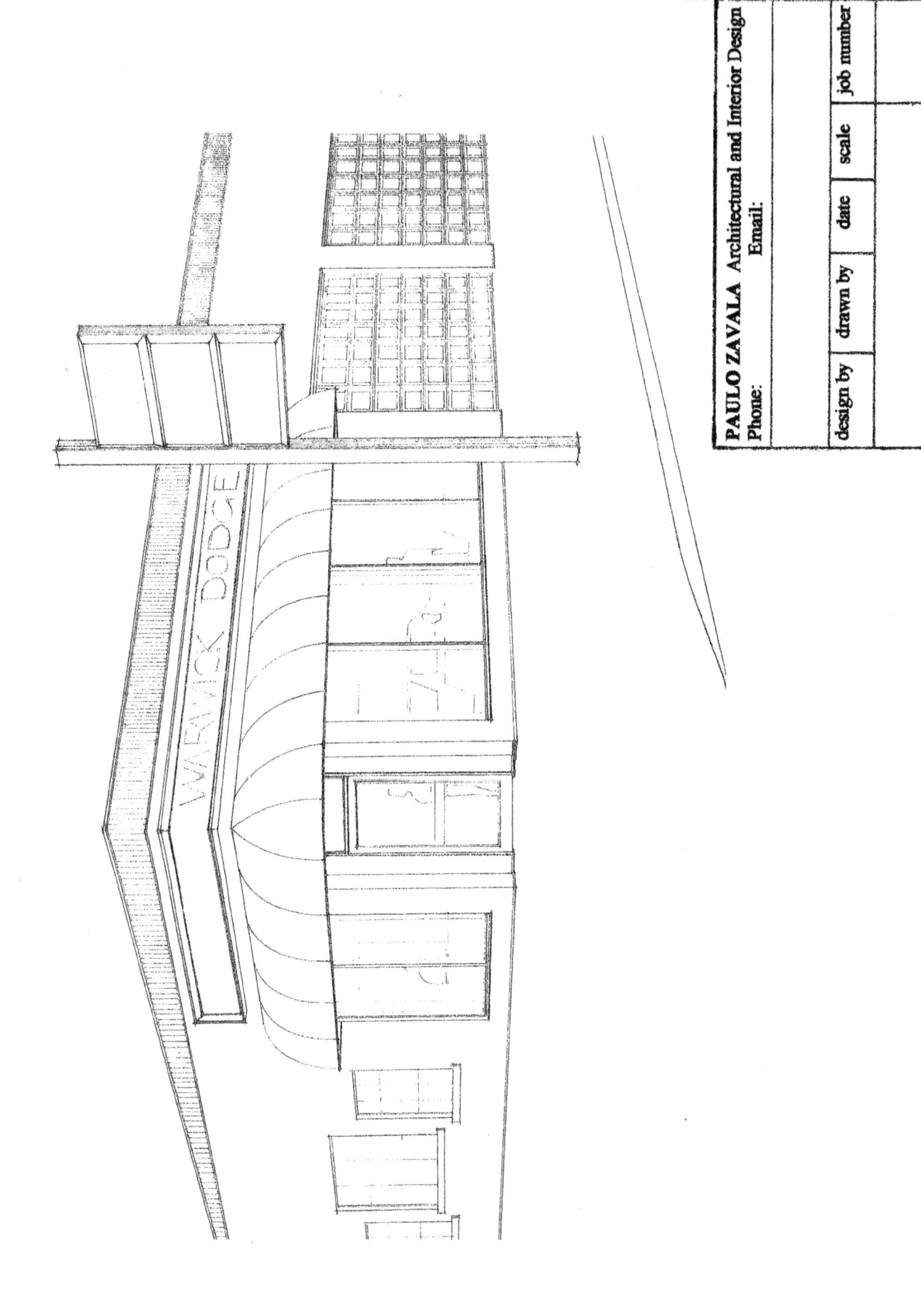

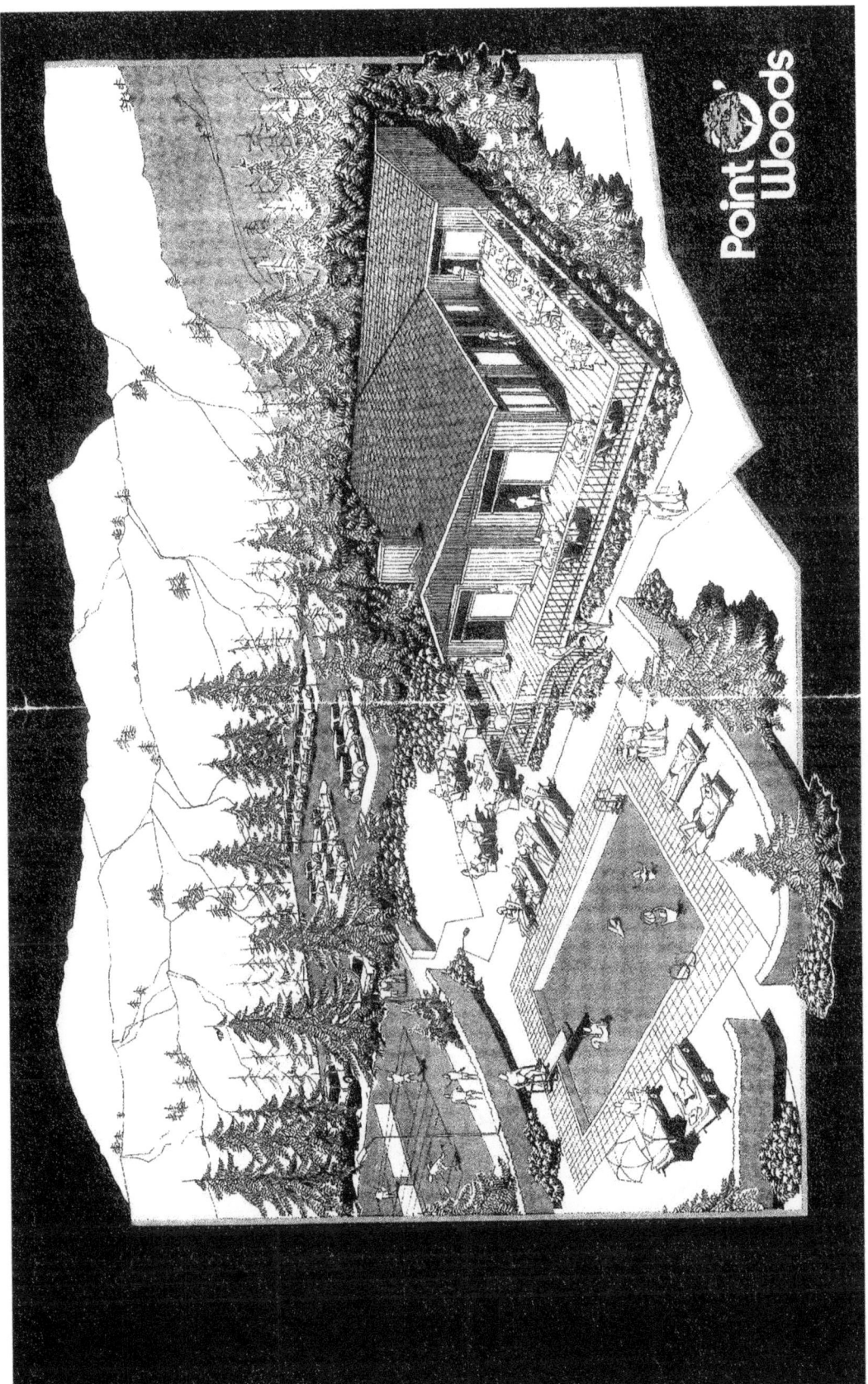

PAULO ZAVALA Architectural and Interior Design
Phone:
Email:

design by	drawn by	date	scale	job number

Point
Woods

Point O'Woods

CALIFORNIA REDWOOD RAISED RANCH

PAULO ZAVALA Architectural and Interior Design
Phone:
Email:

design by	drawn by	date	scale	job number

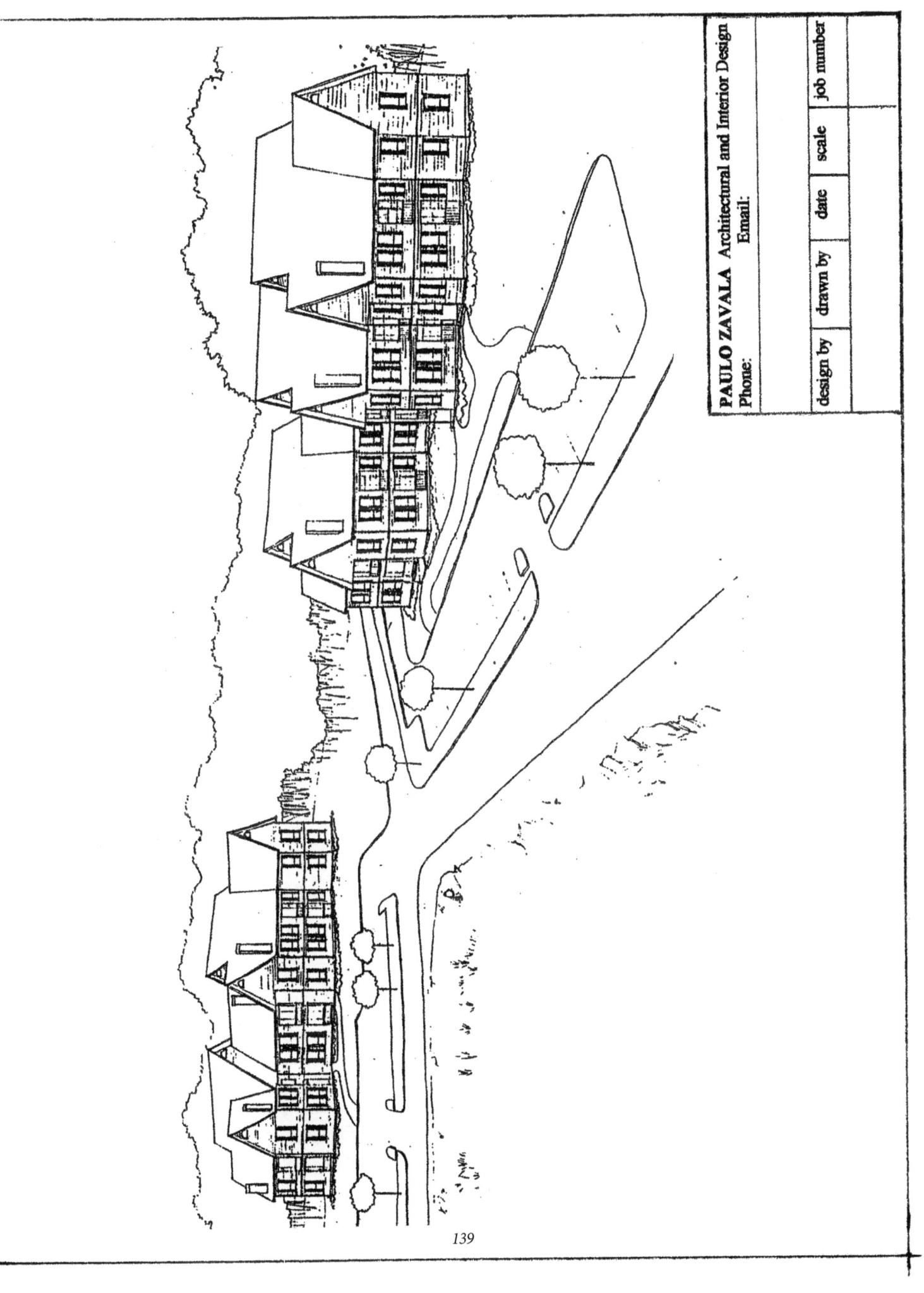

PAULO ZAVALA Architectural and Interior Design
Phone:
Email:

design by	drawn by	date	scale	job number

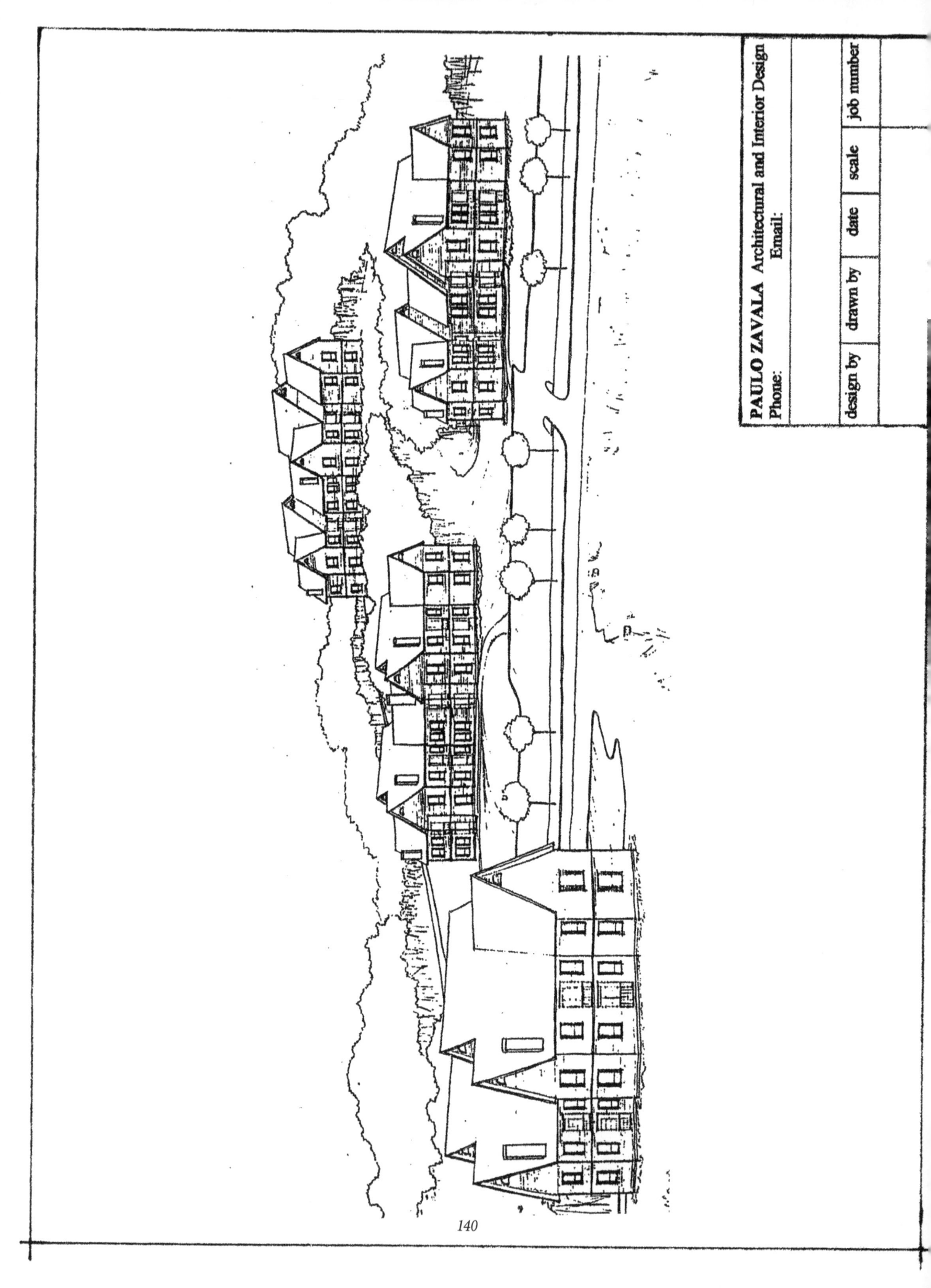

PAULO ZAVALA Architectural and Interior Design
Phone:
Email:

design by	drawn by	date	scale	job number

PAULO ZAVALA Architectural and Interior Design
Phone:
Email:

design by	drawn by	date	scale	job number

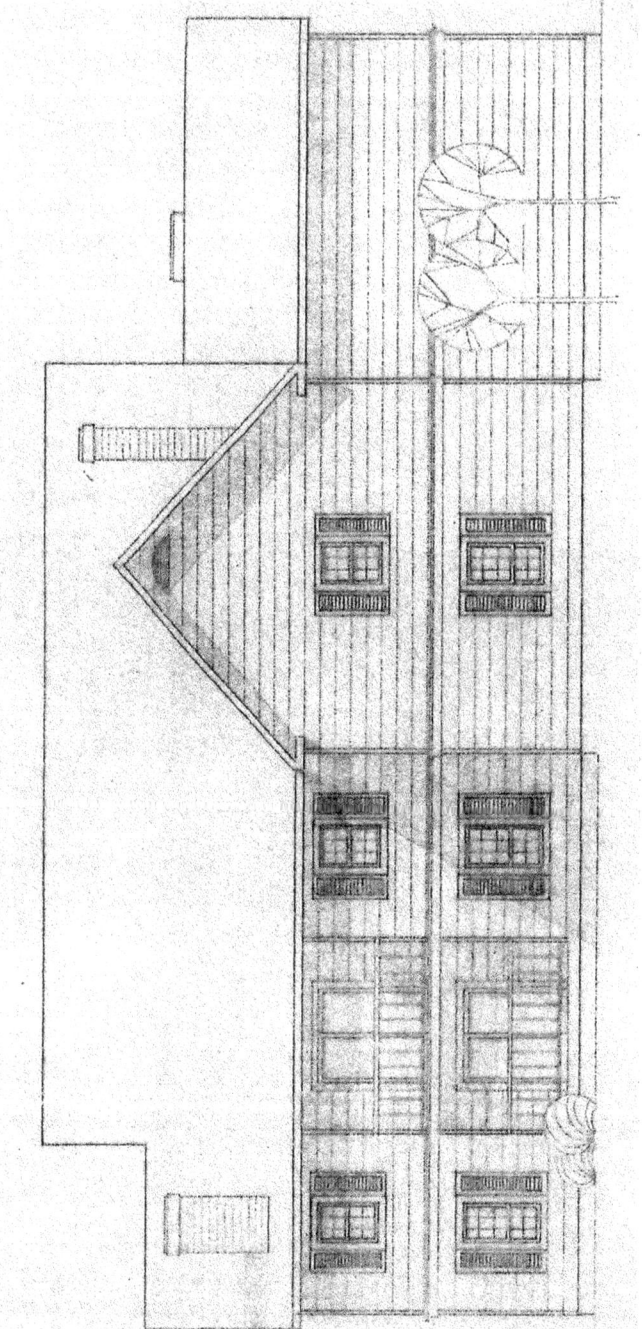

PAULO ZAVALA Architectural and Interior Design
Phone: Email:

design by	drawn by	date	scale	job number

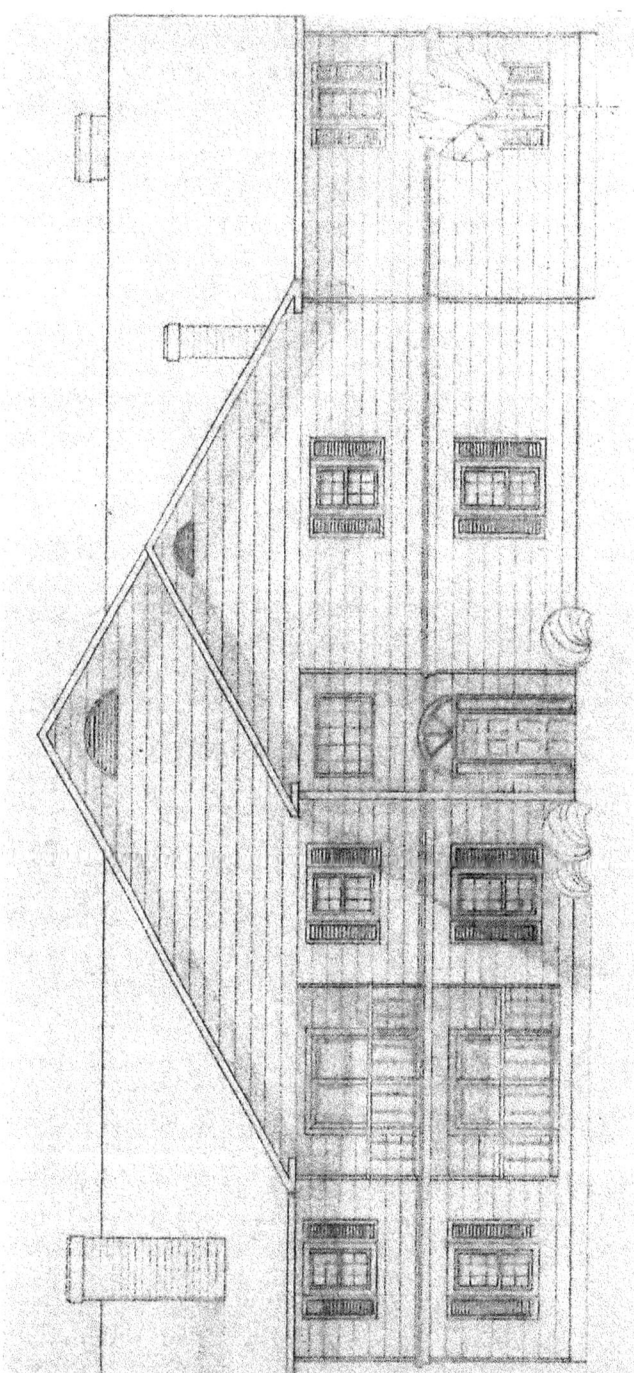

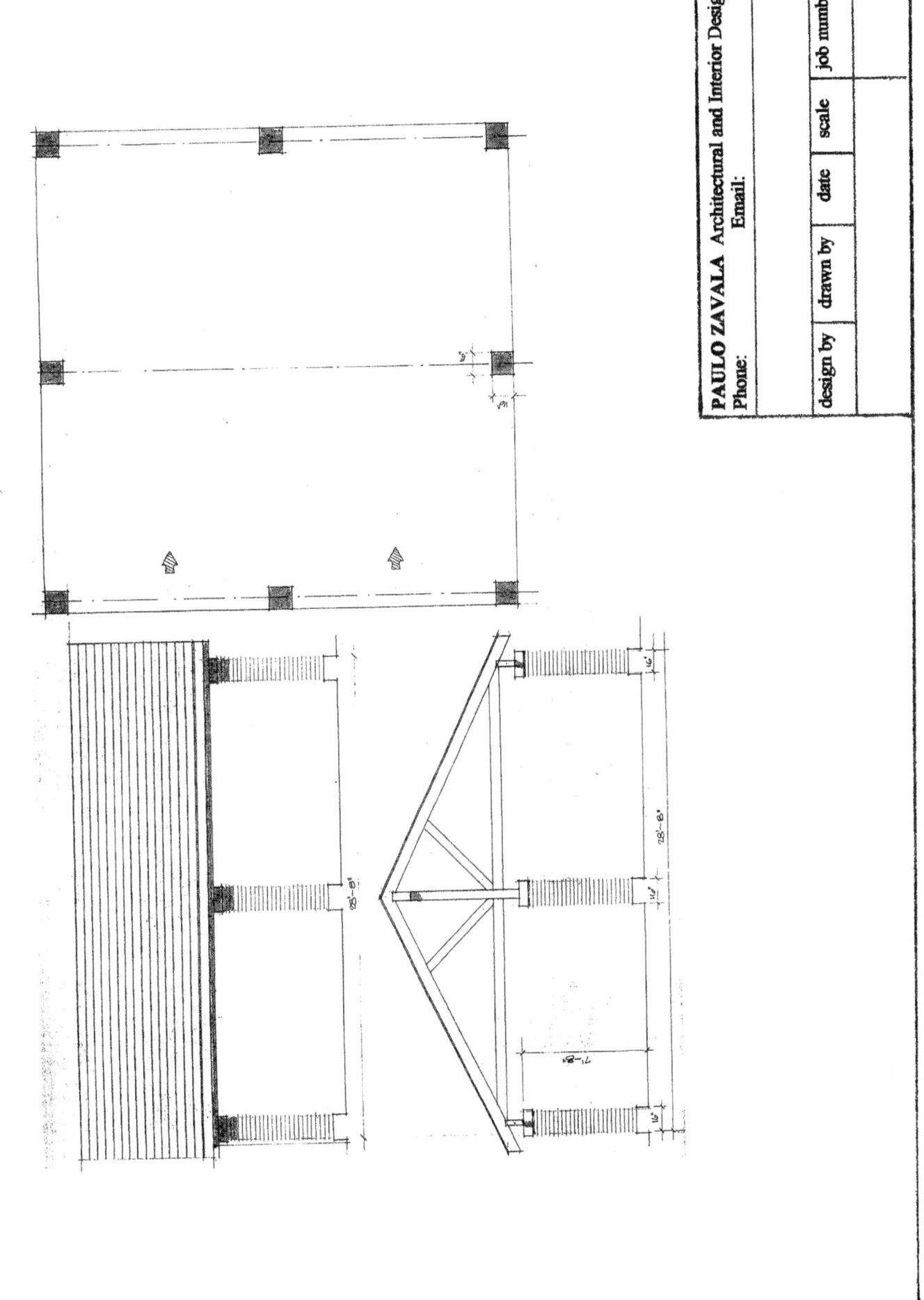

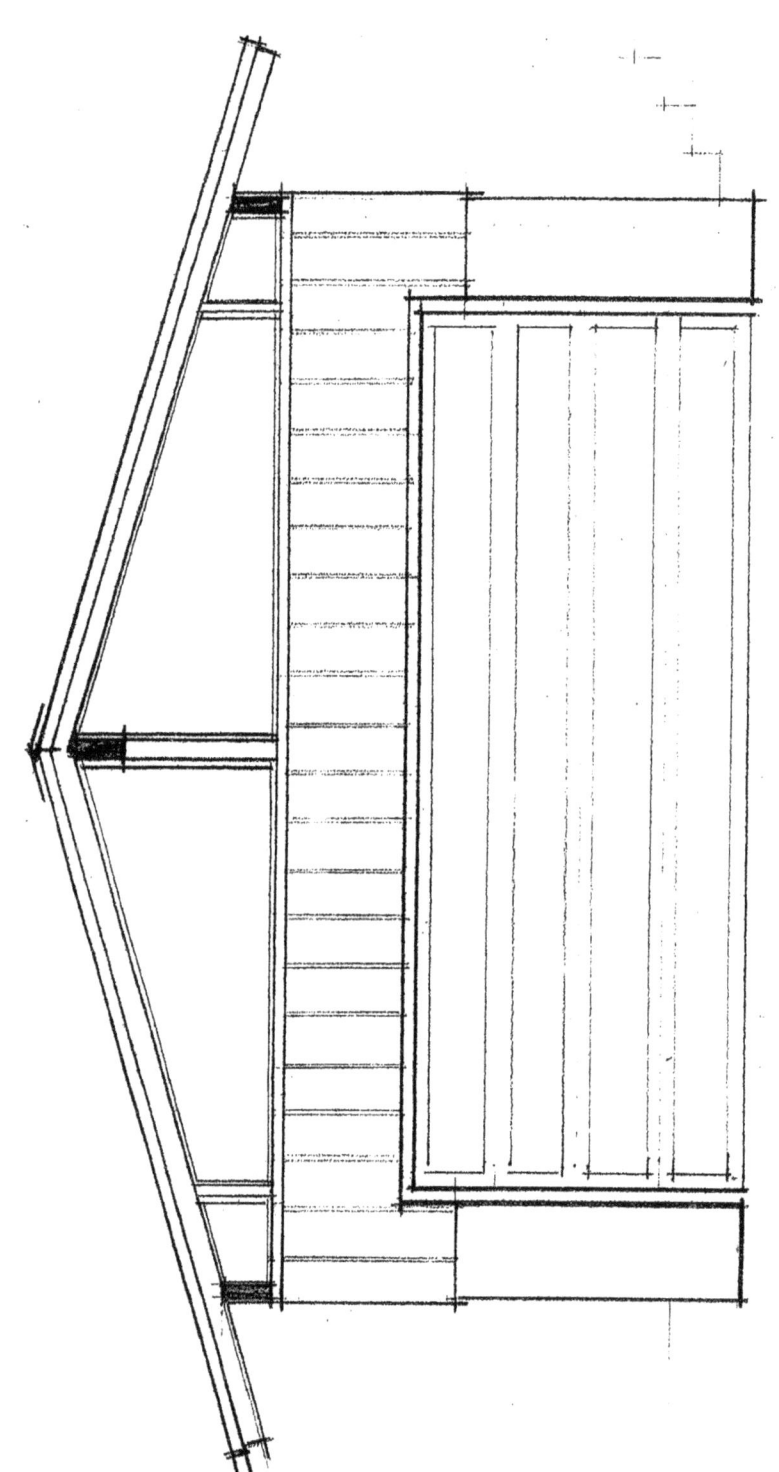

PAULO ZAVALA Architectural and Interior Design
Phone:
Email:

design by	drawn by	date	scale
			job number

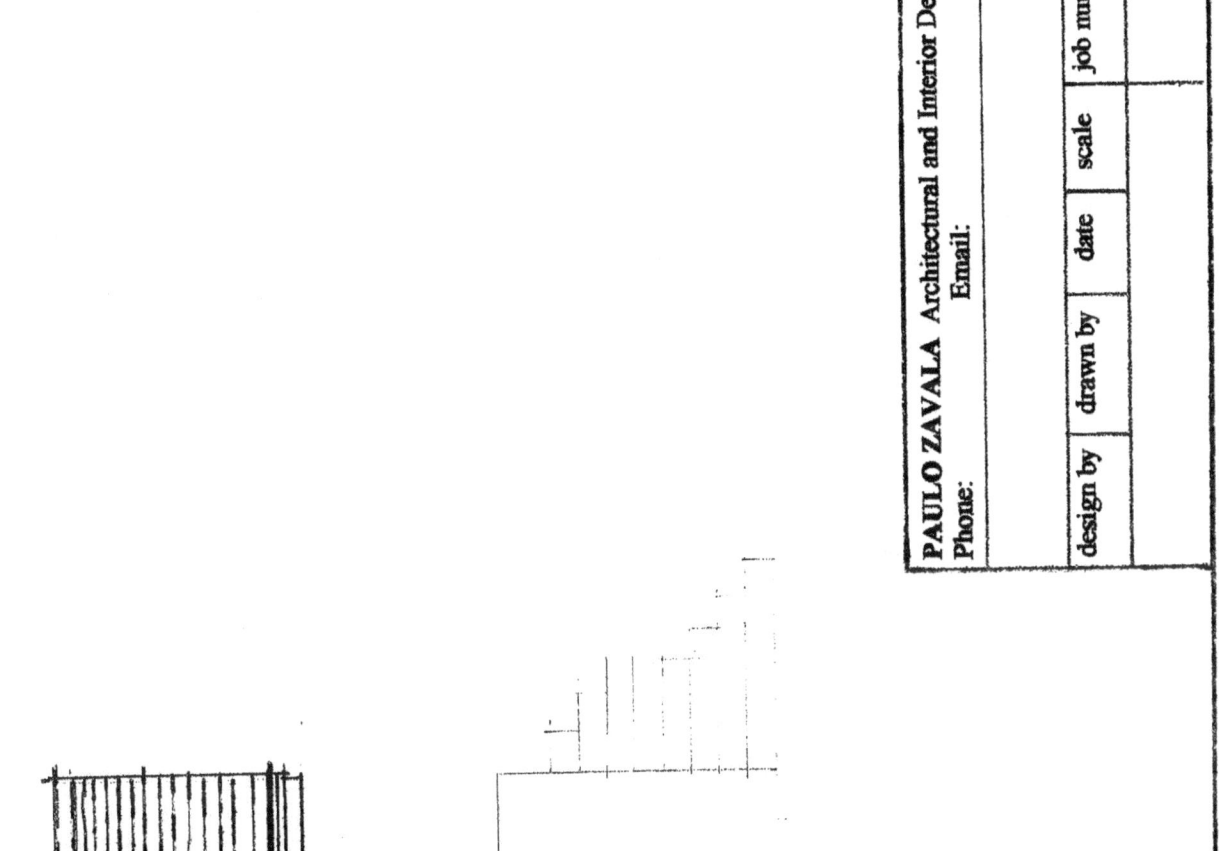

PAULO ZAVALA Architectural and Interior Design
Phone:
Email:

design by	drawn by	date	scale	job number

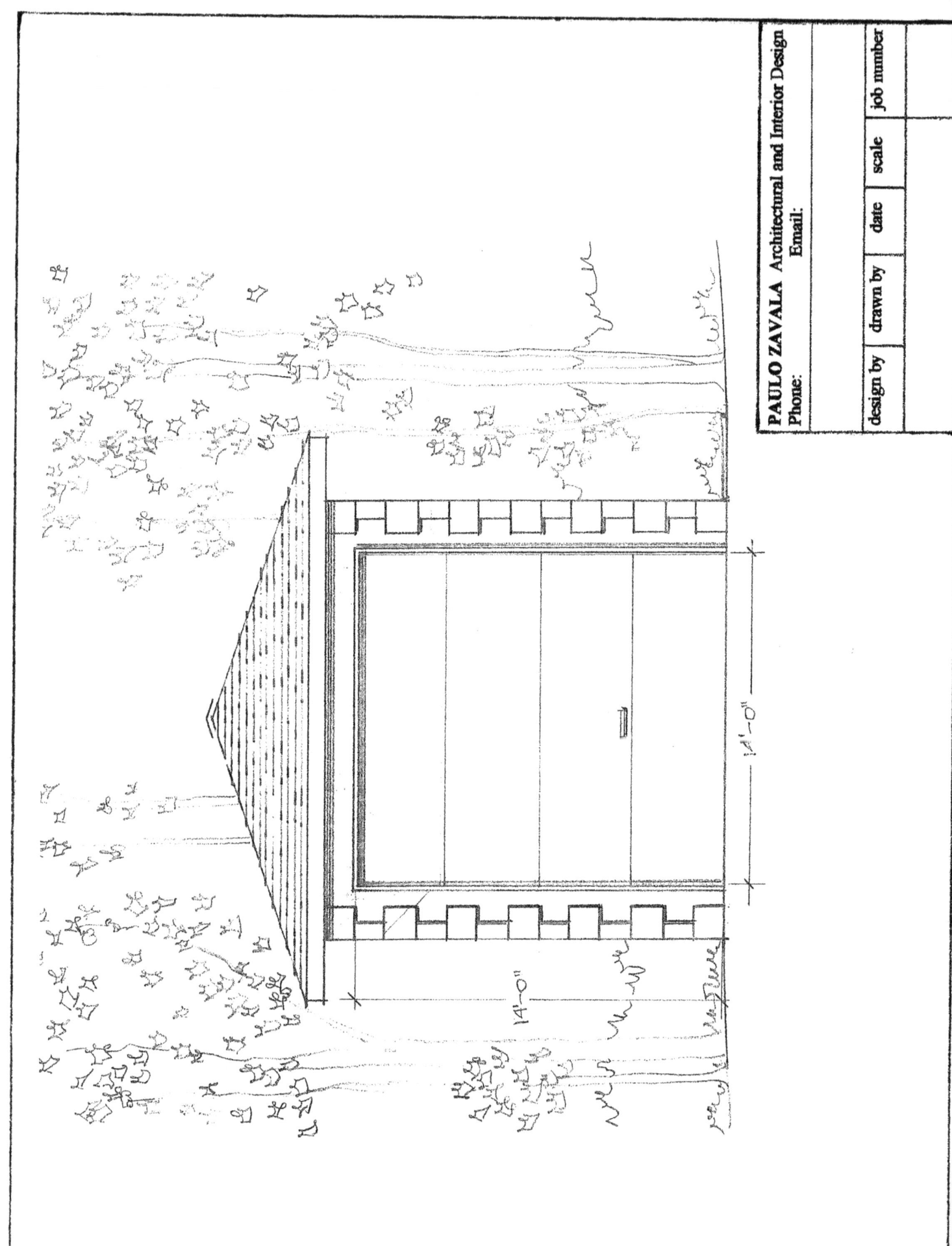

14'-0"

14'-0"

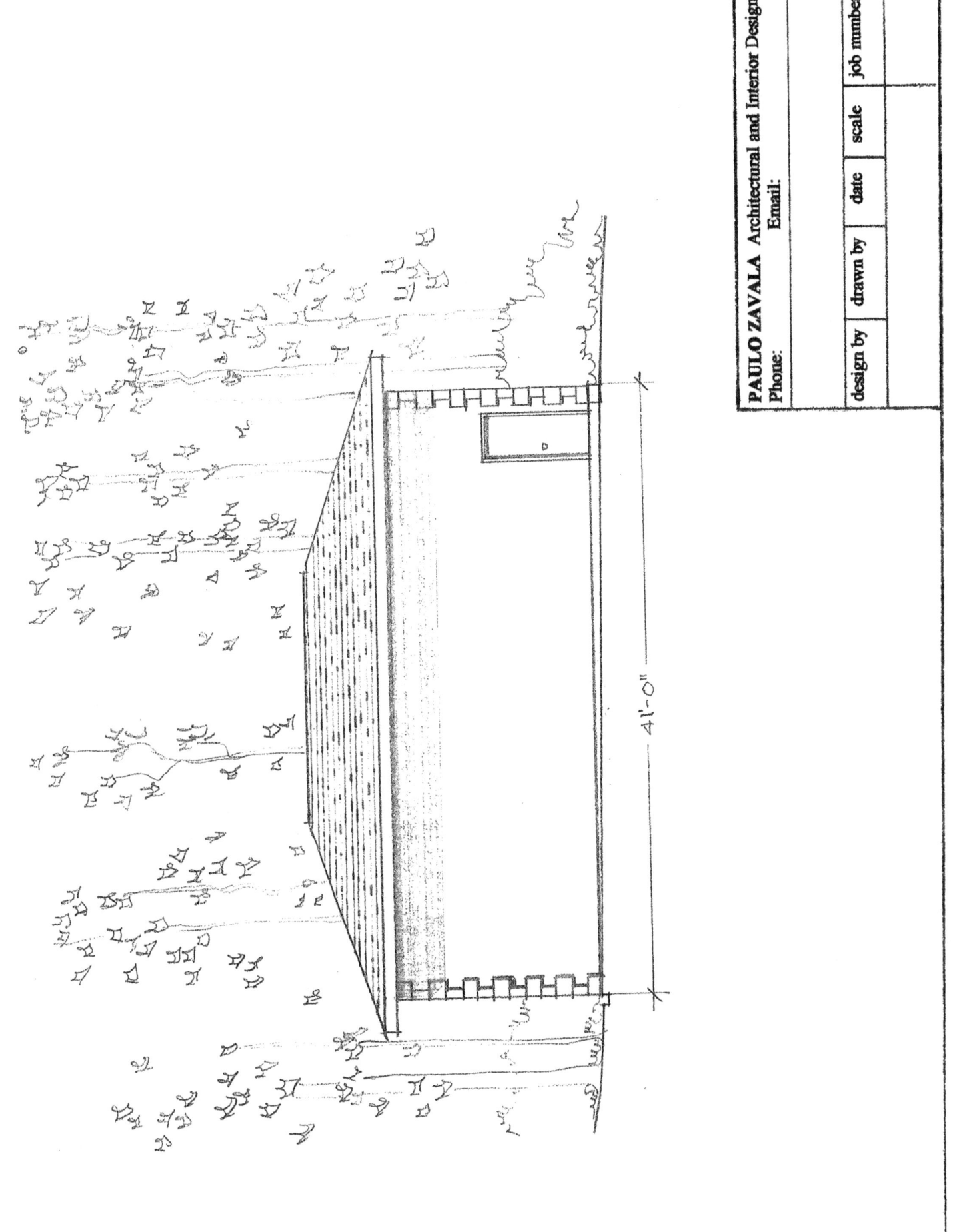

PAULO ZAVALA Architectural and Interior Design
Phone:
Email:

design by	drawn by	date	scale	job number

41'-0"

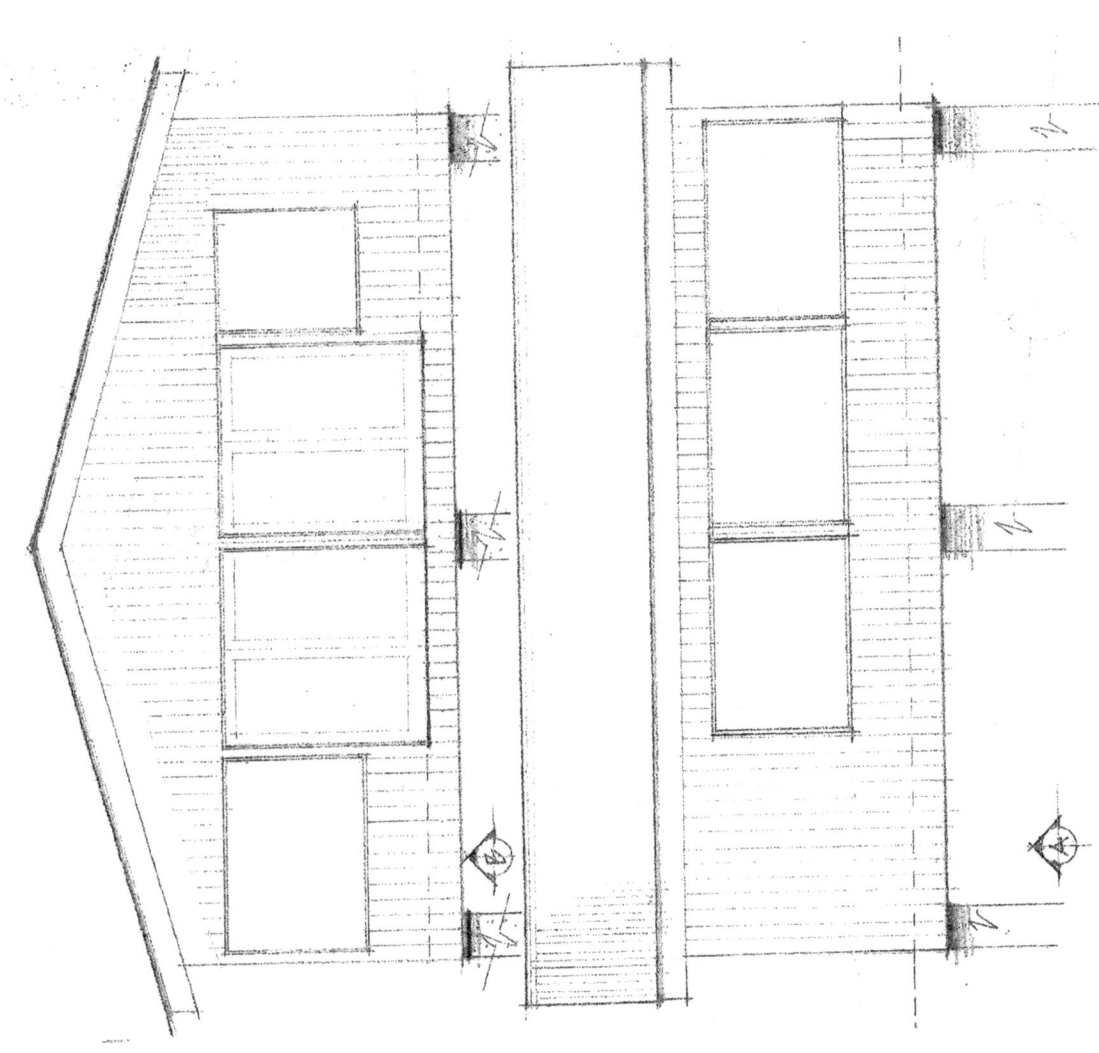

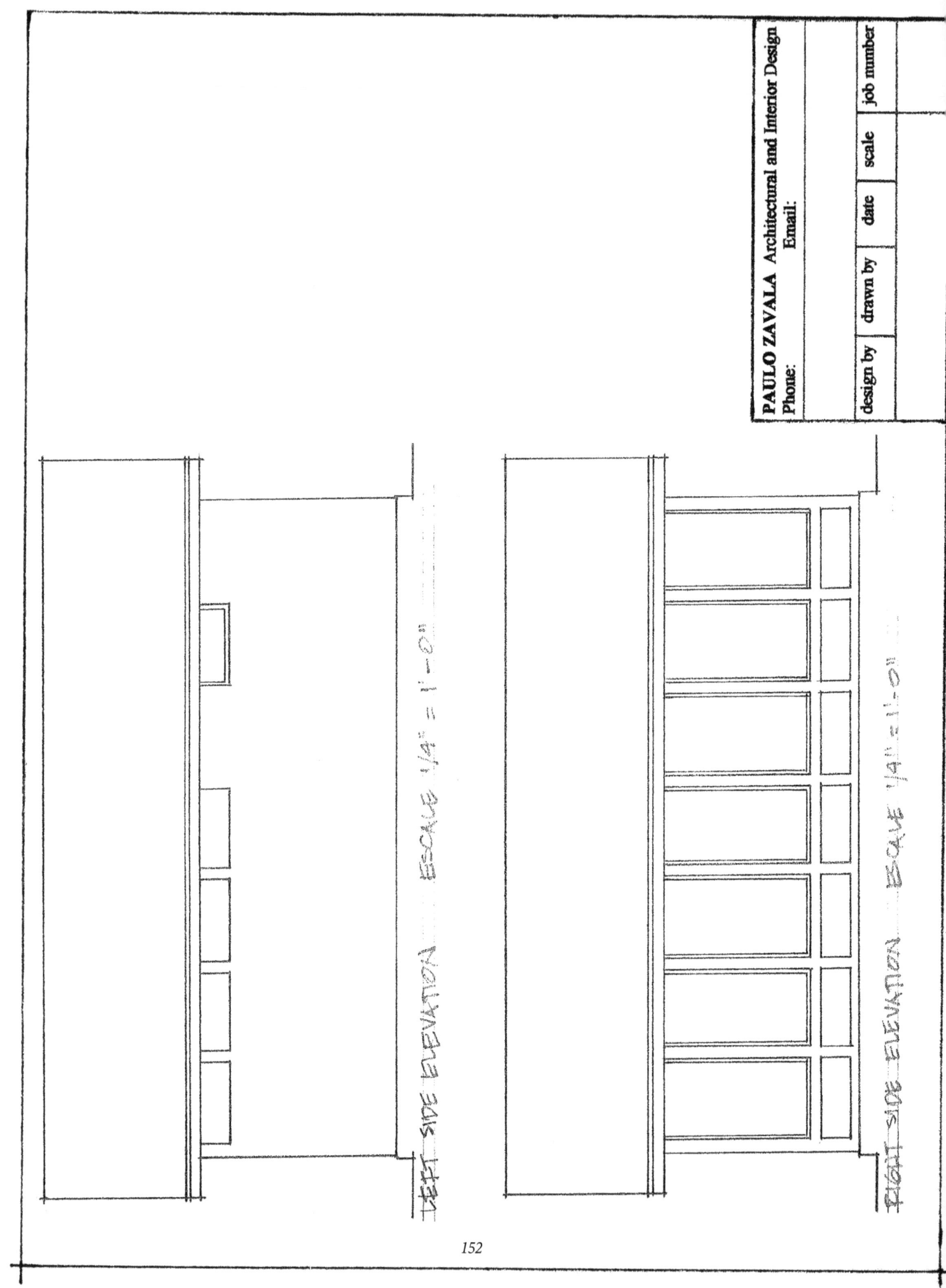

LEFT SIDE ELEVATION   ESCALE 1/4" = 1'-0"

RIGHT SIDE ELEVATION   ESCALE 1/4" = 1'-0"

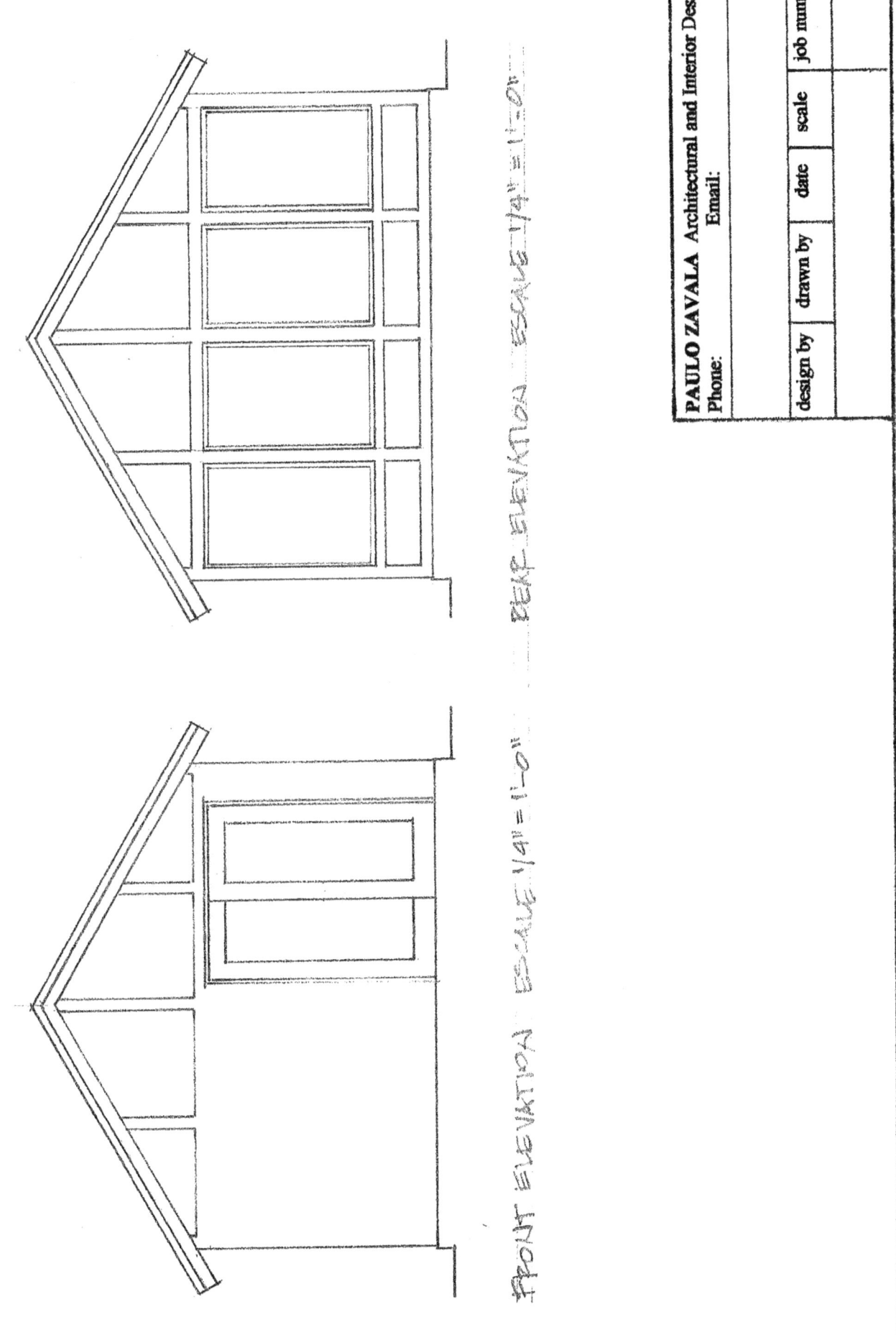

REAR ELEVATION   SCALE 1/4"=1'-0"

FRONT ELEVATION   SCALE 1/4"=1'-0"

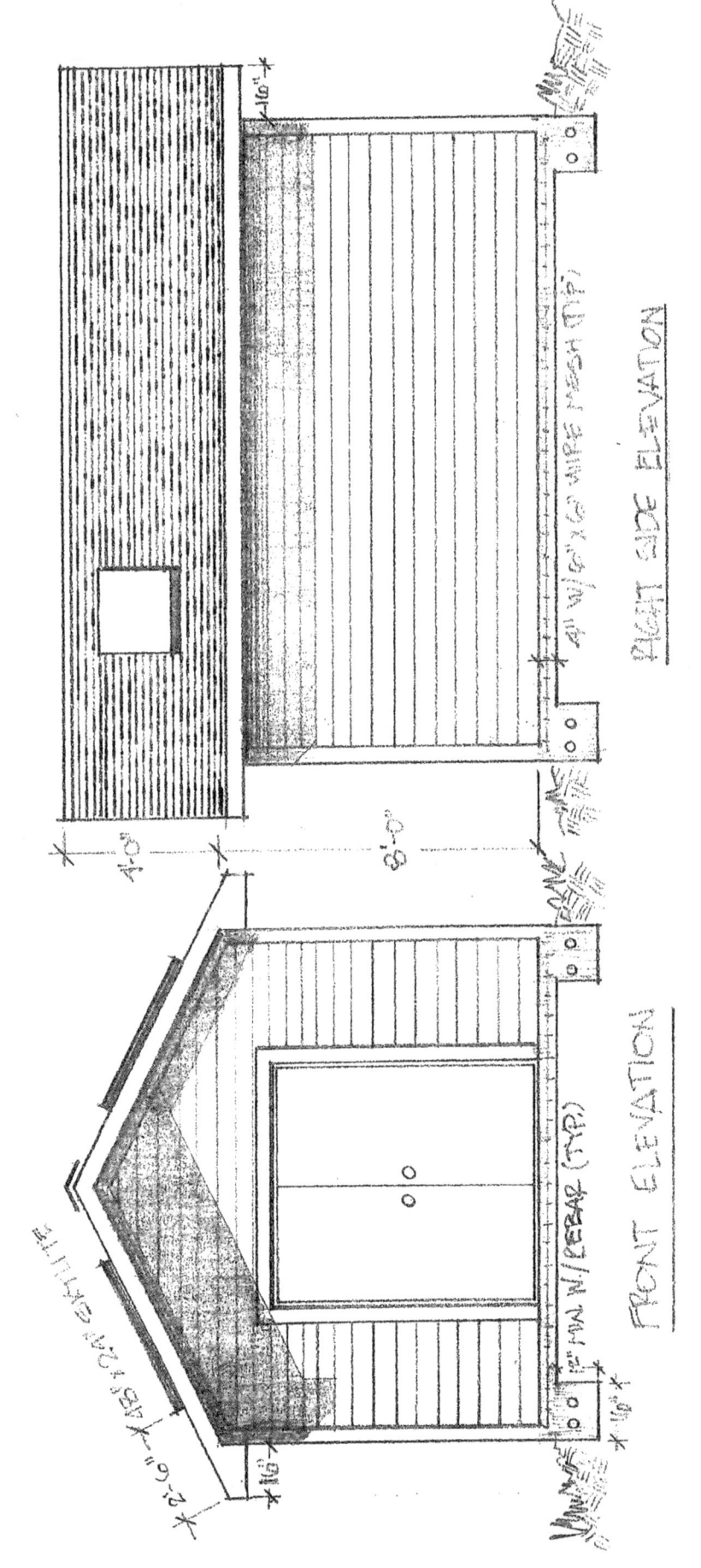

RIGHT SIDE ELEVATION

4" W/ 2'X2' WIRE MESH (TYP.)

FRONT ELEVATION

12" PYL W/ REBAR (TYP.)

PAULO ZAVALA Architectural and Interior Design
Phone:
Email:

design by	drawn by	date	scale	job number

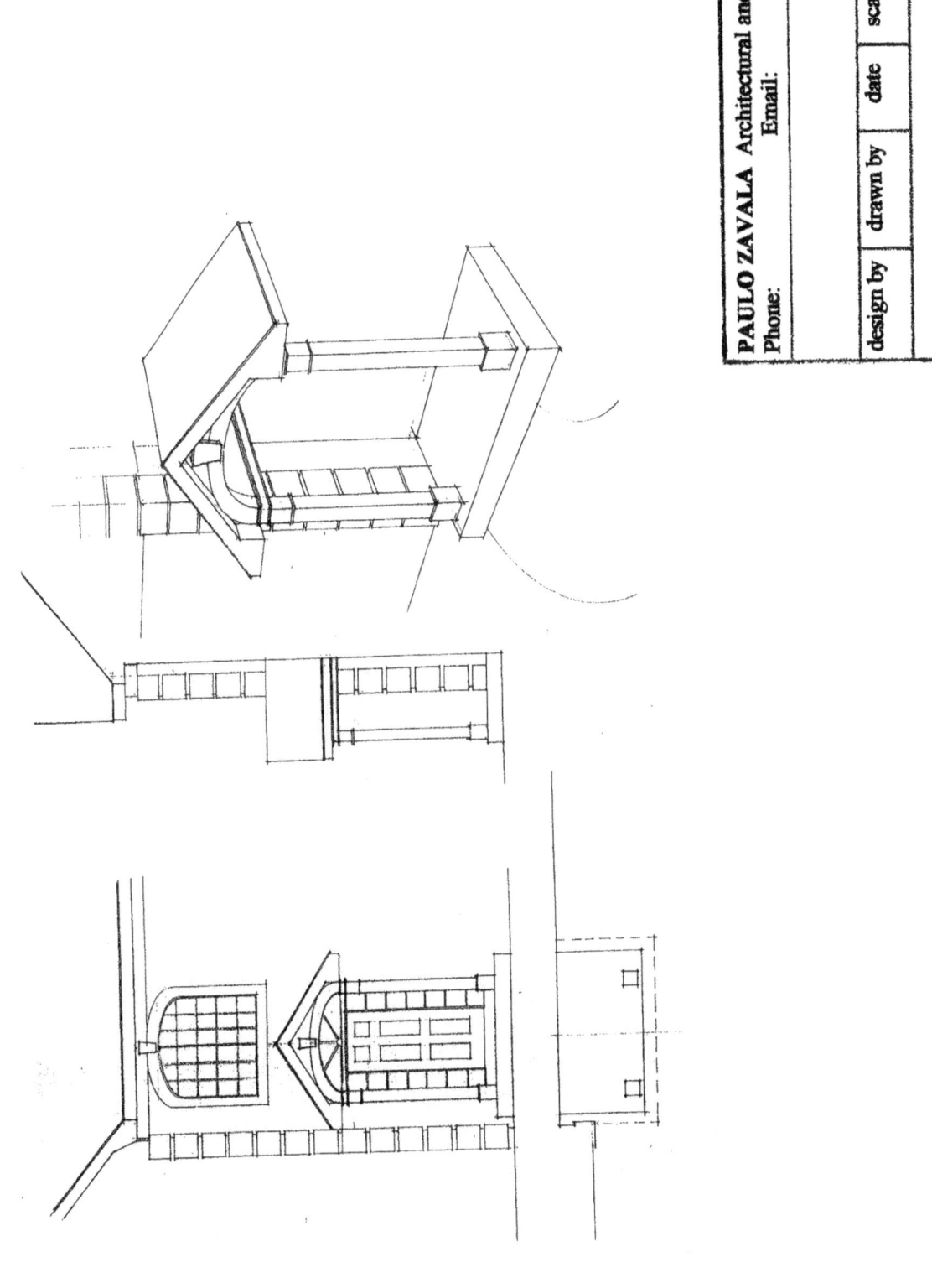

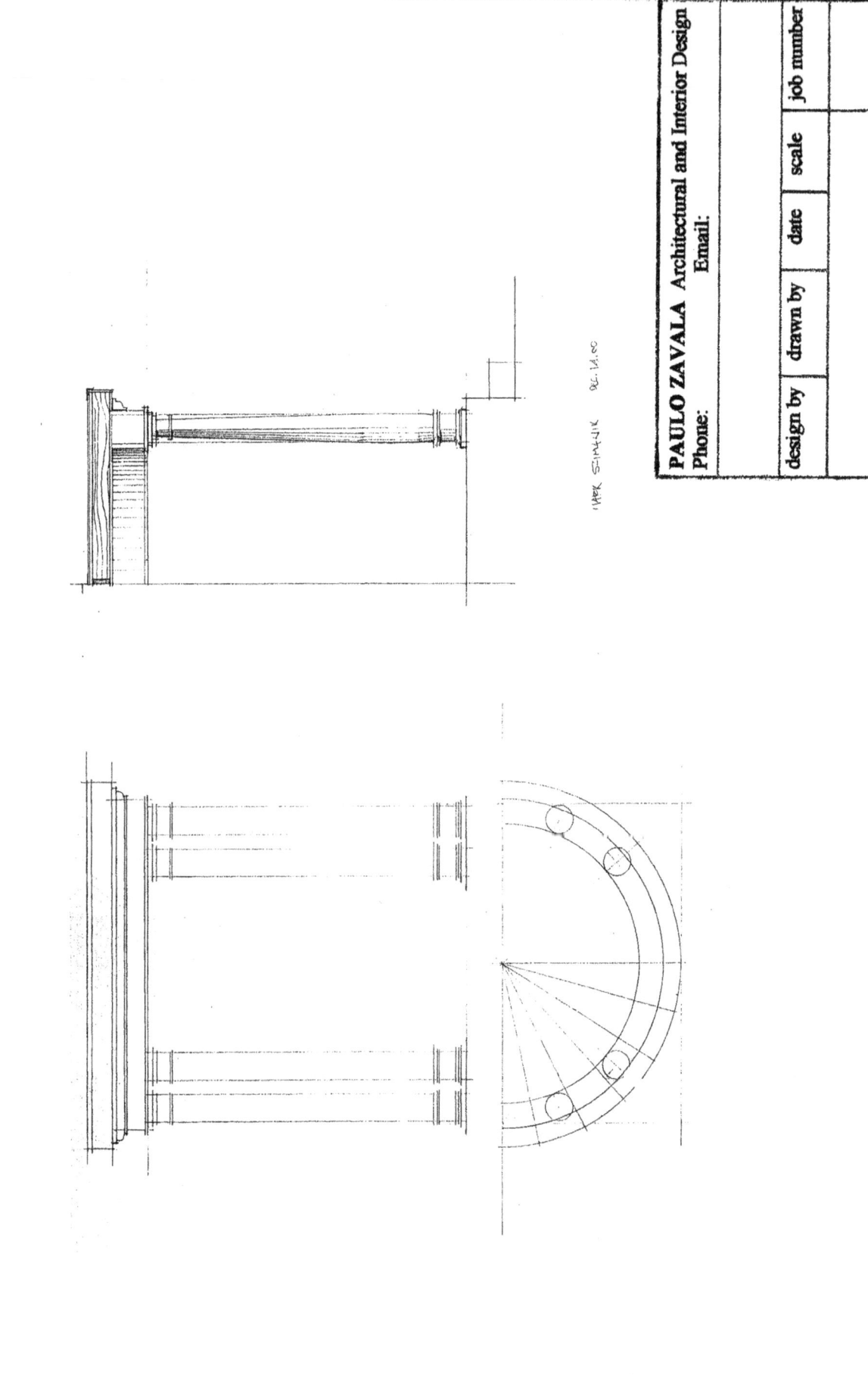

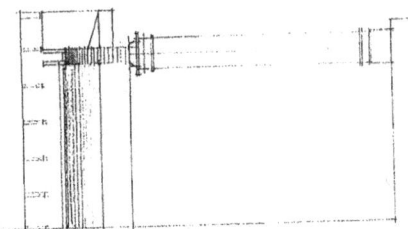

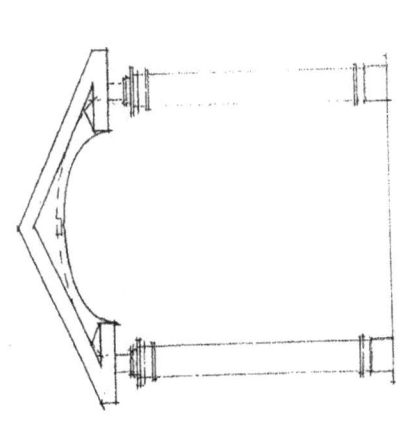

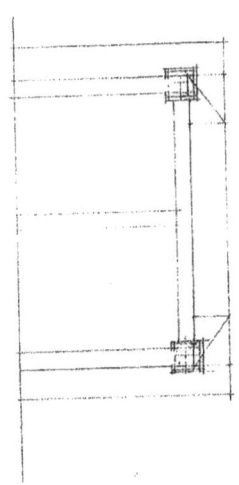

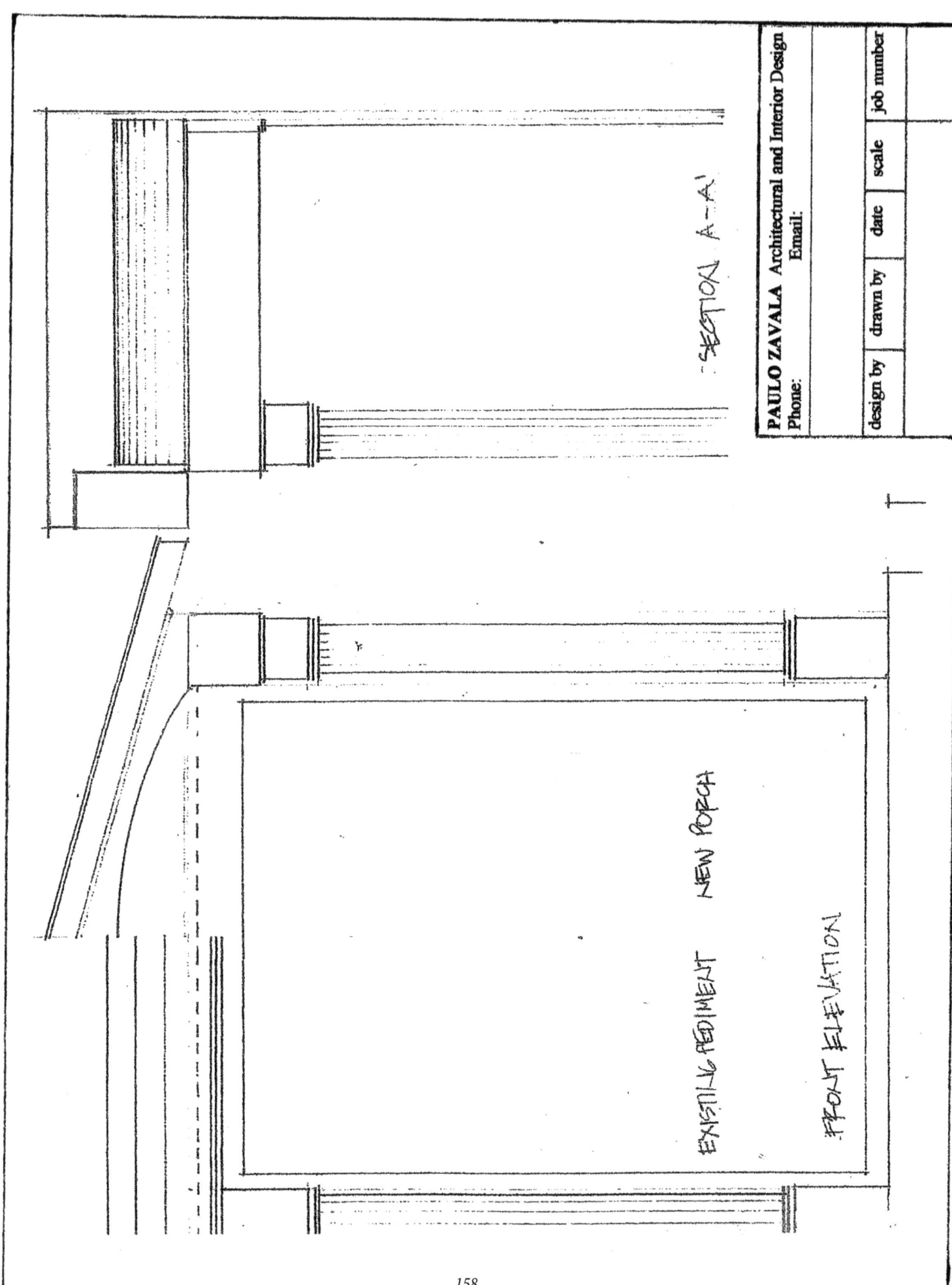

SECTION A—A'

EXISTING PEDIMENT   NEW PORCH

FRONT ELEVATION

PAULO ZAVALA Architectural and Interior Design
Phone:
Email:

design by	drawn by	date	scale	job number

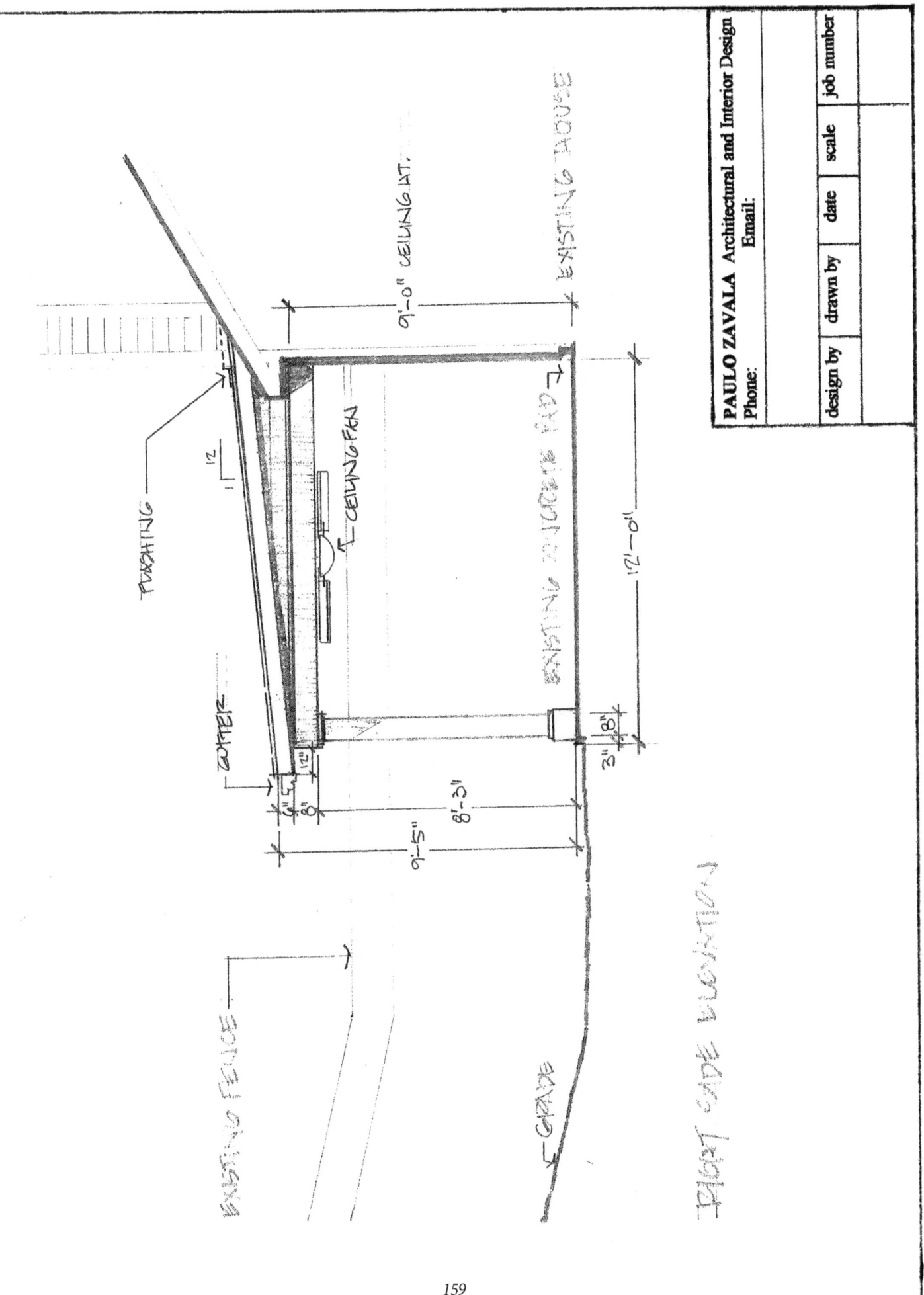

9'-0" CEILING HT.

EXISTING HOUSE

12

FLASHING

CEILING FAN

EXISTING 20 LOCATE FAD

GUTTER

12"

6"
8"

8'-3"

9'-5"

12'-0"

3" 8"

EXISTING FENCE

GRADE

RIGHT SIDE ELEVATION

PAULO ZAVALA Architectural and Interior Design
Phone: Email:

design by	drawn by	date	scale	job number

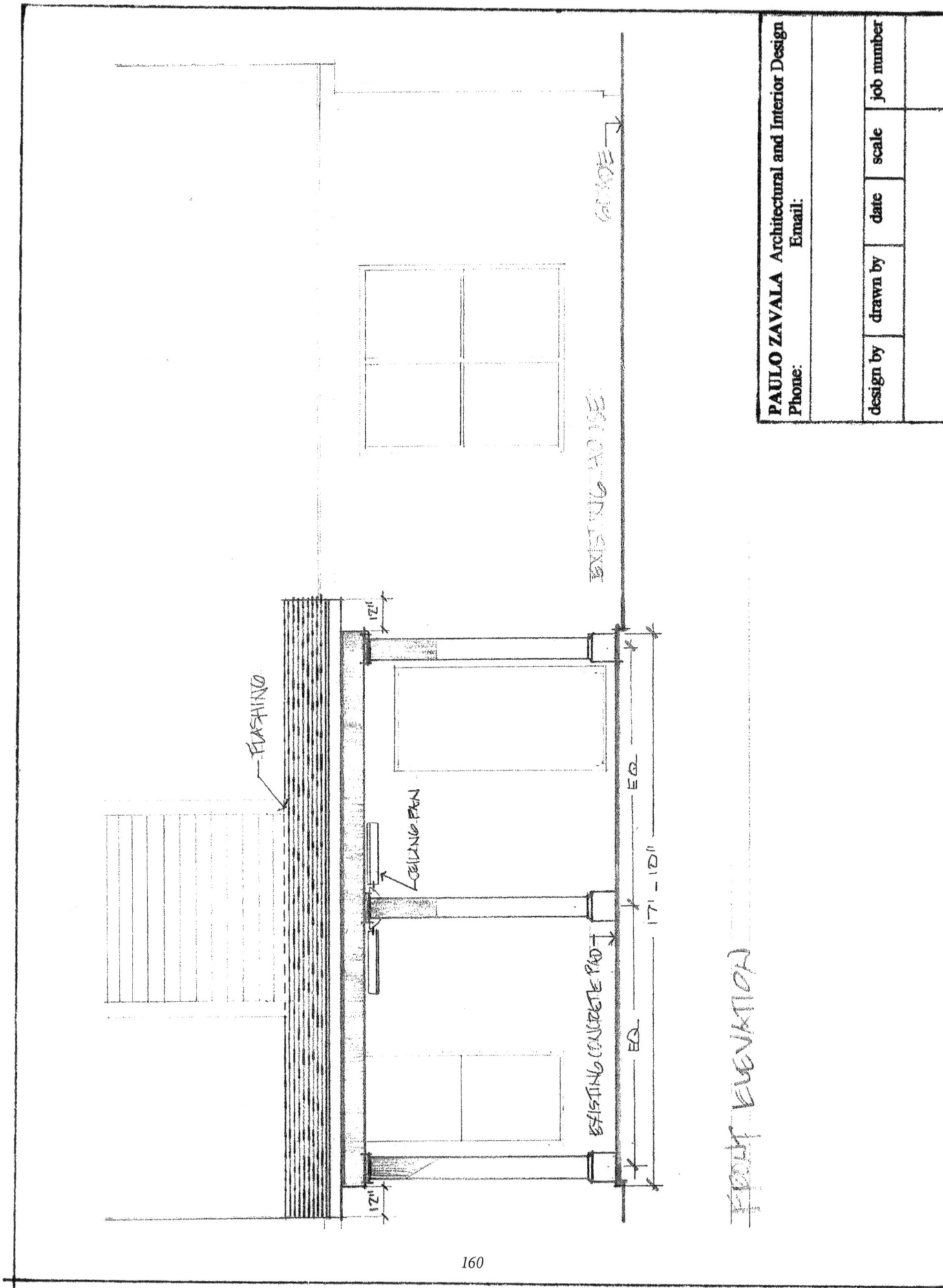

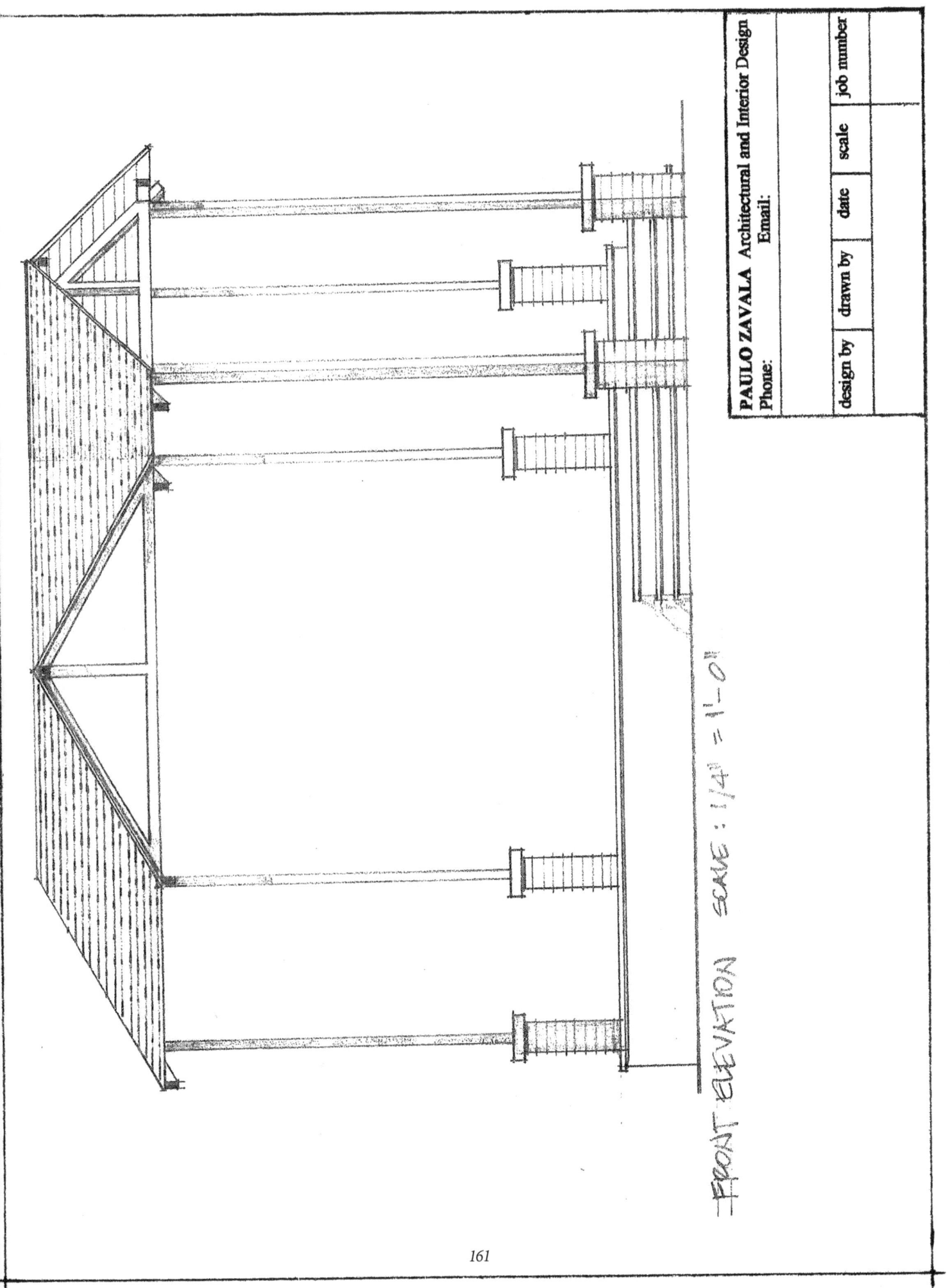

FRONT ELEVATION   SCALE : 1/4" = 1'-0"

PAULO ZAVALA Architectural and Interior Design
Phone: Email:

design by	drawn by	date	scale	job number

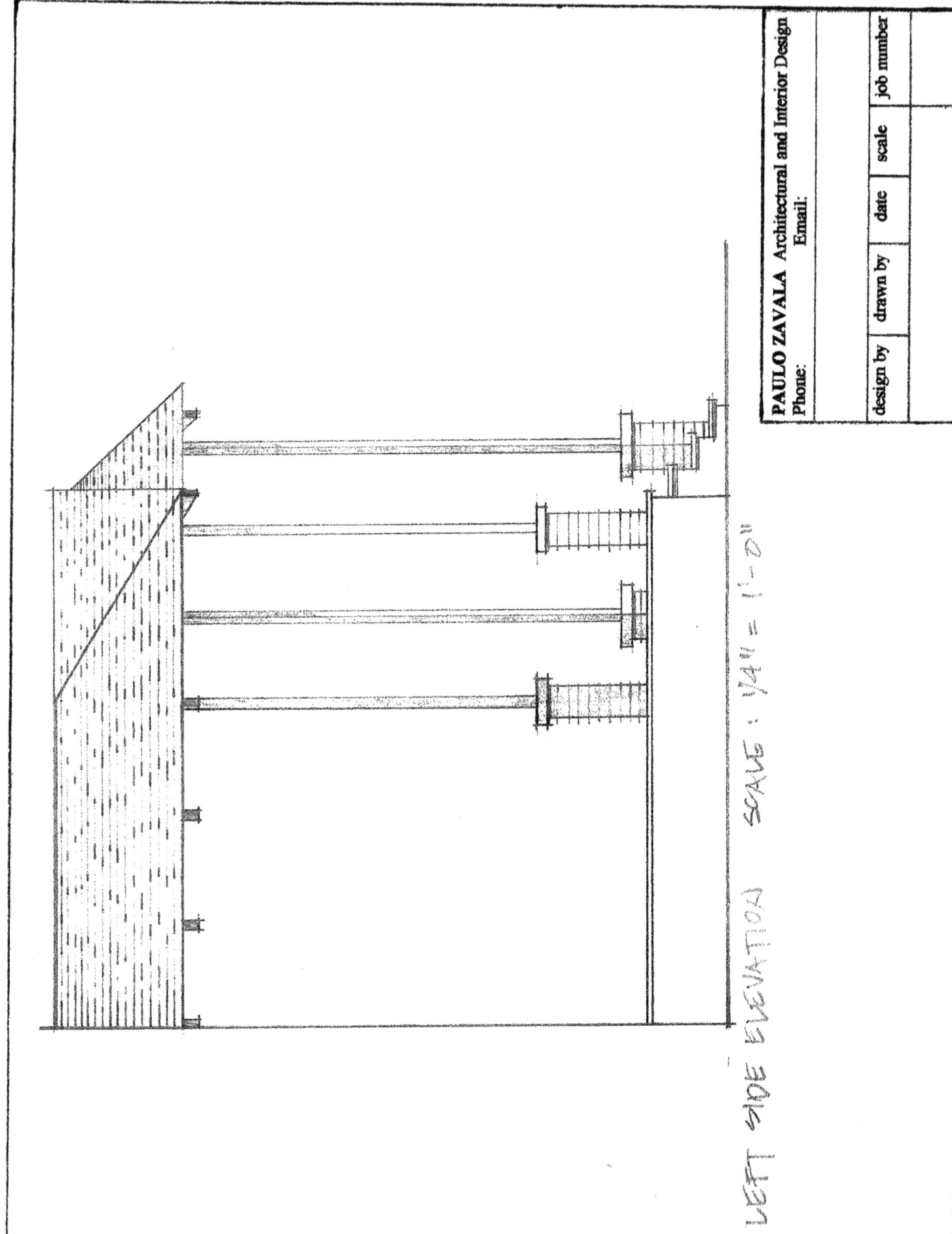

LEFT SIDE ELEVATION   SCALE : 1/4" = 1'-0"

PAULO ZAVALA Architectural and Interior Design
Phone: Email:

design by	drawn by	date	scale	job number

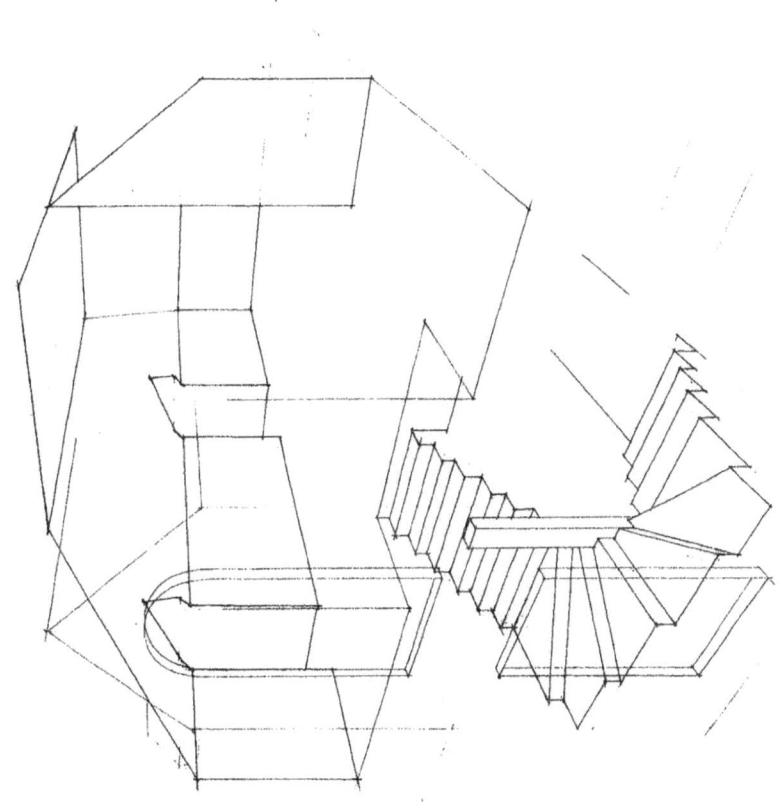

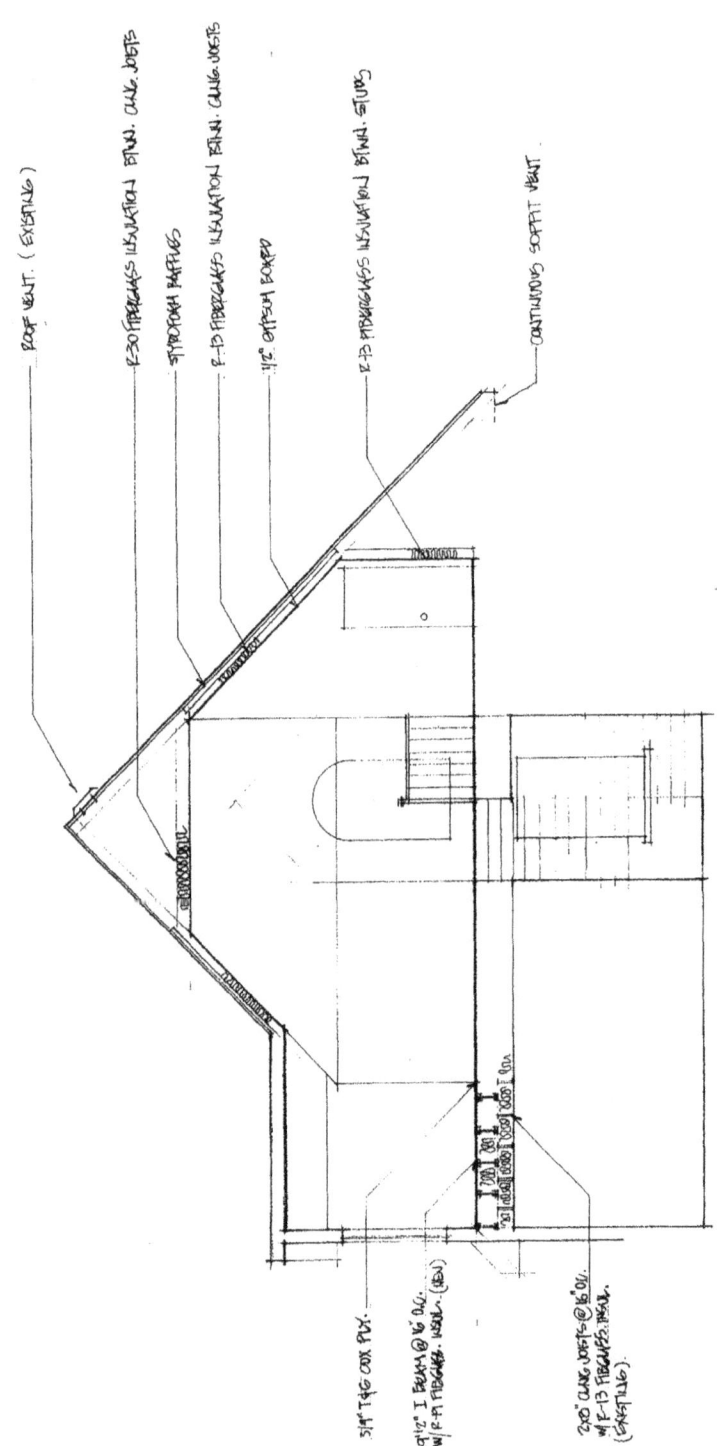

ROOF VENT. (EXISTING)

R-30 FIBERGLASS INSULATION BTWN. CLNG. JOISTS

STYROFOAM BAFFLES

R-19 FIBERGLASS INSULATION BTWN. CLNG. JOISTS

1/2" GYPSUM BOARD

R-13 FIBERGLASS INSULATION BTWN. STUDS

CONTINUOUS SOFFIT VENT

SIM. T&G CDX PLY.

9 1/2" I BEAM @ 16" O.W.
W/ R-19 FIBERGLASS INSUL. (NEW)

2x10 CLNG. JOISTS @ 16" O.W.
W/ R-13 FIBERGLASS INSUL.
(EXISTING)

PAULO ZAVALA Architectural and Interior Design
Phone:
Email:

design by	drawn by	date	scale	job number

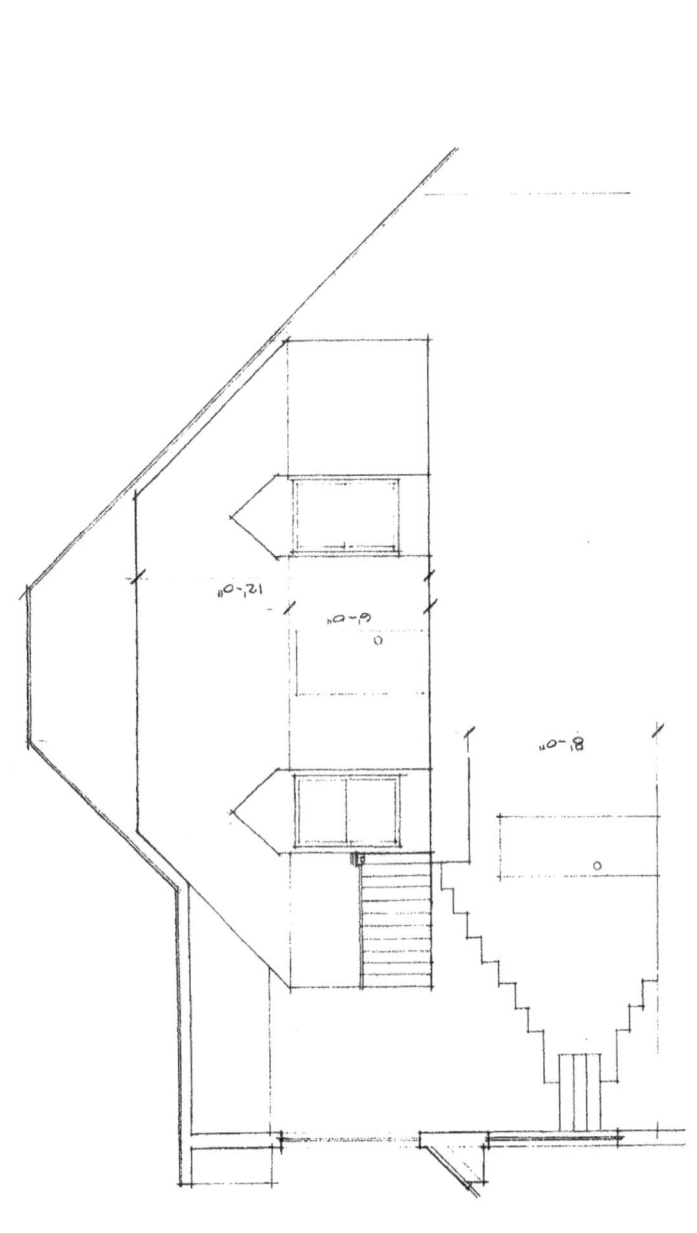

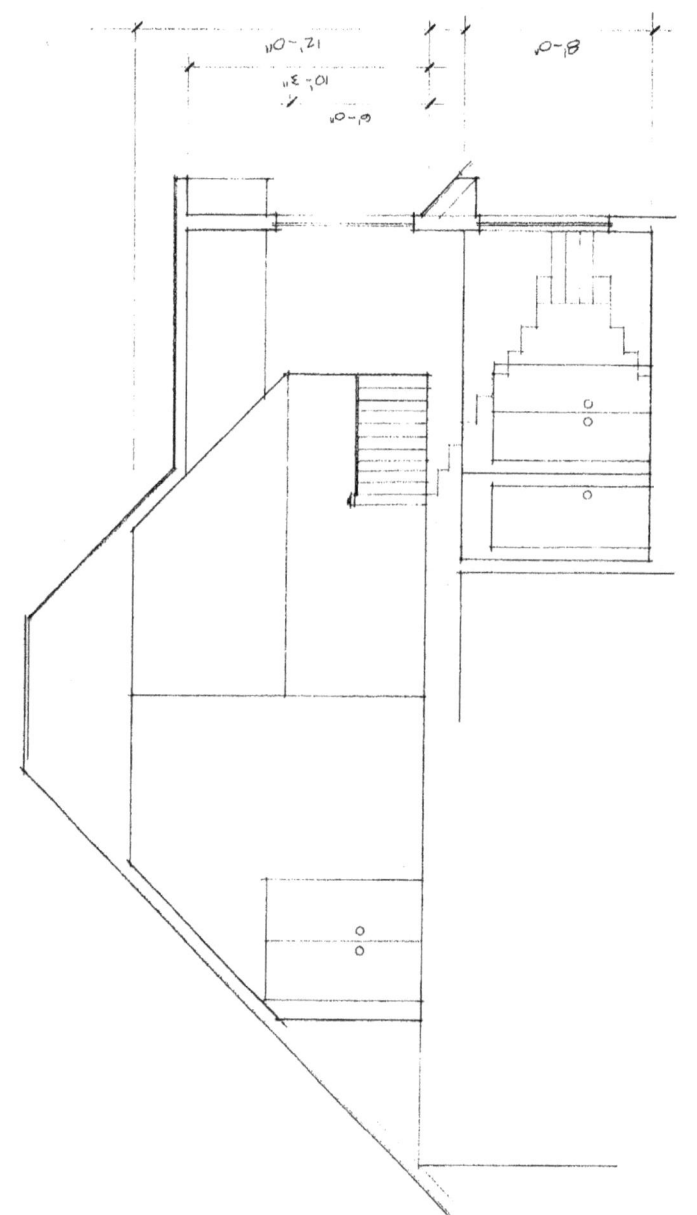

PAULO ZAVALA Architectural and Interior Design

Phone:

Email:

design by	drawn by	date	scale	job number

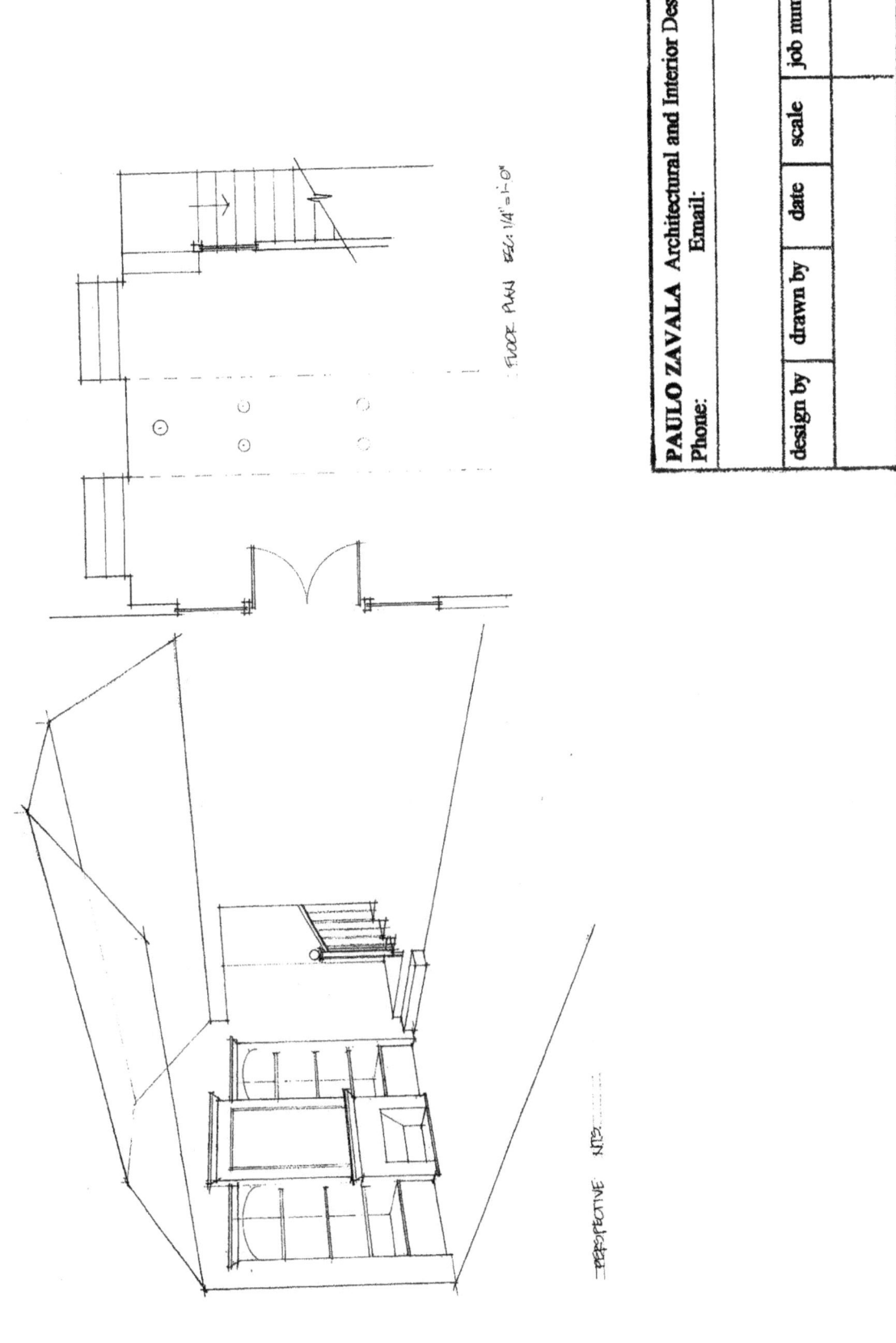

FLOOR PLAN SCALE: 1/4"=1'-0"

PERSPECTIVE N.T.S.

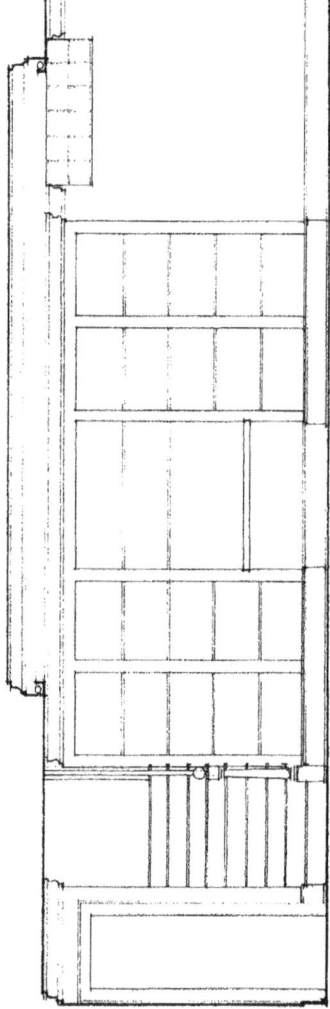

PAULO ZAVALA Architectural and Interior Design
Phone: Email:

design by	drawn by	date	scale	job number

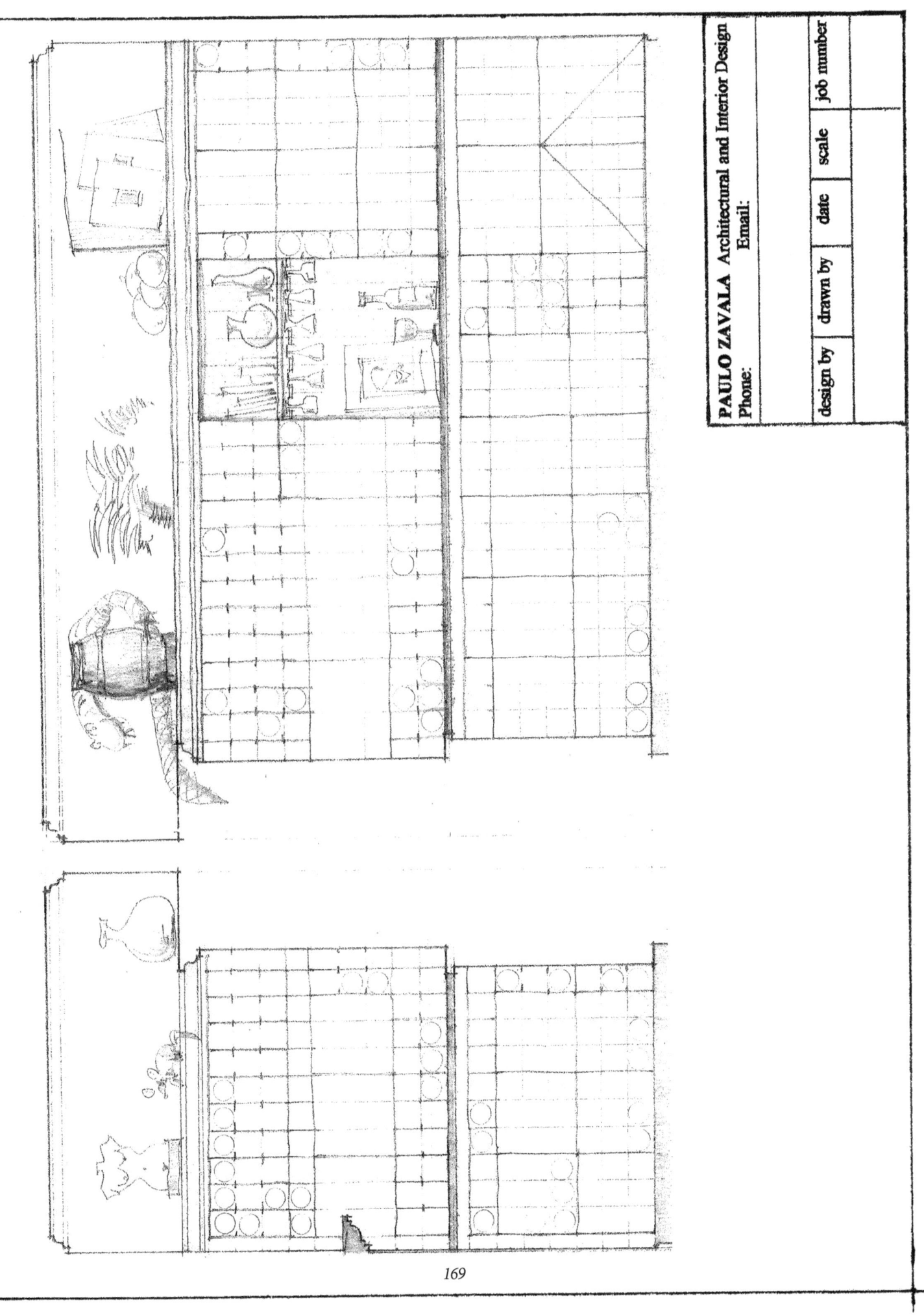

PAULO ZAVALA Architectural and Interior Design
Phone:
Email:

design by	drawn by	date	scale	job number

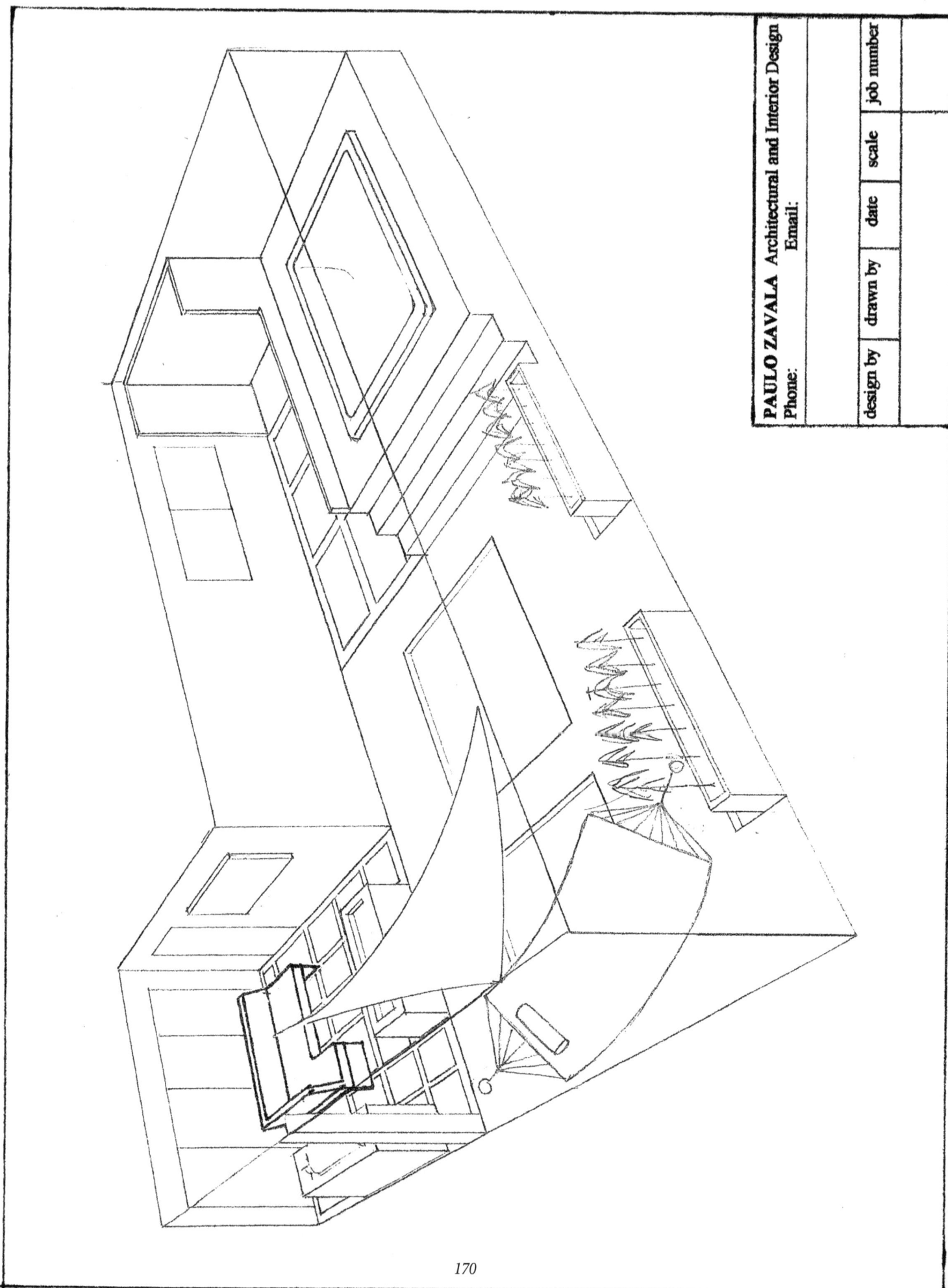

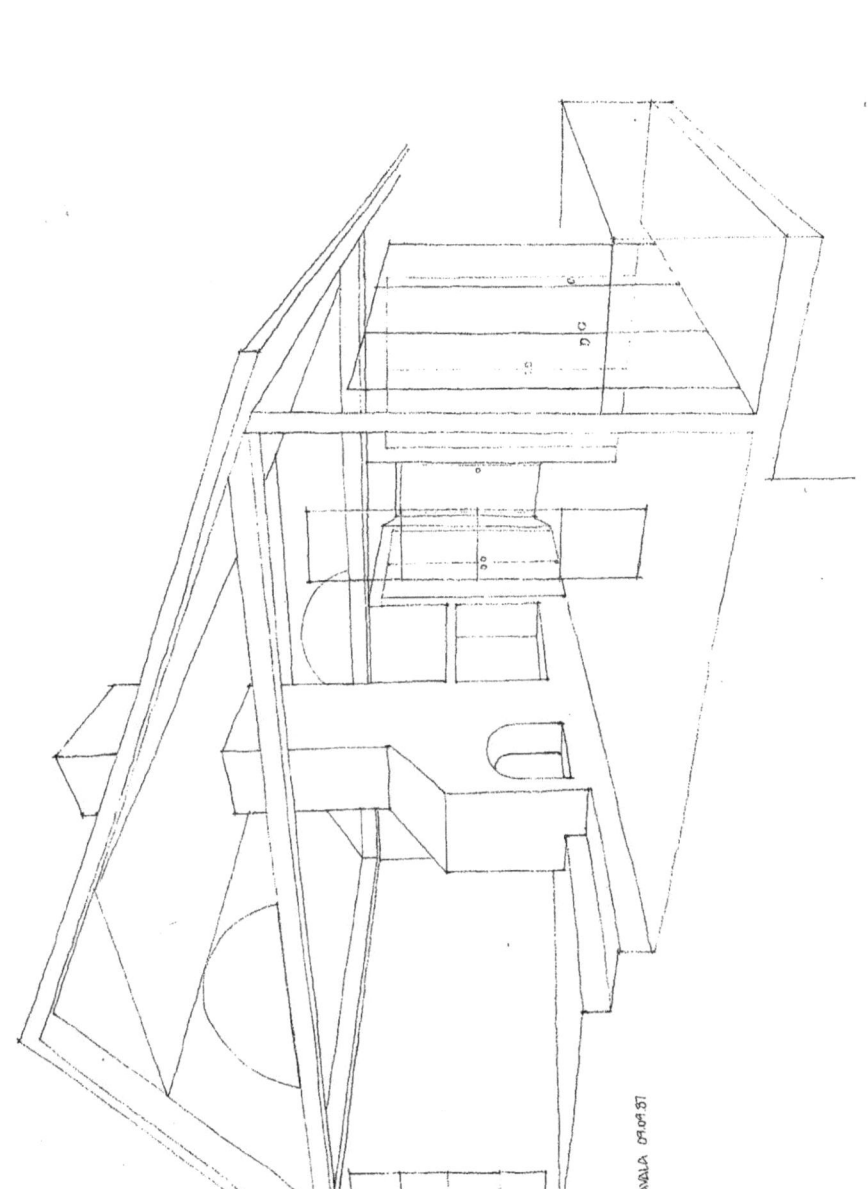

PZAVALA 09.09.87

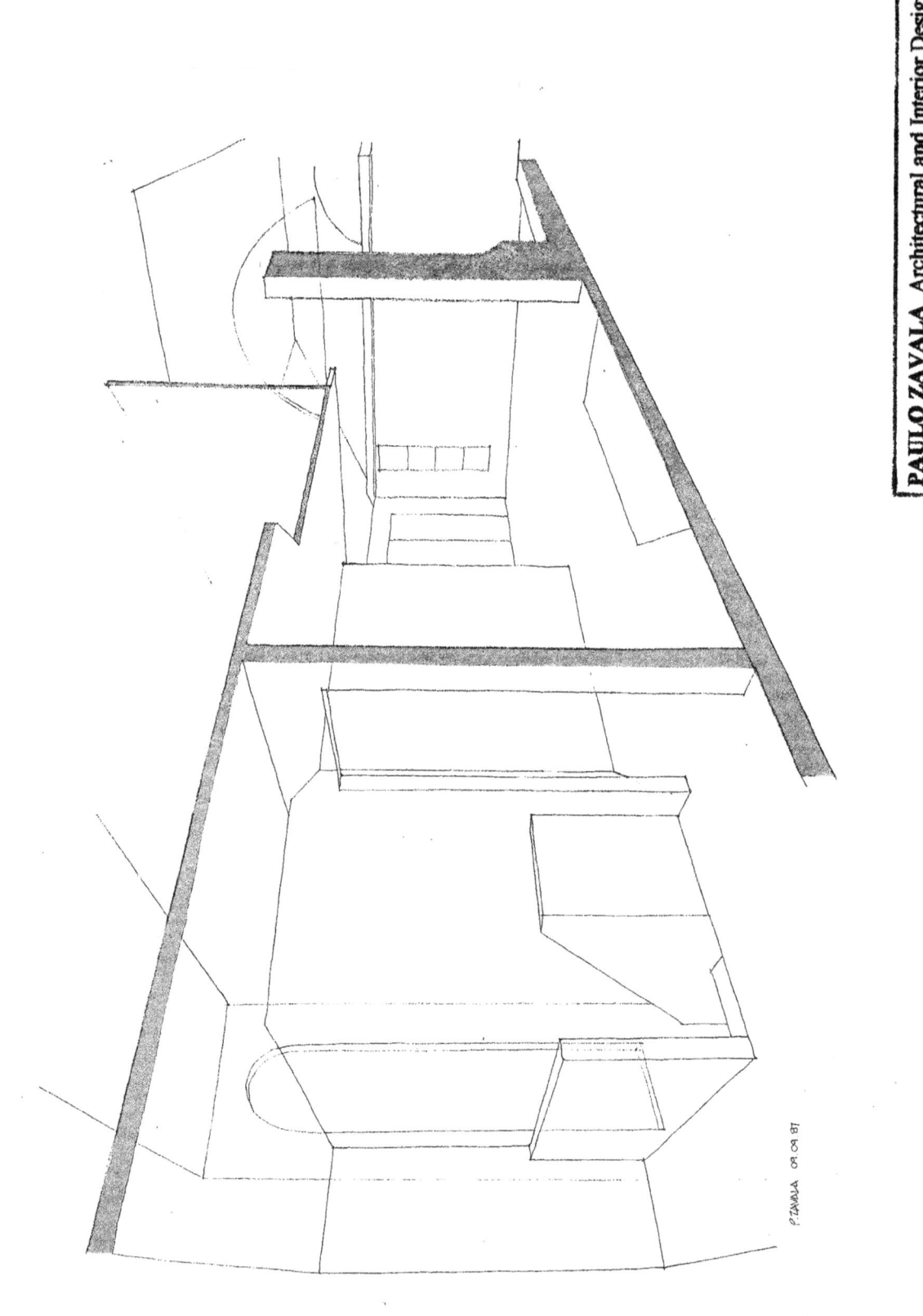

P. ZAVALA 09 09 87

PAULO ZAVALA Architectural and Interior Design
Phone:
Email:

design by	drawn by	date	scale	job number

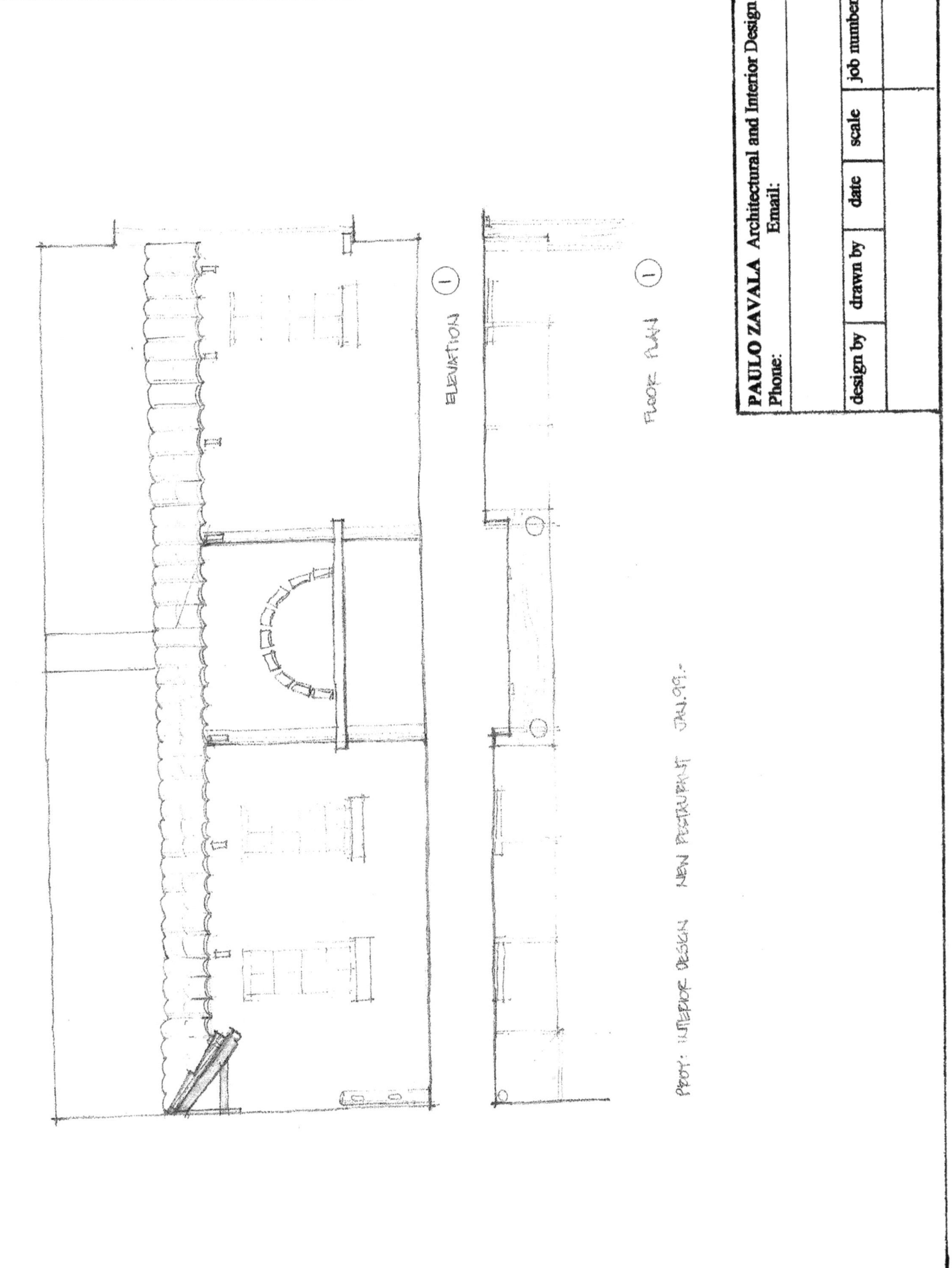

ELEVATION 1

FLOOR PLAN 1

PROY: INTERIOR DESIGN   NEW RESTAURANT   JAN.99.-

PAULO ZAVALA Architectural and Interior Design
Phone: Email:

design by	drawn by	date	scale	job number

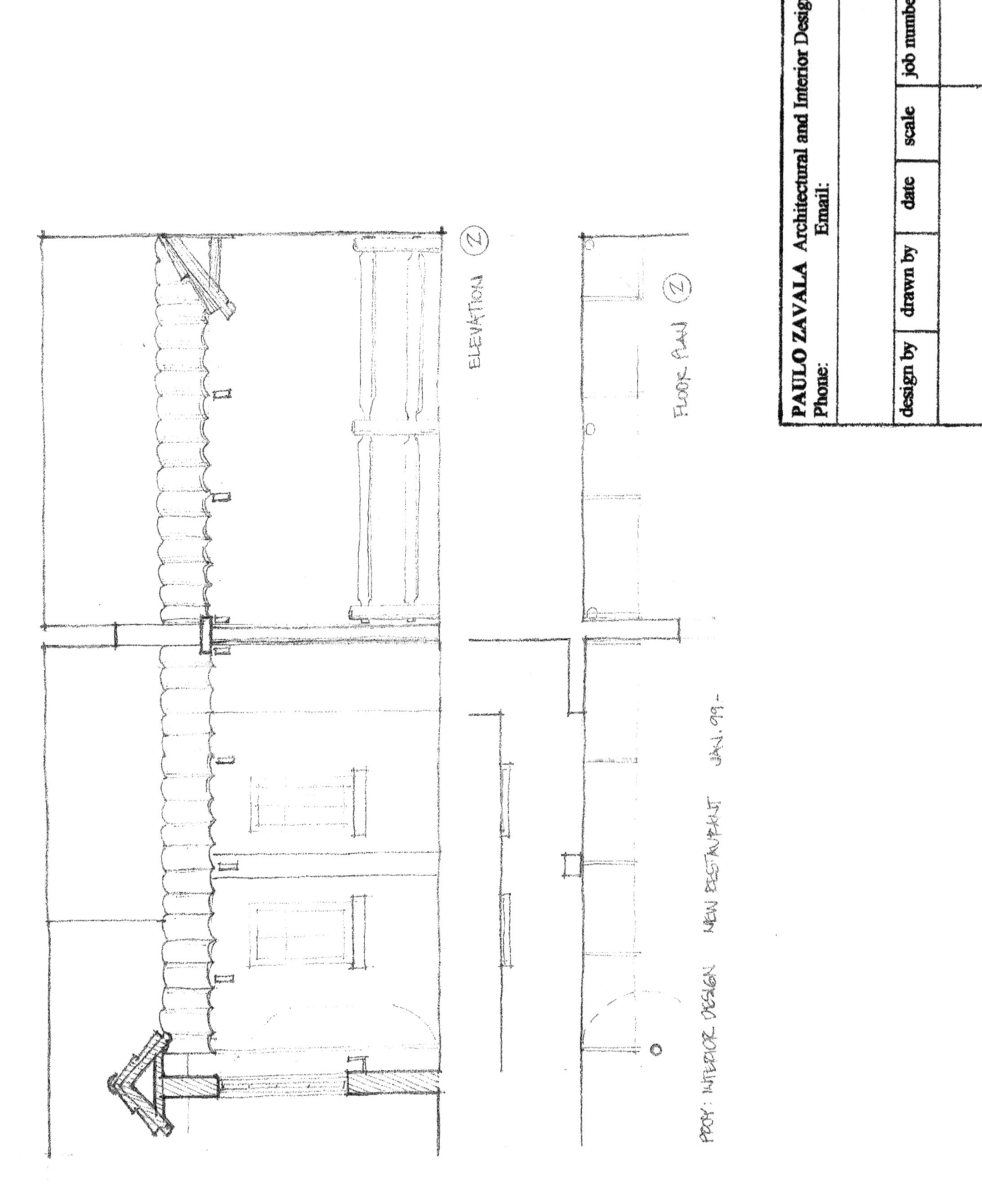

ELEVATION (2)

FLOOR PLAN (2)

PROJ: INTERIOR DESIGN   NEW RESTAURANT   JAN. 99 -

PAULO ZAVALA Architectural and Interior Design
Phone: Email:

design by	drawn by	date	scale	job number

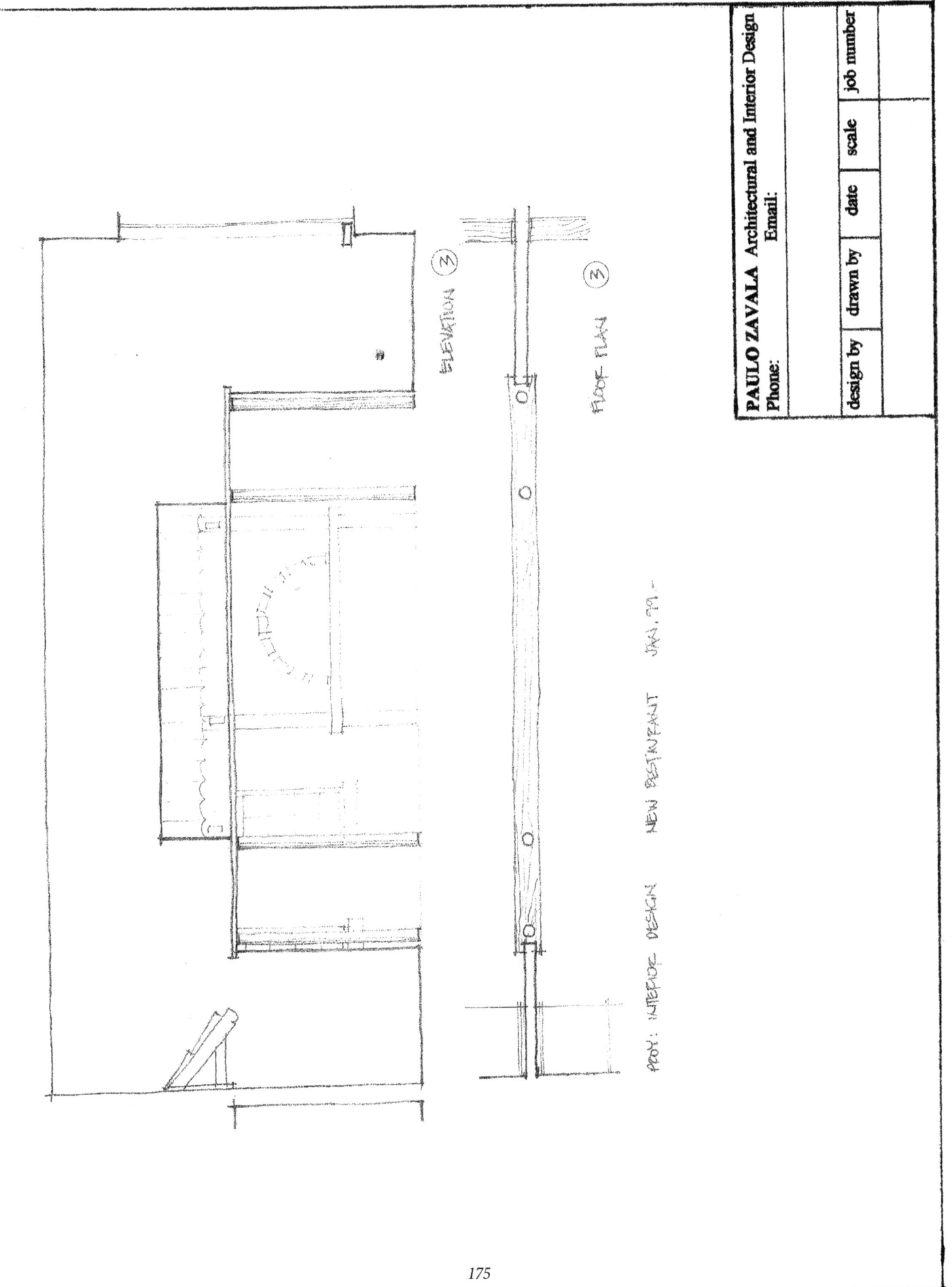

ELEVATION 3

FLOOR PLAN 3

PROY: INTERIOR DESIGN   NEW RESTAURANT   JAN. 79.-

PAULO ZAVALA Architectural and Interior Design
Phone: Email:

design by	drawn by	date	scale	job number

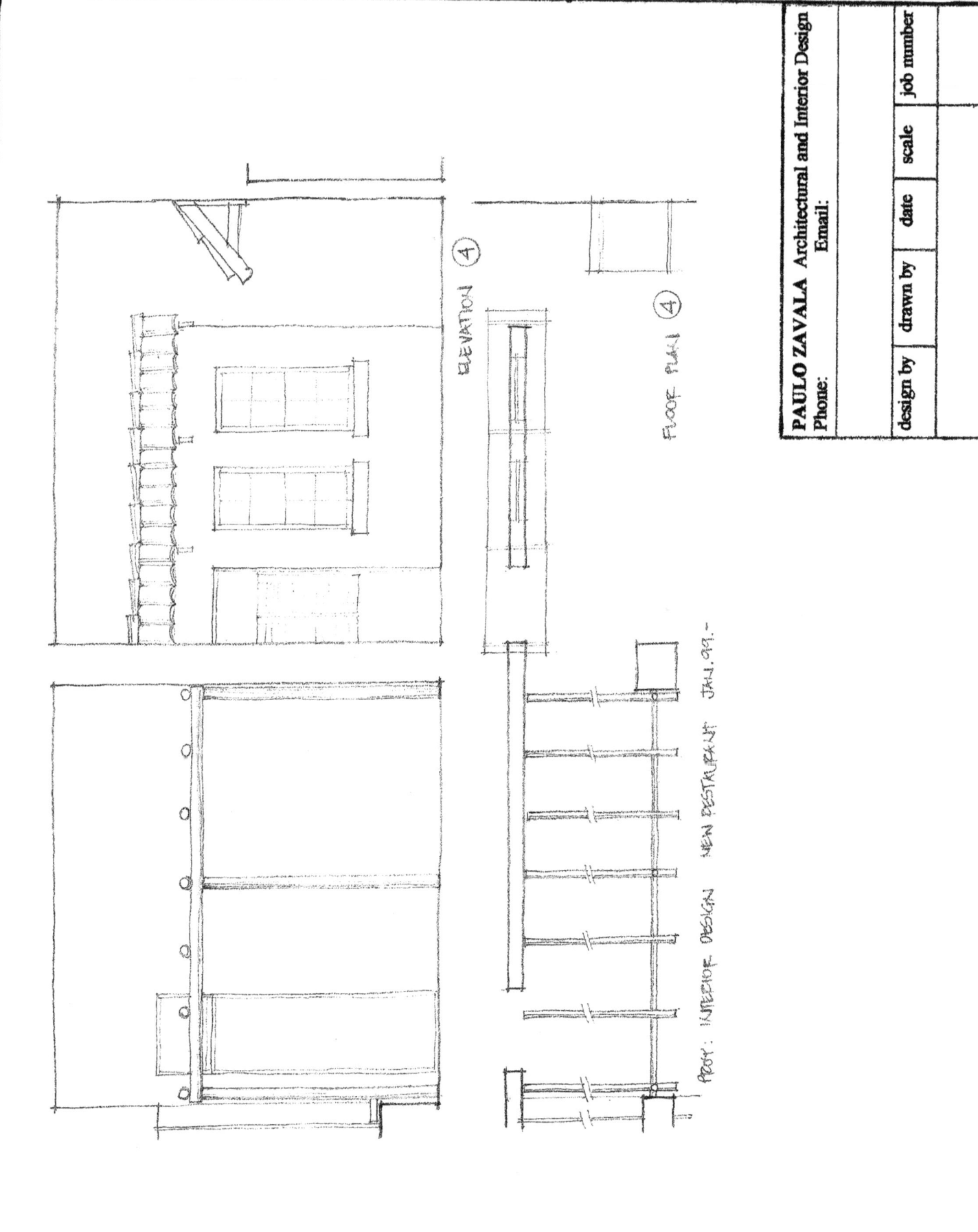

ELEVATION ④

FLOOR PLAN ④

PROY: INTERIOR DESIGN NEW RESTAURANT JAN.99.-

PAULO ZAVALA Architectural and Interior Design
Phone:
Email:

design by	drawn by	date	scale	job number

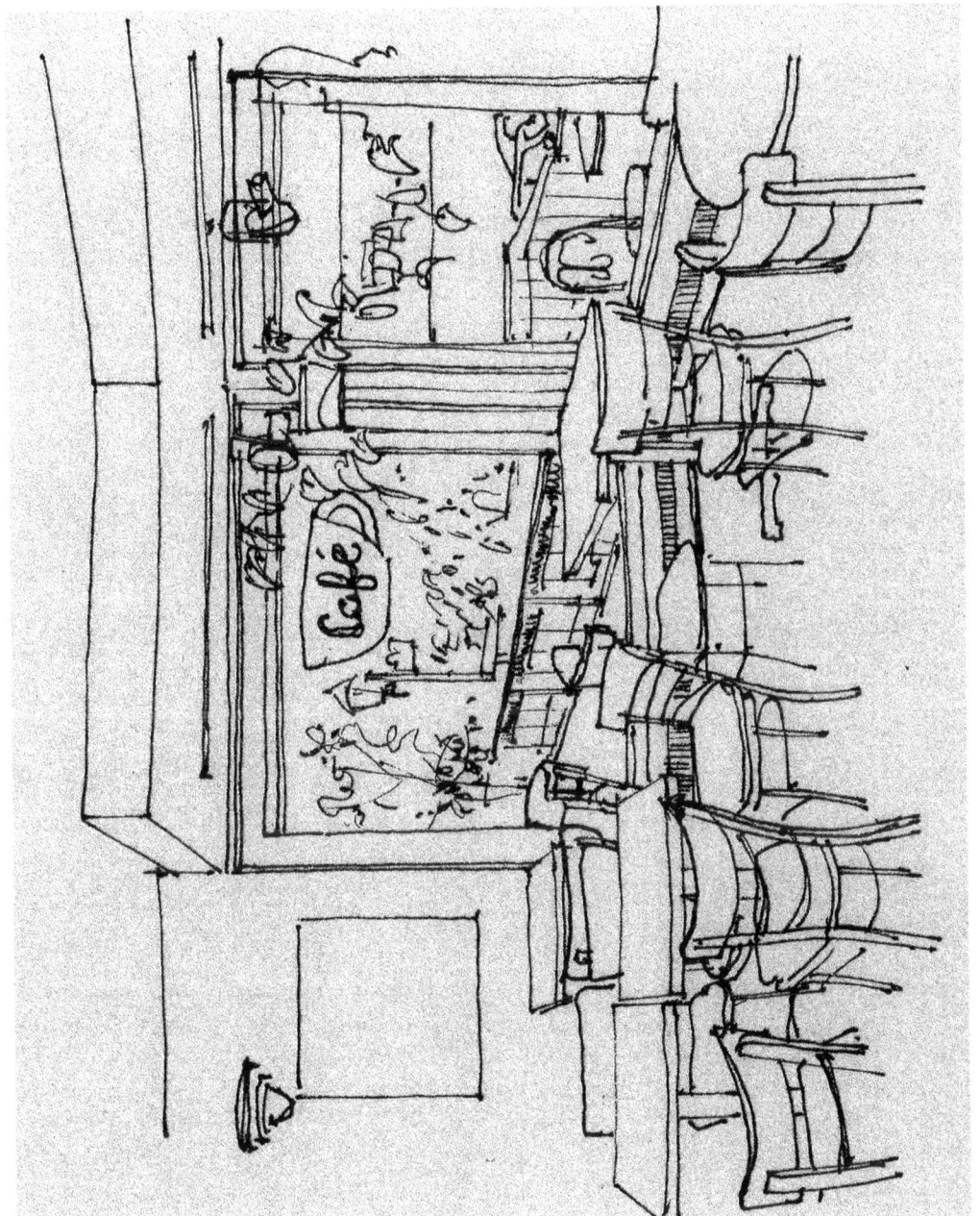

PAULO ZAVALA Architectural and Interior Design
Phone:
Email:

design by	drawn by	date	scale	job number

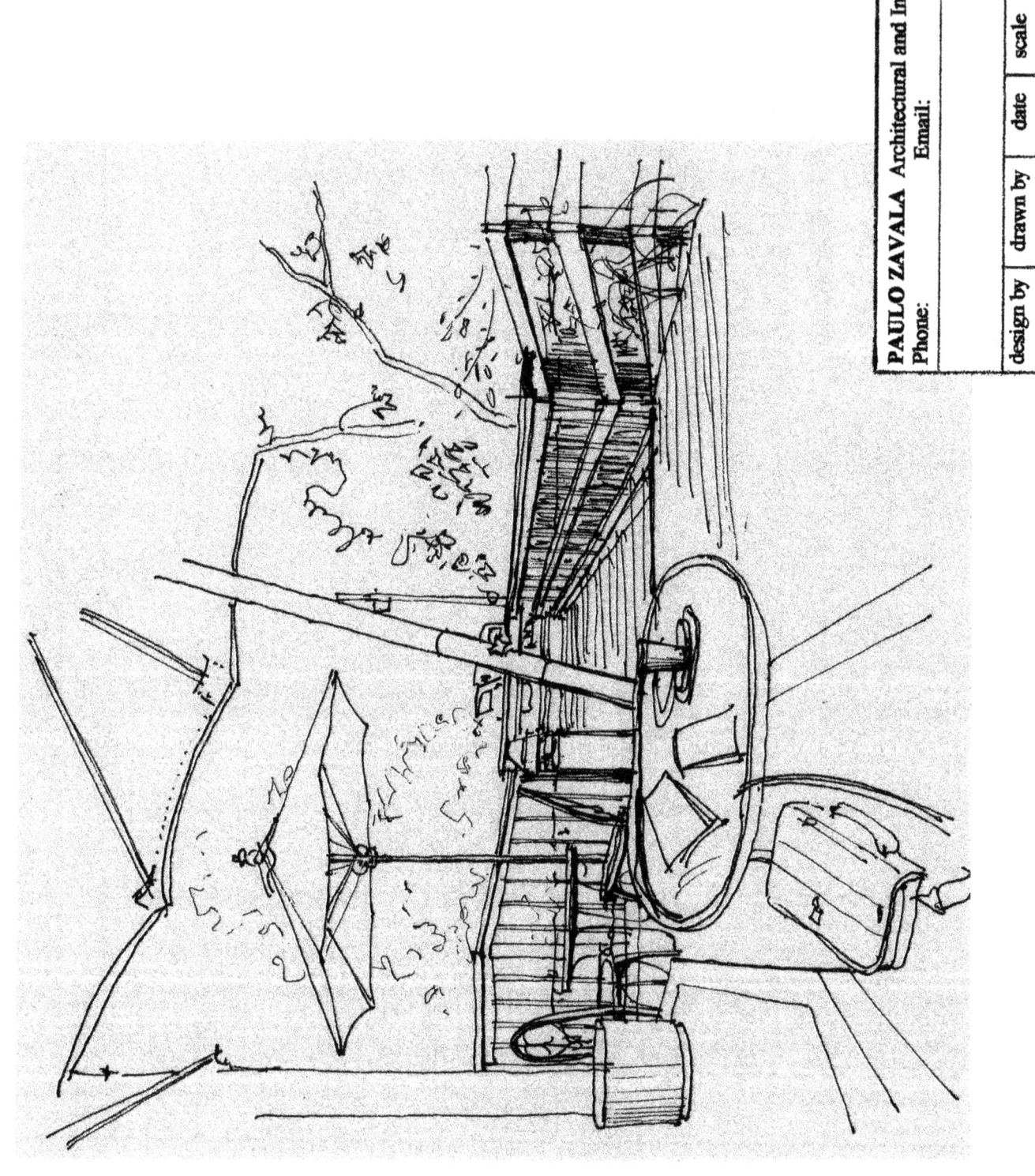

PAULO ZAVALA Architectural and Interior Design
Phone:
Email:

design by	drawn by	date	scale	job number

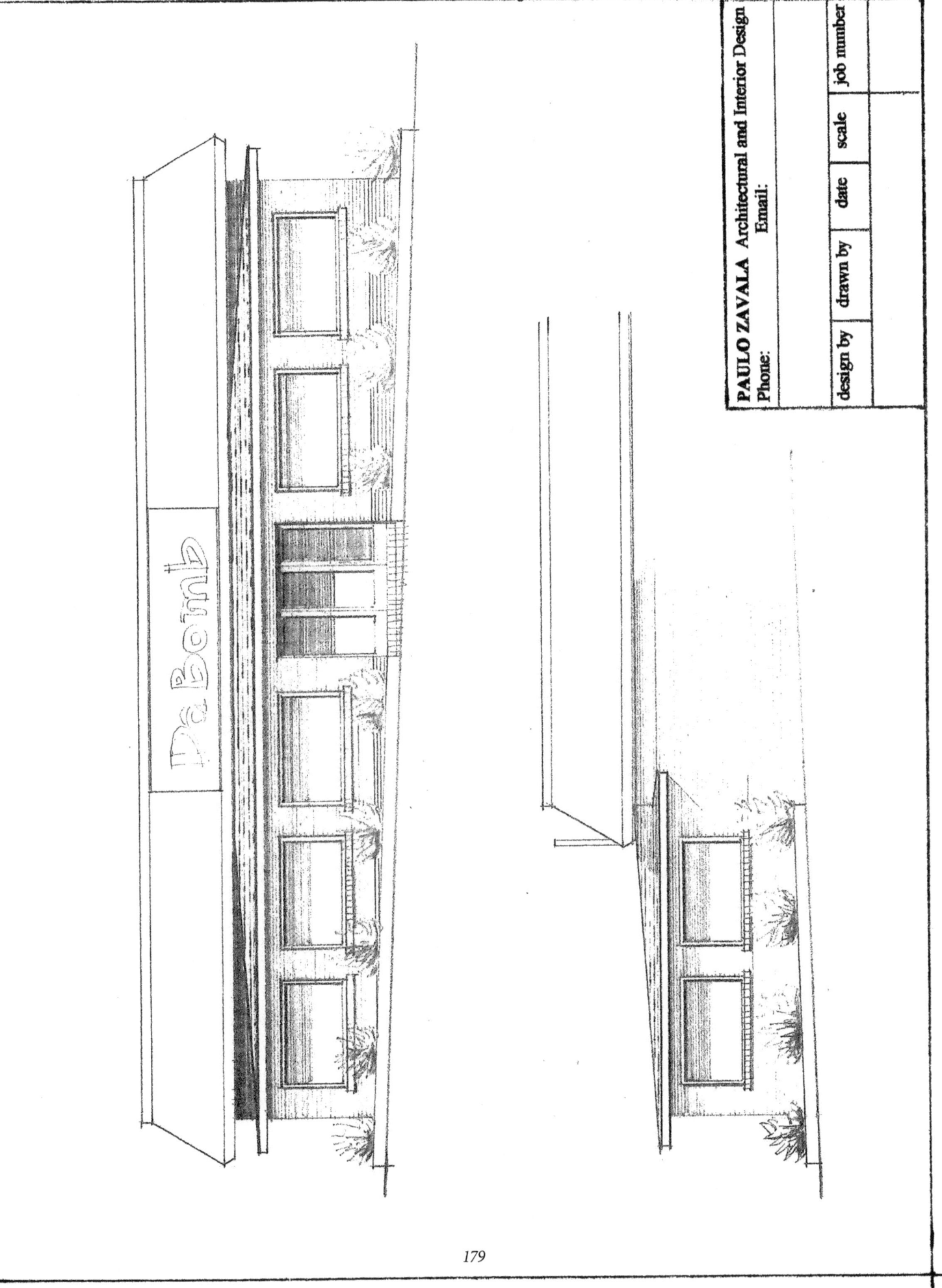